HORNS &

world, Mr. Mennel ex
special insti

THORNS & THISTLES

Frontispiece from George C. Needham,
Street Arabs and Gutter Snipes, 1884

THE UNIVERSITY PRESS OF NEW ENGLAND

Sponsoring Institutions

BRANDEIS UNIVERSITY

CLARK UNIVERSITY

DARTMOUTH COLLEGE

UNIVERSITY OF NEW HAMPSHIRE

THE UNIVERSITY OF RHODE ISLAND

UNIVERSITY OF VERMONT

THORNS & THISTLES

Juvenile Delinquents
in the United States
1825-1940

ROBERT M. MENNEL

Published for
The University of New Hampshire
by
The University Press of New England
Hanover, New Hampshire

1973

FOR GISELA
AND TIMOTHY

ORPHANES, WHO HAVING NOTHING LEFT UNTO THEM, AND BEING DESTITUTE OF ALL RELIEF AND HELP, ARE LEFT TO THEIR OWN DISPOSITIONS, THESE . . . SWARME IN CLUSTERS IN EVERY CORNER AND QUARTER OF YOUR CITIE, AND FOR WANT OF GOOD EDUCATION AND NURTURING, ALSO GROWE TO BE THORNES AND THISTLES

JOHN HOOKER ALIAS *Vowell*
CHAMBERLAIN OF EXETER

ORDERS ENACTED FOR ORPHANS AND FOR THEIR PORTIONS WITHIN THE CITIE OF EXCESTER . . . (1575)

Contents

Abbreviations

AR	*Annual Report*
ASSU	American Sunday School Union
AICP	Association for Improving the Condition of the Poor (New York)
NCCC	National Conference of Charities and Correction
NCET	National Conference on the Education of Truant, Backward, Dependent, and Delinquent Children
NYCAS	New York Children's Aid Society
NYCP	New York Catholic Protectory
NYJA	New York Juvenile Asylum
NYSA&I	New York State Agricultural and Industrial School (Western House of Refuge)
SPP	Society for the Prevention of Pauperism (New York)
SRJD	Society for the Reformation of Juvenile Delinquents (New York)

Preface

JUVENILE DELINQUENCY, according to a recent definition, is "a violation of the law or ordinance by an individual below the legal adult age of the community." Delinquency further describes acts or courses of conduct deemed socially, morally, of physiologically undesirable for children as legally defined, e.g. truancy, disobedience of parents, or the consumption of alcoholic beverages. The age dividing juvenile delinquency from youth crime is usually 18 but at present varies from state to state with the euphemisms "wayward minor" or "youthful offender," often utilized to indicate the adjudication of youths between 16 and 21.[1]

If we regard juvenile delinquency as merely a legal term, the dictionary definition may be adequate. It bears some resemblance to that of the first juvenile court act in Illinois (1899), which categorized delinquency as the violation of "any law of this State or any City or Village ordinance."[2] Like the modern definition, however, the Illinois law gives us little of the social and cultural information which we must have if we are to understand the full meaning of the term. When considered as a violation of mores, juvenile delinquency becomes less a fixed concept and more a description of certain kinds of

1. George A. and Achilles G. Theodorson, *A Modern Dictionary of Sociology* (New York: Thomas Y. Crowell, 1969), p. 106. See also Irving J. Sloan, *Youth and the Law: Rights, Privileges and Obligations* (New York: Oceana Publications, 1970), pp. 55–61. (Sources are generally documented at the end of each paragraph. Publishers are cited only for twentieth–century works.)

2. See Robert H. Bremner et al., eds., *Children and Youth in America,* 3 vols. (Cambridge: Harvard University Press, 1970–), II, 506–11.

behavior by certain children living in certain places. Thus the large number of Irish children in reform schools during the nineteenth century and of Negro children in such institutions today reflect tensions and hostilities operative in the society of each age. In George Rosen's words, "At any given period certain criteria are employed to establish normal human nature as well as any deviation from it." The only way we can really know the meaning of juvenile delinquency is to discover how society over a period of time has attempted to define and combat it.[3]

Public authorities have always taken cognizance of juvenile delinquency, but until recently the control of noncriminal deviance has been ordinarily assigned to the family. The family's task, as Erik Erikson has pointed out, was and is to teach the child "the principle of *law and order,* which in daily life as well as in the high courts of law apportions to each his privileges, his obligations, and his rights."[4] Today, as in the past, we encourage the family in its disciplinary role by exhorting parents to control their children and by substituting higher authority when parental failure leads to disruption of the community. Since the early nineteenth century, we have believed, however, that juvenile delinquency could not be prevented solely by family government. We have developed an array of voluntary and public institutions—community organizations, juvenile courts, and reform schools—which provide special treatment for children accused of criminal offenses and offer services to those whose behavior is considered inimical to society or detrimental to their own welfare, or both. My analysis of efforts to define and prevent juvenile delinquency proceeds, therefore, in the context of this shift from family-centered discipline to an institutionally supported system of care and control. This change evolved as part of the larger change in American life whereby an agrarian commercial country became an urban industrial nation.

The history of juvenile delinquency has not, until recently, at-

3. Rosen, *Madness in Society: Chapters in the Historical Sociology of Mental Illness* (New York: Harper and Row, 1969), p. 164. See also Kai T. Erikson, *Wayward Puritans: A Study in the Sociology of Deviance* (New York: Wiley, 1966), p. 6.

4. *Identity and the Life Cycle* (New York: International Universities Press, 1959), pp. 65–74.

tracted serious attention, perhaps because those scholars and professionals most logically interested in it—juvenile court judges, probation officers, psychiatrists, psychologists, reform school officials, social welfare administrators and social workers and teachers—have been more interested in keeping abreast of current issues in their particular fields than in examining the historical roots of their concerns. This presentist approach is often reflected in the questions that they ask. What new techniques have been devised to facilitate adjudication in the juvenile court? What ideas about adolescent behavior do sociologists and psychologists consider significant? How best can a community organize its resources to prevent juvenile delinquency?

Without denying the significance of these questions, we should be able to acknowledge the additional importance of understanding more fully the history of juvenile delinquency, not necessarily to solve the problem but at least to learn more of its dimensions. This sentiment may sound familiar, because it also informed the outlook of a now departed generation of reformers and social workers, foremost of whom was Grace Abbott (1878–1939), chief of the United States Children's Bureau from 1921 to 1934 and then professor of public welfare administration at the University of Chicago. In 1938 Miss Abbott, with the aid of her sister Edith and Sophonisba P. Breckinridge, published *The Child and the State* (1938), a two–volume documentary history of public policy toward children in America since 1600. Concentrating on legislative, judicial, and administrative actions affecting apprenticeship, child labor, child welfare, delinquency, and family law, this work helped to train students in schools of social work and public health and served as a reference for historians and administrators of voluntary and government programs for children.

In 1964 Drs. Martha M. Eliot and William M. Schmidt, both of the Harvard School of Public Health (Dr. Eliot had also been chief of the Children's Bureau 1951–1957), became convinced that an enlargement of Miss Abbott's work would serve the needs of scholars and professionals in work with children in many fields. After receiving a grant of financial support from the federal government, which was administered by the American Public Health Association, they initiated a revision and updating of *The Child and the State* under the editorship of Robert H. Bremner of The Ohio State University. Initial research and the collection of documents proceeded from 1967 until 1969 at the Charles Warren Center for American Studies. Harvard University. The new Child and State Project resulted in the publication of *Children and Youth in America* by Harvard University Press.

As an associate editor of *Children and Youth in America*, I collected and interpreted documents relating to the history of juvenile delinquency in the United States, and in this capacity I began an analysis of the subject, the results of which are presented in the following chapters. Opening with a brief discussion of initial efforts to define delinquency in the pre-industrial Anglo-American world, the study next examines the houses of refuge, the first institutions founded specifically to reform juvenile delinquents. The subsequent development of preventive "child saving" philanthropies and of state reform schools, both beginning in the midnineteenth century, are the subjects of Chapter two. Later in the century, new scientific explanations of human origins and concepts modified ideas about the causes of juvenile delinquency: these developments and their implications for reform schools are discussed in the third and fourth chapters. The last two analyze the bases for contemporary study and treatment of delinquency, i.e., establishment of the juvenile court, and the researches of psychiatrists and social scientists during the first third of the twentieth century.

Generally, this is an analysis of informed opinion—a discussion of the theories and feelings of some of the significant men and women who devoted their lives to the care of delinquents and the prevention of delinquency. Of course, "informed opinion" must take into account the unvarnished recollections of the boys and girls who, for one reason or another, were called delinquents. Their testimony, although hard to obtain, especially in the nineteenth century, is also included.

Librarians and their staffs at The Ohio State University and Harvard University were helpful to me at all stages of research and writing. Other institutions and libraries were equally considerate. These include The Library of Congress, the Boston Public Library, the Massachusetts State House Library, the New York Public Library, the New York State Library (Albany), the New-York Historical Society, the Newberry Library (Chicago), the Chicago Historical Society, the University of Chicago Library, the Social Welfare History Archives (University of Minnesota), the Schlesinger Library (Radcliffe), the Children's Mission (Boston), the Olin Library (Cornell), the Syracuse University Library, the Lyman School for Boys (Westborough, Mass.), the Ohio Historical Association, and the Rutherford B. Hayes Memorial Library (Fremont, Ohio).

I wish especially to acknowledge the assistance of Robert H. Bremner. As friend and mentor, he provided constant encouragement and advice for which I shall always be indebted. At the Charles Warren Center I benefited greatly from the friendship and guidance of Martha Eliot, and William Schmidt, and of Oscar Handlin, director of the Center.

Subsequent research was made possible by grants from the Central University Research Fund of the University of New Hampshire. For this support I wish to thank the Graduate Council and especially Trevor Colbourn, dean of the Graduate School, and William H. Drew, associate dean. My colleagues, Darrett B. Rutman and Charles E. Clark, made suggestions which helped to clarify my writing during the revision process.

Other scholars aided me at different stages of the work. Gerald N. Grob was kind enough at a busy time to read and criticize drafts of the first three chapters; Clarke A. Chambers, James Leiby, and Charles E. Strickland took time out from their research to read earlier versions of the manuscript and give me the benefits of their knowledge. Mark H. Haller, Joseph F. Kett, and Peter G. Slater also made valuable observations on particular points. I profited greatly from conversations with Mrs. Karl De Schweinitz, William H. Knox, Lloyd H. Ohlin, Leonard Schneiderman, Thorsten Sellin, and Miriam Van Waters.

My wife Gisela typed and edited the manuscript several times. Without her devoted support, I should never have completed the work.

In recent years, a number of books, articles, and dissertations have been completed on the history of childhood and adolescence in America. Some of these have dealt perceptively with juvenile delinquency or related topics. In addition to noting these studies in appropriate places, I have included them in the Note on Sources which follows the text. In some cases, these studies appeared too late for inclusion into the body of this work. Nevertheless, it is rewarding to note fresh scholarly interest and activity relating to the history of juvenile delinquency, and it is my hope that this work adds to the accomplishments of contemporaries.

R.M.M.

Durham, New Hampshire
August 1972

Introduction

CHILDREN HAVE always misbehaved and committed crimes, but only since the eighteenth century has the term "juvenile delinquency" been used to describe these illegal or unacceptable acts. The words imply specially organized governmental or voluntary responses. In the early modern world, such efforts were not indicated, because the security and continuity of society depended almost entirely upon family government. Peter Laslett, in his study of preindustrial England, has recalled an era "when the whole of life went forward in the family, in a circle of loved, familiar faces." Similarly, Bernard Bailyn and John Demos have shown that the family in early colonial America assumed the powers and responsibilities of guiding the child to civilized living: "It introduced him to the world; and in so doing reinforced the structure of its own authority." The control and punishment of children, like apprenticeship, education, and health care, was the responsibility of family government.[1]

The scope of the socializing task was enormous when children constituted a substantial portion of the whole population. Laslett, citing census figures for 1695 and 1821, estimates that more than a quarter of the population of England and Wales was under nine years of age and just less than half under twenty. J. Potter suggests a similar distribution for the American colonies. There were few families which did not have small children constantly under foot, and

1. Peter Laslett, *The World We Have Lost: England Before the Industrial Age* (New York: Charles Scribner's Sons, 1965), p. 21. Bernard Bailyn, *Education in the Forming of American Society* (Chapel Hill: University of North Carolina Press, 1960), p. 16. John Demos, *A Little Commonwealth: Family Life in Plymouth Colony* (New York: Oxford, 1970), pp. 146, 183–84.

the care and governance of those who survived infancy was provided only by great sacrifices.[2]

Family governments were not everywhere the same. In urban settings, family government had been traditionally characterized by a system of apprenticeship according to which masters furnished food and lodging and taught handicraft trades to their sons and other young men. In return, these youths subordinated themselves to the moral as well as vocational discipline of their masters for legally stipulated periods of time, in France three to five years, in England usually seven years. Municipal guilds controlled access to trades and supervised relations between masters and apprentices and, in this manner, attempted to regulate the number of future masters and householders.

This system never worked perfectly, but by the midsixteenth century it was beginning to crack noticeably. Early enclosures of rural land combined with civil strife brought forced migrations of families and individuals into the cities of England and Europe; others, seeking commercial gain or adventure, came willingly. Few of the newcomers were familiar with the highly structured system of trade and apprenticeship, and urban merchants were not anxious to integrate them into it. Quite the contrary, for in legislation such as the Elizabethan Statute of Artificers (1562), urban householders sought to restrict certain trades to their own children while at the same time binding rural families to the countryside.[3]

Laws, however, could not stem the tide of urban migration. Apprentices and other newcomers violated laws with increasing impunity, entering trades as they desired. The corporate basis of town life—the guilds and the system of family government which underlay them—began to weaken. In the migratory process, some families, often but not always the families of newcomers, disintegrated, casting loose their members as deprived individuals in a society of families.

---

2. Laslett, pp. 103–106. J. Potter, "The Growth of Population in America, 1700–1860," in D. V. Glass and D. E. C. Eversley, eds., *Population in History: Essays in Historical Demography* (Chicago: Aldine, 1965), pp. 631–88.

3. *Encyclopedia of Social Sciences*, II, 144–47. See also O. Jocelyn Dunlop and Richard D. Denman, *English Apprenticeship and Child Labour: A History* (New York: Macmillan, 1912), and Lawrence Stone, "Social Mobility in England, 1500–1700," *Past and Present* 32 (1966), 16–55.

Congregating in groups, the unkempt children and youths began to attract particular attention. John Howes's survey of London in the midsixteenth century worried over two thousand persons in need of relief, of which three hundred were "fatherless children." Thorsten Sellin has noted similar concern in Dutch and French cities. F. DeCalvi's *History of Thieves* (1640) claimed that the French Civil Wars had caused "the sons of many good families to seek their livelihood by finesse and craft or other illicit ways."[4] Nor did the problem abate with the passage of time. In 1732 the Lord Mayor of London complained that "divers Poor Vagrant Children are suffered to skulk in Nighttime, and lie upon Bulks, Stalls, and other Places in the Public Streets of this City, whereby many of them perish by the Extremity of the Weather, and other Inconveniences ensue."[5] Like conditions obtained in American cities in the later eighteenth century. A Philadelphia newspaper commented: "The custom of permitting boys to ramble about the street by night, is productive of the most serious and alarming consequences to their morals. Assembled in corners, and concealed from every eye, they can securely indulge themselves in mischief of every kind."[6]

In these circumstances of want and petty thievery, public authorities employed apprenticeship as their principal device of social control. But this was a different sort of apprenticeship from that used by masters of skilled callings. Destitute and delinquent children were "bound out," not to learn specific trades, but to serve individual householders in generalized tasks—usually farming for boys and "domestic economy" for girls. The purpose of Elizabethan appren-

4. Howes is quoted in Ivy Pinchbeck and Margaret Hewitt, *Children in English Society,* 2 vols. (London: Routledge & Kegan Paul, 1969–), I, 126. Thorsten Sellin, *Pioneering in Penology: The Amsterdam Houses of Correction in the Sixteenth and Seventeenth Centuries* (Philadelphia: University of Pennsylvania Press, 1944), pp. 19, 41–42, and Sellin, "A 'History of Thieves': Crime in Seventeenth-Century France," offprint of *Liber Amicorum in Honour of Professor Stephan Hurwitz LL.D.* (Copenhagen: Juristforbundets Forlag, 1971), pp. 447–60.

5. Quoted in Wiley B. Sanders, ed., *Juvenile Offenders for a Thousand Years: Selected Readings from Anglo-Saxon Times to 1900* (Chapel Hill: University of North Carolina Press, 1970), p. 40.

6. *Dunlap's American Daily Advertiser* (August 5, 1791), in Sanders, p. 325. See also Carl Bridenbaugh, *Cities in Revolt: Urban Life in America, 1743–1776* (New York: Oxford, 1955), pp. 98–133, 299–305.

ticeship laws, according to a commentator of the period, "was not for the education of boys in arts but for charity to keep them and relieve them from turning to roguery and idleness, so a man's house was, as it were, a Hospital in that case, rather than a shop of trade."[7] In colonial Massachusetts and Virginia, apprenticeship served similar ends—relieving the public from charges of supporting dependent children while at the same time providing them with maintenance and supervision more than training them in a particular calling. Indeed, the American colonies directly supported the English apprenticeship system by receiving and indenturing poor and delinquent children whom parish officials declared part of "the surcharge of necessitous people" and sentenced to be transported. Children whose parents supposedly encouraged them to pick pockets and commit crimes were the most likely candidates for transportation.[8]

In England as well as America public authorities subordinated themselves to the householder who was expected to administer punishment when appropriate to all the young people under his roof, servants and children alike. Public laws ordered parents to teach their children and servants "the laws against Capital offenders" and supported them in the reasonable exercise of their disciplinary function. Punishment was still more of a domestic than a public matter. In Massachusetts, for example, children whose delinquencies brought them before magistrates were often remitted to their own families for a court-observed whipping. Local government pronounced the reproof, but the family enforced it.[9]

Outside of the family, institutional provisions for delinquent children were not extensive. The Amsterdam House of Correction

7. Quoted in Dunlop and Denman, p. 252; spelling modernized.

8. Pinchbeck and Hewitt, I, 105–107. Bremner, *Children and Youth in America,* I, 115–21. Abbot E. Smith, *Colonists in Bondage: White Servitude and Convict Labor in America, 1607–1776* (Chapel Hill: University of North Carolina Press, 1947), pp. 147–51. Children were usually transported to Virginia or Maryland. After the American Revolution, some English children were transported to Australia; see below, p. 41.

9. Bremner, *Children and Youth in America,* I, 39. Ariès and Rosen have both noted that youthful misbehavior along with other kinds of deviation—insanity, bodily deformity, even some adult criminality—were accommodated as integral features of daily life by pre–industrial, family–centered society. See Philippe Ariès, *Centuries of Childhood: A Social History of Family Life* (New York: Vintage Books, 1965), pp. 315–28, and Rosen, pp. 139–77.

(1595) received "young persons who had got on the wrong path and are headed for the gallows," and the Hospice de St. Michael (1704) in Rome provided a separate apartment where "children who cause sorrow to their parents . . . are lodged, nourished, entertained, instructed and chastised in the most marvellous manner." In Elizabethan London, the House of Bridewell had a children's side "to train up the beggar's child in virtuous exercise, that of him should spring no more beggars" and a number of provincial towns followed London's example.[10]

Generally, however, early institutions for children did not discriminate among types. A number of institutions were originated for children who were simply referred to as "needy." Christ's Hospital (London), generously supported by John Howes and other local householders, opened its doors in 1552 to the orphaned, destitute, and delinquent children of the city. With its imitators in other cities, Christ's provided Tudor-Stuart England with a fabric of institutions founded by private generosity but designed as expressions of communal responsibility and vital supplements to family government. Similar institutions existed in colonial America but not until the eighteenth century and then on a more limited scale. In 1729 the Ursulines established at New Orleans the first orphanage within the present boundaries of the United States, and a decade later George Whitefield began to lay plans for the Bethesda, Georgia, orphanage (1740), which he modeled after August Francke's institution in Halle, Germany. The organizing purpose, as in England, was to nurture children carefully and amply, for the future stability of society depended at least in part upon the children's ability to function as responsible householders. Generous in outlook but limited and largely voluntary in scope, early modern philanthropy existed compatibly with public authority which gave moral if not fiscal support.[11]

10. Sellin, *Pioneering in Penology,* pp. 39–43, and "The House of Correction for Boys in the Hospice of St. Michael in Rome," *Journal of the American Institute of Criminal Law and Criminology* 20 (1930), 533–53; Pinchbeck and Hewitt, I, 132–36.

11. Wilbur K. Jordan, *Philanthropy in England, 1480–1660* (New York: Russell Sage, 1959), pp. 178–79, 224–25, and Jordan, "The English Background of Modern Philanthropy," *American Historical Review* 66 (1961), 401–408. Robert H. Bremner, *American Philanthropy* (Chicago: University of Chicago Press, 1960), pp. 22–23.

Family government remained the mainstay of social control, although by 1700 the family's inability to accommodate and discipline its young was becoming more apparent. The shrill tone of numerous colonial laws threatening parents with punishment for failing to catechize, employ, and govern their children and apprentices was one indication of disharmony. A Virginia journal of 1690 laid the "utter Rewing [ruin] and undoing" of one apprentice to his negligent family.[12] In England, too, it was acknowledged by 1700 that apprenticeship often failed to teach or control children. Nor did the policy of transportation to the colonies bring much relief in terms of juvenile mendicancy and misbehavior to the parishes which employed it.[13] Deterioration proceeded unevenly, evidence of failure appearing in England and on the Continent before it surfaced in America, in cities more than in the countryside and, as would be expected, among orphans, vagrants, and servants more than among children who lived regularly with their parents. The desertion of apprentices increased noticeably. In 1758 a Virginian observed: "Few of those poor children now serve out their Time, and many of them are driven by Neglect or Cruelty, into such Immoralities as to render them the objects of publick Justice."[14]

These youths were responding to opportunity as well as fleeing from abuse. Craftsmen and merchants began to see them as workers valuable for their labor and little else. These masters had neither the time nor the inclination to regard apprentices as members of the family—a development not entirely unwelcome to the children but one which left them at the mercy of public authorities when they committed crimes.[15]

The tendency to view children as economic units affected both

12. Quoted in Marcus W. Jernegan, *Laboring and Dependent Classes in Colonial America, 1607–1783* (Chicago: University of Chicago Press, 1931), p. 163. For examples of colonial laws admonishing parents, see Bremner, *Children and Youth in America*, I, 39–42.

13. Pinchbeck and Hewitt, I, 109, 123. Max Beloff, *Public Order and Popular Disturbances, 1660–1714* (New York: Oxford, 1938), pp. 31–33, 154–56.

14. Quoted in Guy F. Wells, *Parish Education in Colonial Virginia* (New York: Columbia University Press, 1923), pp. 79–80. See also Raphael Semmes, *Crime and Punishment in Early Maryland* (Baltimore: Johns Hopkins Press, 1938), pp. 80–118.

15. E. P. Thompson, *The Making of the English Working Class* (New York: Pantheon Books, 1964), pp. 306–309, 333–36, associates the decline of the family with the rise of the factory system in the early nineteenth century:

public policy and organized benevolence. As society's primary design became the promotion of individual and national wealth, philanthropy became miserly and minimized the scope of institutional care in order to spur poor children to work. Institutions like Christ's Hospital, whose ample care for children had been predicated on the need to ensure the future integrity of the family and the community, were increasingly regarded as abettors of crime and sloth because of their supposed generosity. The value of work, which had once been stressed because it encouraged social stability, now was urged because of its economic profitability.[16] Institutional life was to change accordingly, as John Locke explained in his *Report for the Reform of the Poor Law* (1697):

> The children of the labouring people are an ordinary burden to the parish, and are usually maintained in idleness, so that their labour is also generally lost to the public, till they are twelve or fourteen years old. . . . The most effectual remedy for this . . . is, that working schools be set up in each parish, to which the children of all such as demand relief of the parish, above three and under fourteen years of age . . . shall be obliged to come.[17]

In England, some early parish workhouses and almshouses, especially those with attached charity schools run by benevolent societies, did try to provide children with adequate care. Charity schools, however, had limited appeal because their evangelical anti-Catholicism obscured the material benefits and educational opportunities that were also offered. In time, however, most English and American institutions followed Locke's plan too literally, scrimping on food and clothing and exploiting inmates, young and old, unmercifully. For abandoned infants, the public almshouse became, in the words of

---

"There had been a time when factories had been thought of as kinds of workhouses for pauper children . . ."—a viewpoint indicative of the family's failure to care for some children even before 1800.

16. Pinchbeck and Hewitt, I, 131–32, 310–11. The London Marine Society (1756), which was organized to train destitute and delinquent boys as recruits for the Royal Navy, soon restricted its admission to "boys of good character"; see Sanders, pp. 52–56.

17. Quoted in Pinchbeck and Hewitt, I, 309. A similar attitude informed the operation of the Hôpital-Général in Paris (1657); see Leon Bernard, *The Emerging City: Paris in the Age of Louis XIV* (Durham, North Carolina: Duke University Press, 1970), pp. 145–55.

English philanthropist Jonas Hanway, "the greatest sink of mortality in these Kingdoms."[18]

The new "philanthropic" attitude, already characterized by increasing distrust of the traditional practice of remanding deviants and paupers to the family, was also opposed to the existing use and definition of penal institutions. Before 1750 jails were regarded as detention facilities for adult persons awaiting trial or places to incarcerate political and religious offenders and debtors. Persons found guilty of ordinary crimes such as stealing were usually released after being punished physically, sometimes brutally. Focusing on the barbarity of branding and mutilation and on the irrationality of prescribing extremely severe punishments for petty crimes, Enlightenment writers like Cesare Beccaria, Jeremy Bentham, and Charles Montesquieu argued for more humane and predictable penal codes. Their pleas were supplemented and dramatized by the work of such pioneer prison inspectors as Elizabeth Fry and John Howard in England, Thomas Eddy in New York, and Philadelphians Caleb Lownes, Roberts Vaux, and Benjamin Rush. Although these reformers were known primarily for their exposition of the degrading conditions in most prisons of the time, they became, in the course of their work, enthusiastic about the benefits of specially organized incarceration, particularly for young persons convicted of crimes. John Howard, for example, was "delighted" in 1778 following his visit to a correctional establishment for juvenile offenders in Rome.[19]

Traditional penal codes posed special problems for public officials

18. Pinchbeck and Hewitt, I, 177. On charity schools see Mary G. Jones, *The Charity School Movement: A Study of Eighteenth Century Puritanism in Action* (Cambridge: Cambridge University Press, 1938).

19. D. L. Howard, *John Howard: Prison Reformer* (New York: Archer House, 1963), pp. 71–72. A review of penal reform in colonial and early national America is Harry Elmer Barnes, "The Historical Origin of the Prison System in America," *Journal of the American Institute of Criminal Law and Criminology* 12 (1921), 36–51. Michael Kraus, "Eighteenth Century Humanitarianism: Collaboration Between Europe and America," *Pennsylvania Magazine of History and Biography* 60 (1936), 270–86, and Frank Thistlethwaite, *The Anglo-American Connection in the Early Nineteenth Century* (Philadelphia: University of Pennsylvania Press, 1959), pp. 76–102, explore the trans-Atlantic connections between penal reformers. On the uses of imprisonment before the modern period, see Ralph B. Pugh, *Imprisonment in Medieval England* (Cambridge: Cambridge University Press, 1968).

and philanthropists interested in helping delinquent children. Biblically derived statutes such as those in colonial Massachusetts provided harsh punishment, even death, for delinquent and disobedient children, but these laws were for all intents and purposes useless because they were almost never applied.[20] By the late eighteenth century, English common law was being widely used to describe what constituted crimes by children, but it too proved an unsatisfactory guide to actual punishment. Blackstone's *Commentaries* (IV, 1795) categorized the child under seven years of age as incapable of crime. The child between seven and fourteen was also presumed to be incapable of felony, but "if it appear to the court and jury, that he . . . could discern between good and evil, he may be convicted and suffer death."[21] Under these guidelines, juries were reluctant to condemn children either to death or to jail, where, it was commonly believed, adult inmates schooled them for future crimes. Thomas Buxton, reporting on a visit to the Bristol Gaol in 1818, wrote: "I counted eleven children—children hardly old enough to be released from a nursery—hardly competent to understand the first principles of moral obligation—here receiving an education which . . . must eminently qualify them for that career which they are doomed to run."[22] Cognizance of these conditions often led juries to acquit youths with a finding of "lack of knowledge" as the reason for their crimes.[23]

20. Bremner, *Children and Youth in America,* I, 37–39, 307. Lawrence H. Gipson, *Crime and Its Punishment in Provincial Pennsylvania,* Lehigh University Publication 108 (1935).

21. William Blackstone, *Commentaries on the Laws of England,* 12th ed., 4 vols. (London, 1795), IV, 23. David Flaherty, "Law and the Enforcement of Morals in Early America," *Perspectives in American History* 5 (Cambridge, Mass., 1971), 207–208, has pointed out the close relationship between Mosiac and common law in the colonial world: "The New England colonists specifically listed Biblical authority for statutes in their law codes and firmly believed that the English common law was grounded on the law of God."

22. Quoted in Sanders, p. 101.

23. Bremner, *Children and Youth in America,* I, 309–12, 313–14. Anthony Platt, *The Child Savers: The Invention of Delinquency* (Chicago: University of Chicago Press, 1969), pp. 183–202, discusses this tendency as it continued in the nineteenth century. His survey of fourteen cases involving the criminal responsibility of children (1806–1882) concluded that unless the child was black, guilty findings were seldom returned despite evidence proving intent to commit a crime.

Few special institutions for juvenile delinquents were founded in the late eighteenth century, but the few that were opened reflected in their operation both the spirit of calculated philanthropy and the sharpening of distrust between social classes. A case in point was the school for the children of convicts and other delinquent children, established by the London Philanthropic Society in 1788. An early pamphlet tells us that the Society was founded "for the Prevention of Crimes, and for a reform among the Poor; by training up to Virtue and Industry the Children of Vagrants and Criminals and such who are in the Paths of Vice and Infamy." The organizing purpose was to promote virtue and industry rather than charity:

> It was proposed to establish a fund, not to be sunk in gratuities without any return, not to be a perpetual current from the purses of the rich to the miseries of the poor . . . the object in short to unite a spirit of charity with the principles of trade, and to erect a temple of philanthropy on the foundations of virtuous industry.

In pursuit of this object the boys and girls worked ten hours a day in shoemaking, tailoring, and housekeeping.[24]

Thus, during the eighteenth century, juvenile delinquency slowly ceased to mean a form of misbehavior common to all children and became instead a euphemism for the crimes and conditions of poor children. Rising distrust of the ability of poor families to raise their own children fused with dissatisfaction with the operation of the law as it affected delinquent children. These developments combined to result in organized activity to prevent juvenile delinquency. The founders of the New York House of Refuge, the first reform school established in the United States, made this comment on what they regarded as both a moral and judicial dilemma posed by the presence of children in criminal court.

> If acquitted, they returned destitute to the same haunts of vice from which they had been taken, more emboldened to the commission of crime, by their escape from present punishment. If convicted, they were cast into a common prison with older culprits to mingle in conversation and intercourse with them.[25]

24. Sanders, pp. 70–77.

25. New York Society for the Reformation of Juvenile Delinquents (SRJD), *AR* (1826), pp. 3–4.

To these men and to other concerned citizens, the key to the solution of delinquency seemed to lie in the development of more institutions. A system of social control would have to be developed apart from the family which would discipline homeless, vagrant, and destitute children—the offspring of the poor. Ideally, this system would avoid the cruelty of sending children to jail, but it would nonetheless ensure that they were suitably corrected and reformed.

THORNS & THISTLES

CHAPTER 1

Houses of Refuge, 1825–1860

THE FIRST ORGANIZED efforts to treat juvenile delinquency as a distinct social problem centered around the founding and development of houses of refuge in New York, Boston, and Philadelphia during the 1820s. A house is not a home, as Polly Adler has told us. In the context of juvenile punishment, the word "house" identifies a milestone in the shift from family-centered discipline to institutional treatment administered by society. One connotation of "refuge" derives from the Book of Moses, where six cities of refuge were designated to harbor persons who had committed crimes under mitigating circumstances. "Refuge" implies and was on occasion explicitly linked to the idea of asylum, an institution that necessarily had to exist apart from the troubles and temptations of society in order to work its reformative or protective purposes. Houses of refuge for children were sealed-off institutions; the motivation for their founding was social awareness and concern that family discipline was no longer sufficient to control the neglected and abandoned children living in the larger seacoast cities.[1]

The New York House of Refuge, the first of these institutions, opened on New Year's Day, 1825, under the management of a group

1. On the biblical meaning of refuge see *Proceedings and Addresses at the Laying of the Cornerstone of the New House of Refuge at Glen Mills, Pennsylvania, October 17, 1889* (Philadelphia, 1889), p. 26. David J. Rothman, *The Discovery of the Asylum: Social Order and Disorder in the New Republic* (Boston: Little, Brown, 1971) argues that reformers in the Jacksonian age should be remembered not just for creating insane asylums, penitentiaries, and houses of refuge but also for their great faith that these institutions could fully cure or reform inmates.

of philanthropic citizens constituted as the Society for the Reformation of Juvenile Delinquents. The next year the Boston City Council, following the recommendation of Mayor Josiah Quincy, established the Boston House of Reformation. Also in 1826 a group of prominent Philadelphians received a state charter to found a refuge which they opened in 1828. For a quarter of a century the activities of these three institutions defined institutional treatment of juvenile delinquents.[2]

The philanthropists who founded houses of refuge were, in general, descendants of established families and prosperous members of the merchant or professional classes. In New York they included Cadwallader D. Colden (1769–1834) and Stephen Allen (1766–1852), both former Mayors of the City, Thomas Eddy (1757–1827), the Quaker prison reformer known as the "Howard of America," John Griscom (1774–1852), also a Quaker and a noted chemist and educator, and such other reputed citizens as Isaac Collins, Charles Glidden Haines, and John Pintard. Edward Livingston (1764–1836), Mayor of New York City 1800–1803, had moved to Louisiana by the 1820s and took no direct part in the founding of the New York Refuge. His penal code for Louisiana (1824), however, included plans for a "School of Reform" which provided guidelines for the actual organizers of the institution.

The Philadelphia House of Refuge resulted from the efforts of a disparate group of reformers whose plans were given shape by Isaac Collins, who moved from New York to Philadelphia in 1828. Among the managers of the Philadelphia Refuge were Roberts Vaux (1786–1836), a Quaker and leader of the Philadelphia Society for Alleviating the Miseries of the Public Prisons; Alexander Henry (1766–1847), first President of the American Sunday School Union; and

2. The refuges in New York and Philadelphia were private corporations; the Boston House of Reformation was a public institution. The two refuges received public funds to augment institutional operating revenue, but their internal affairs were subject to minimal state control. Corporation members elected managers who could serve an indeterminate period of time, and these managers appointed and controlled the administrators of the institutions. Managers submitted annual reports to the legislature, and delegations from the legislature paid pro forma visits to the institutions. The Boston City Council directly supervised the House of Reformation by appointing its directors and providing most of its operational expenses. Citizens of Baltimore incorporated a refuge in 1831, but lack of funds delayed its opening until 1851.

Paul Beck, Jr., Thomas P. Cope, and Robert Ralston, all of whom were active in the ASSU. John Sergeant (1779–1852), congressman and advocate of the United States Bank, was the first president of the refuge, while Sarah Grimké (1792–1873), abolitionist and feminist, served on the Ladies Committee. In Boston, Mayor Josiah Quincy (1772–1864) was largely responsible for founding the local house of reformation. His work was enthusiastically supported by his successors, notably Theodore Lyman, Jr. (1792–1849), mayor from 1831 to 1835.

Clifford Griffen has characterized early nineteenth-century philanthropists as conservative reformers—men who regarded themselves as the only legitimate heirs to the ideas and traditions of colonial theocrats and of the Federalist founding fathers.[3] Defining themselves as God's Elect, they felt duty bound to develop charitable organizations in the secular sphere in His name. Benevolent activity was part of their moral stewardship—their trusteeship to relieve the suffering of the needy and to correct the behavior of the deviant. John Griscom spoke for conservative reformers when he accepted "the blessed Redeemer as the only source of our justification." He defined his (and their) philanthropic motive as "a constantly enlarging love to our fellow creatures . . . and the desire we feel to do all the good we can in our day and generation."[4]

3. Clifford S. Griffen, "Religious Benevolence as Social Control, 1815–1860," in David B. Davis, ed., *Ante-Bellum Reform* (New York: Harper and Row, 1967), pp. 81–96. See also Griffen, *Their Brothers' Keepers: Moral Stewardship in the United States, 1800–1865* (New Brunswick, N.J.: Rutgers University Press, 1960), pp. 23–43, and W. David Lewis, "The Reformer as Conservative: Protestant Counter-Subversion in the Early Republic," in Stanley Coben and Lorman Ratner, eds., *The Development of an American Culture* (Englewood Cliffs, N.J.: Prentice-Hall, 1970), pp. 64–91. Sydney V. James traces the activism of Quaker reformers to the Revolutionary War when the Friends repudiated their aloofness from non-Quaker society. They embraced a variety of social causes (pacifism, antislavery, Indian education, and penal reform) while not taking sides in the conflict. James, "The Impact of the American Revolution on Quakers' Ideas About Their Sect," *William and Mary Quarterly,* 3d ser. 19 (1962), 360–82, and James, *A People Among Peoples: Quaker Benevolence in Eighteenth Century America* (Cambridge: Harvard University Press, 1963).

4. John H. Griscom, *Memoir of John Griscom* (New York, 1859), p. 395. Dr. John H. Griscom was John Griscom's son and a pioneer sanitary reformer. John H. Griscom's study, *The Sanitary Condition of the Laboring Population of New York* (New York, 1845) detailed for the first time the wretched

Early nineteenth-century philanthropists also undertook charitable work for their own protection. They feared imminent social upheaval resulting from the explosive mixture of crime, disease, and intemperance which they believed characterized the lives of poorer urban residents. Without relieving the poor of responsibility for their condition, these philanthropists saw, in their benevolences, ways of avoiding class warfare and the disintegration of the social order. The French Revolution reminded them, however, that the costs of class struggle were highest to advantaged citizens like themselves. Nonetheless, fear of Armageddon did not inhibit these stiff and austere men from displaying condescension toward the poor. "Ah, how vainly and foolishly are the lives of the multitude . . . spent in this world," sighed John Griscom.[5]

The reformism of Griscom and his associates was defined by their belief in their own unique qualifications to govern society and to manage social and political change. In politics they were usually Federalist and, later, Whig, and were therefore repelled by the increasingly powerful Jacksonian dogma that dictated wider popular participation in public affairs. Some refuge managers, most notably Stephen Allen, president of the Society for the Reformation of Juvenile Delinquents, 1832–1852, provide exceptions to the political categorization. Allen was a poor boy who became a wealthy businessman and an active supporter of Andrew Jackson, Martin Van Buren, and Tammany Hall. John Pintard's view of the Democratic party was more typical: "My very soul sickens at the name Jackson," he wrote his daughter.[6]

---

sewage and drainage conditions which prevailed in the city's rapidly developing slums, thus helping to initiate a municipal public health movement.

5. Griscom, *Memoir of John Griscom*, p. 395.

6. On Allen see Robert S. Pickett, *House of Refuge, Origins of Juvenile Reform in New York State, 1815–1857* (Syracuse, N.Y.: Syracuse University Press, 1969), pp. 4, 166–67. "Letters of John Pintard to His Daughter Eliza Noel Pintard Davidson, 1816–1833," *Collections* of the New-York Historical Society, 4 vols. (1938–1941), IV, 19. Party labels do not seem to have affected personal relationships between refuge managers. Allen, for example, enjoyed the esteem of Pintard, Griscom, and other New York managers in opposite political parties. See John C. Travis, ed., "Memoirs of Stephen Allen," unpublished MS (1927) in The Papers of Stephen Allen, New-York Historical Society.

Operating in rapidly developing urban societies, these frankly elitist men could no longer enforce their policies as holders of key positions in church and government, from which their ancestors had traditionally supervised community affairs. Rather, they believed that the maintenance of their authority now depended upon founding a host of benevolent societies, each devoted to a particular cause. Thomas Eddy, for example, in addition to superintending the Newgate Prison, participated in the government of the New York Lunatic Asylum, the American Bible Society, the African Free School Society, and the Public School Society. As already noted, Alexander Henry and other founders of the Philadelphia Refuge were active in the American Sunday School Union, one of several interdenominational Bible societies dedicated to spreading orthodox Protestantism through the distribution of tracts and the establishment of Sunday schools in outlying areas and new states.[7]

These philanthropists did not rely solely upon houses of refuge to reform delinquent children. Any organization ministering to the needs of poor and homeless children could be and was construed as valuable in preventing youthful misbehavior, which in the view of founders of a Sunday school in New Jersey could be flagrant: "No sooner were schools commenced in destitute places than a change was visible in the morals of the children and the inhabitants of the neighborhood. Profane swearing, intemperance, and Sabbath breaking which formerly prevailed to an alarming extent, in a great measure ceased."[8] Organizers of the African Free School Society and the New York High

---

7. On the interlocking nature of early nineteenth-century philanthropy see also Moses Beach, *Wealth and Pedigree of the Wealthy Citizens of New York City* (New York, 1842). The Public School Society of New York was led by nearly the same group of men as those who founded the New York Refuge. See William O. Bourne, *History of the Public School Society of New York* (New York, 1870). Page Smith, *As a City upon a Hill: The Town in American History* (New York: Knopf, 1966), p. 174, describes the spread of voluntary philanthropic organizations as "an effort to recapture that sense of personal involvement which had been so strong in the original covenanted community."

8. Quoted in Edwin Wilbur Rice, *The Sunday School Movement and the American Sunday School Union, 1780–1917* (Philadelphia: Philadelphia Sunday School Union, 1917), p. 67. Charles R. Keller, *The Second Great Awakening in Connecticut* (New Haven: Yale University Press, 1962), p. 133, notes that the ASSU gradually abandoned its special concern for destitute children and became an adjunct to churches serving middle-class families.

School boasted that none of their graduates had ever been in court.[9] Like Sunday schools, these institutions were established to inculcate children with the values of hard work, orderliness, and subordination and thereby ensure their future good behavior.

Conservative reformers conceived of the particular problem of law and order in a manner befitting their self-conferred mandate. Policing the city was *their* personal responsibility, as much as it was the job of an organized and uniformed constabulary. Josiah Quincy himself led citizen posses against riotous mobs, and refuge managers personally arrested the children they deemed in need of institutional care. Mayor Colden, reporting little serious crime in New York City in 1818, was, like Quincy, opposed to the development of a police force. Such an organization, according to their reasoning, might become an instrument of despotism, as it had in Europe.[10]

What else explains the rise of philanthropic interest in the problem of juvenile delinquency? We must note again the increasing concern of citizens with the indiscriminate institutionalization of children, particularly the practice of sending vagrant and delinquent youths to almshouses and jails where they were confined with adult offenders. John Pintard characterized state prisons generally as "the present plan of promiscuous intercourse where little Devils are instructed to become great ones and at the expiration of their terms turn out accomplished Villains." A committee of Philadelphians denounced the city's policy of sending children convicted of crimes to the municipal almshouse, "where they are liable to acquire bad habits and principles, and lay the foundation for the career of worthlessness and improvidence, 'which terminates often in the gaol; often in the peniten-

9. Charles C. Andrews, *The History of New York African Free-Schools* . . . (New York, 1830), pp. 46–47. Griscom, *Memoir of John Griscom,* p. 209.

10. Roger D. Lane, "Urbanization and Criminal Violence in the 19th Century: Massachusetts as a Test Case," in Hugh D. Graham and Ted R. Gurr, eds., *Violence in America: Historical and Comparative Perspectives,* a Staff Report to the National Commission on the Causes and Prevention of Violence, 2 vols. (Washington, D.C.: Government Printing Office, 1969), II, 363–64. James F. Richardson, *The New York Police: Colonial Times to 1901* (New York: Oxford, 1970), pp. 7, 14–15. On Quincy see Edmund Quincy, *Life of Josiah Quincy* (Boston, 1867), pp. 394–95, and Roger D. Lane, *Policing the City: Boston, 1822–1855* (Cambridge: Harvard University Press, 1967), p. 20.

tiary, and not seldom at the gallows.' "[11] Of course, this skeptical view of institutions extended beyond concern for children confined within them to encompass an increasingly sharp debate on the place of the adult penitentiary in American society.[12]

Sentiment against incarcerating children with adults did not immediately translate itself into efforts to found special reformatory institutions for children. Beginning in 1812 and at regular intervals thereafter, Reverend John Stanford proposed the establishment of a separate institution in New York for juvenile offenders. His plan was always defeated, in the last instance (1821) by Mayor Stephen Allen, later president of the SRJD. Noting that some of the New York penitentiary children had been transferred to the almshouse, where they were being taught and cared for by the older paupers, Allen concluded of Stanford's plan that "neither the urgency of the case requires it, nor will the finances of the city admit of it."[13]

The proximity of delinquent children and adult criminals concerned philanthropic citizens less than the presence of children in almshouses. Beginning in the 1820s, municipal officials, perhaps influenced by the ideas of charity reformers like J. V. N. Yates of New York,

11. "Letters of John Pintard," II, 338. *Report of the Committee Appointed by the Board of Guardians for the Poor of the City and Districts of Philadelphia to Visit the Cities of Baltimore, New York, Providence, Boston and Salem* (Philadelphia, 1827), pp. 32–33.

12. By the 1820s, adult penitentiaries enjoyed mixed reputations. The chaotic histories of such early institutions as the Newgate [New York] prison had caused some penal reformers to advocate imprisonment only for the most recalcitrant offenders. W. David Lewis, *From Newgate to Dannemora: The Rise of the Penitentiary in New York State, 1796–1848* (Ithaca: Cornell University Press, 1965), describes this shift of attitude in terms of the decline of the Quaker belief in the potential goodness of all men and the subsequent rise of harsh neo-Calvinistic concepts of criminality which required precisely regulated prison routines in order to remind individual prisoners of their irredeemable wickedness. In contrast, David Rothman, *The Discovery of the Asylum*, sees penal reformers of the era enthusiastically embracing various and elaborate systems of institutionalization in the hope of effecting wide-scale reformation. Earlier penitentiaries, according to Rothman, were casually organized because of the general belief that proper laws more than institutions were the chief means of reforming or controlling lawbreakers. See also Orlando F. Lewis, *The Development of American Prisons and Prison Customs, 1776–1845* (Albany: J. Lyon, 1922), pp. 38–63.

13. Charles G. Sommers, *Memoir of the Reverend John Stanford* (New York, 1835), pp. 272–77. New York City, *Minutes of the Common Council*, XI (1821), 722–23.

increasingly rejected applications of individuals and families for "outdoor" relief—that is, for various kinds of public assistance while remaining at home. Believing that outdoor relief promoted pauperism by making aid too easy to obtain and, conversely, not shameful enough to receive, officials relegated the destitute to local almshouses or "poor farms." There, officials reasoned, life might be austere but paupers could engage in productive labor, earn their own keep and, by virtue of the rigorous routine, become anxious to leave the institution and seek gainful employment. This scenario depended for its success upon the presence of able-bodied male adults, but, in practice, almshouses were filled mostly with disabled and senile persons and, to a lesser degree, with women and children. Even in an ideal almshouse children had no place. The institutions which actually evolved soon came to symbolize the persistence of pauperism in society, and the presence of children there seemed only to guarantee a future supply of paupers and deviants.[14]

Pauperism then was the enemy; juvenile delinquency, like intemperance, ignorance, and gambling, was a symptom. In order to combat the many facets of pauperism, Griscom, Eddy, and other philanthropists formed in 1817 the (New York) Society for the Prevention of Pauperism (SPP), which embarked upon a comprehensive propaganda program, attacking taverns, pawn brokers, immigrants, lotteries, houses of ill fame, and gambling dens. The SPP also condemned charitable organizations that failed to verify the poverty of alms seekers, thus supposedly encouraging the growth of an indolent class. With so many obvious causes of adult pauperism at hand, children initially received only passing notice, although in 1820 the SPP did suggest that the Bellevue city prison should provide its youthful inmates with a separate room.[15]

As Raymond Mohl has shown, the SPP failed to influence the passage of state or municipal legislation drawn to suppress drinking and gambling and to plan public employment for the poor. Thus the

14. On the Yates Report see Bremner, *Children and Youth in America,* I, 631, 633–35.

15. SPP, *AR* (1820), pp. 2, 31–36. For the activities of a similar organization in Baltimore, see Blanche D. Coll, "The Baltimore Society for the Prevention of Pauperism, 1820–1822," *American Historical Review* 61 (1955), 77–87.

society turned to the prevention of pauperism in the next generation by investigating both children in jail and destitute children of the city who seemed likely to end there. In its fourth annual report (1821) the SPP warned, "Thousands of children are growing up in this city, destitute of that superintendence over their minds and morals, so indispensable to render them a valuable acquisition to society." In 1818–1819 John Griscom had visited a number of European institutions devoted to the reform of refractory children and had been particularly impressed by an institution for the children of prisoners and for other destitute and delinquent children which was founded by the London Philanthropic Society in 1788. Griscom influenced the SPP to concentrate upon the reform of children, and in 1822 the group issued its *Report on the Penitentiary System in the United States,* which called for "the erection of new prisons for juvenile offenders." "These prisons," said the report, "should be rather schools for instruction, than places of punishment, like our present State Prisons where the young and the old are confined indiscriminately. The youth confined there should be placed under a course of discipline, severe and unchanging, but alike calculated to subdue and conciliate. A system should be adopted that would prove a mental and moral regimen." In 1823 the SPP began to investigate possible sites for such an institution and in the spring of 1824 received a state corporation charter under a new name, the Society for the Reformation of Juvenile Delinquents.[16]

"These prisons should be . . . schools for instruction"—the irony of this statement would plague refuge founders as they attempted to define the role of their institutions. Were refuges to be, in John Griscom's words, jails for "juvenile convicts"?[17] Were they to be extensions of Sunday schools, or shelters for children who were more

16. Raymond A. Mohl, Jr., "Poverty, Public Relief and Private Charity in New York City, 1783–1825" (Ph.D. diss., New York University, 1967), pp. 315–25. SPP, *AR* (1821), p. 11. John Griscom, *A Year in Europe,* 2 vols. (New York, 1823), I, 121–23. SPP, *Report on the Penitentiary System in the United States* (New York, 1822), pp. 59–60. See also Sanders, *Juvenile Offenders for a Thousand Years,* pp. 70–90.

17. Griscom, *Memoir of John Griscom,* p. 163. Edward Livingston used similar terminology in outlining his proposed School of Reform: "The convict at the time of his discharge . . . shall be comfortably clad." See Bremner, *Children and Youth in America,* I, 677.

destitute than delinquent? After studying the physical plans of the refuges, one would have to conclude that the penological model was foremost in the minds of the founders. The managers of the Philadelphia Refuge declined to utilize the old Prune Street apartment of the Arch Street Prison but, as the following description shows, their specially constructed refuge hardly resembled a school house:

> The main edifice is 92 feet in length. Its centre contains convenient apartments for a library, and for the use of the Managers and the families of the officers of the institution. The wings, which are of consequence thus entirely separate from each other, comprise the respective dormitories of the male and female pupils, and their several spacious halls for schools. Each lodging room, of which there are eighty-six in either wing, is calculated for entire solitude, being 7 feet in length, and 4 feet in breadth, furnished only with a small bedstead and shelf; but well lighted and ventilated, and exposed at all times to absolute superintendence and inspection. Workshops are constructed in the extensive area, which is surrounded by a lofty wall.[18]

While enclosing boys and girls within "a lofty wall," the Philadelphia managers were insisting that their institution was "*an asylum* for friendless and unfortunate children, *not a prison* for young culprits."[19] A. H. Grimshaw, a later essayist, illustrated the desire of philanthropists to treat neglected instead of delinquent children when he exclaimed: "I would not wait till the child grows large enough to commit some overt act, to be actually delinquent. I would snatch him as a 'brand from the burning.' I would rescue him from the yearning gulf of poverty, drunkenness and crime, into which he is about to fall." Perhaps the English visitor James Dixon had the last word when he characterized the New York Refuge as "half prison and half school . . . under the management of Methodists."[20]

18. Philadelphia Refuge, *AR* (1829), pp. 4–5. As the description implies, refuge managers took considerable pride in the physical magnitude of their institutions. Incarcerated children must have been at least partially aware of this emotional investment when they expressed their reaction to confinement by burning or otherwise damaging the refuges. On incendiarism in the institutions, see below, pp. 28, 61–62.

19. Philadelphia Refuge, *AR* (1859), p. 10. In 1852 a new Philadelphia Refuge had been completed, with walls running to heights between 21 and 32 feet and enclosing an area measuring 685 × 400 feet.

20. A. H. Grimshaw, "An Essay on Juvenile Delinquency," in Edward Everett Hale, T. V. Moore, and A. H. Grimshaw, *Prize Essays on Juvenile Delinquency*

If the distinctions which refuge managers made between juvenile delinquents and children "about to fall" were unclear, the reason may be that their refuges were competing for inmates with other institutions founded explicitly to care for deserted, orphaned, or abused children. The Boston Female Asylum (1800), the New York Orphan Asylum (1806), the Boston Asylum and Farm School for Indigent Boys (1814), and the Baltimore Manual Labor School (1847) were but a few of the early preventive institutions. Charles Dickens, visiting the Boylston School in 1842, noted that it housed "indigent boys who have committed no crime, but who, in the ordinary course of things, would very soon be purged of that distinction if they were not taken from the hungry streets and sent here." The directors of the Boylston School, on the other hand, represented the attitude of the preventive institutions by refusing to accept children convicted of crimes.[21]

Refuges accepted destitute and orphaned children as well as youths convicted of felonies in state and local courts. The Boston House of Reformation received "all children who live an idle or dissolute life, whose parents are dead or if living, from drunkenness, or other vices, neglect to provide any suitable employment or exercise any salutary control over said children." An illustration of the encompassing nature of refuge incorporation statutes is that of the first sixteen children admitted to the New York House of Refuge, nine had not committed a punishable offense.[22]

Refuge founders may have been confused about the type of child best suited for their care, but they agreed unanimously that the greatest cause of both destitution and delinquency was parental neglect. Occasionally, parents voluntarily committed their own children to the refuge, but more often they saw incarceration as a usurpation of their

---

(Philadelphia, 1855), p. 148. James Dixon, *Personal Narrative of a Tour through a Part of the United States and Canada* (New York, 1849), p. 45.

21. Charles Dickens, *American Notes and Pic-nic Papers* (Philadelphia, n.d.), p. 34. Boston, Common Council, *City Doc.* 14 (1841), pp. 18–21. See Dorothea L. Dix, *Remarks on Prisons and Prison Discipline,* 2d ed. (Philadelphia, 1845), pp. 92–94, for an extract of a Boston Asylum and Farm School report. See also Bremner, *Children and Youth in America,* I, 726–29.

22. Boston law in Bremner, *Children and Youth in America,* I, 681. Joseph Curtis, *Examination of Subjects Who Are in the House of Refuge in the City of New York* (Albany, 1825), pp. 3–17.

parental rights.[23] Thus, refuge managers sought to strengthen by legal means the parental power of their institutions in order to rebut claims that they were illegally depriving children of their liberty or cruelly separating them from natural parents. Because refuges received children who had been convicted in state and local courts, the legal definition of institutional parental power also defined the parental power of the state *(parens patriae)*. In this instance, the significant legal case (that is, the case which provided precedent for future disputants) was a Pennsylvania decision in 1838. Mary Ann Crouse's father attempted to free her from the Philadelphia House of Refuge on a writ of habeas corpus. The State Supreme Court denied his claim, saying, "The right of parental control is a natural, but not an unalienable one." The decision continued:

> The object of the charity is reformation, by training its inmates to industry; by imbuing their minds with principles of morality and religion; by furnishing them with means to earn a living; and, above all, by separating them from the corrupting influence of improper associates. To this end, may not the natural parents, when unequal to the task of education, or unworthy of it, be superseded by the *parens patriae,* or common guardian of the community? . . . The infant has been snatched from a course which must have ended in confirmed depravity; and, not only is the restraint of her person lawful, but it would be an act of extreme cruelty to release her from it.[24]

French penologists Alexis de Tocqueville and Gustave de Beaumont had reached a similar conclusion on the rights of refuge children during their tour of American penal institutions in 1831: "The children," they wrote, "were not the victims of persecution, but merely deprived of fatal liberty."[25]

Refuge philanthropists found other ways of expressing their hostility toward the parents of juvenile delinquents. In 1822 the future man-

---

23. SRJD, *AR* (1827), p. 33.

24. *Ex parte* Crouse, 4 Wharton (Pa.) 9 (1838).

25. Gustave de Beaumont and Alexis de Tocqueville, *On the Penitentiary System in the United States,* trans. Francis Lieber (Philadelphia, 1833), p. 115. Dickens, after a visit to the Boston House of Reformation, reflected dryly on this theme: "I saw [the children] in their school, where they sang a chorus in praise of Liberty: an odd, and, one would think, rather aggravating theme for prisoners" *(American Notes and Pic-nic Papers,* p. 34).

agers of the New York Refuge wrote: "The parents of these children are, in all probability, too poor, or too degenerate, to provide them with clothing fit for them to be seen in at school; and know not where to place them in order that they may find employment, or be better cared for." Josiah Quincy condemned "thoughtless and abandoned parents" of "idle and vicious children," while the Philadelphia Refuge denounced "the debased and besotted parent." Indeed, founders of the New York Refuge designed their institution to punish the habits of the parent as well as those of the child: Stephen Allen lobbied the state legislature successfully to divert to the refuge a portion of the state's revenue from a tax on theater licenses. The legislature also taxed the taverns of New York City in order to support the refuge.[26]

The origins of these parents were as suspect as their habits. As early as 1801, Thomas Eddy had warned that West Indian and European lower-class immigration would result in an uncontrollable younger generation. The depression of 1819 threw many native Americans out of jobs just as sizable numbers of foreigners began to emigrate. This coincidence led many citizens to blame the immigrant not only for the depressed economic conditions but also for social ills. *Niles' Weekly Register,* a barometer of early American opinion, grew increasingly cool during the 1820s toward newcomers and their children. The New York legislature apparently believed that the immigrant was a significant cause of juvenile delinquency, for it allotted a varying amount of the state's immigrant head tax to the refuge.[27]

The depression of 1837 exacerbated the nativism aroused by hard times in 1819. Nativist citizens demanded that Congress exclude

26. SRJD, *Memorial to the Legislature of New York . . . on the Subject of Erecting a House of Refuge, for Vagrant and Depraved Young People* (New York, 1824), pp. 9–10. *Report of the Committee on the Subject of Pauperism and a House of Industry in the Town of Boston* (Boston, 1821), pp. 3–4, 8–9. Philadelphia Refuge, *AR* (1838), p. 18. Stephen Allen to Walter Bowne, March 17, 1824, and Stephen Allen to John Morss, April 1, 1824, Allen MS.

27. Thomas Eddy, *An Account of the State Prison or Penitentiary House in the City of New York* (New York, 1801), pp. 85–86. *Niles' Register* 24 (April 26, 1823), 113; 30 (July 29, 1826), 377; 32 (July 21, 1827), 344. New York State contributed annually between six and eight thousand dollars of the immigrant tax to the refuge but occasionally contributed more when capital outlays (new buildings, major repairs) were high.

foreign-born paupers, complaining in one petition that "they immediately become burdensome to our citizens, exhausting the accumu-
lated funds which had been raised . . . by the various charitable
institutions in our country, for the use of our own unfortunate and
destitute citizens." By this time, refuges were publishing yearly records
of the nativity of both the children and their parents, and the pre-
ponderance of Irish children reflected the Irish migration to America
which was then beginning. Refuge managers viewed the plight of
these poor peasants and their children in an unsympathetic light. In
1835 Boston Mayor Theodore Lyman, Jr., warned, "we shall have
among us a race that will never be infused into our own. . . . Their
children will be brought up in ignorance and idleness."[28] Stephen
Allen commented that the "tide of emigration . . . while it enriches
our country, leaves much of its refuse in our city. Pauper families,
and even felons, are not infrequently sent over to us as a cheap way
of disposing of them . . . thus swelling the number of houseless,
friendless and lawless youth, drifting loose upon society."[29]

Immigrant youths were not the only children specially condemned
by refuge managers. White female delinquents and Negro delinquents
of both sexes also suffered from acute forms of prejudice. Girls were
usually committed to refuges because of alleged promiscuity. A New
York report found Mary Ann P. "quite sluttish, and wanting of ambi-
tion" and that Catherine A. had "been acquainted with men."[30]
Rigidly separated from male delinquents, girls spent their time doing
institutional chores—cooking, sewing, and washing—under the watchful eye of a matron. Weekly visits from the management's ladies'
committee did little to relieve the routine. The ladies admonished
girls individually, heard them recite scriptural verses, and sometimes
spoke wishfully to the assembled group on the benefits of dying young.
On September 8, 1825, for example, a New York lady "addressed the
girls, feelingly on the necessity of a preparation for death and men-

---

28. *Foreign Paupers and Naturalization Laws,* 25th Cong., 2d sess. (1838),
House Report 1040, pp. 1, 1067. Boston, Common Council, *City Doc.* 19
(1846), pp. 10–11. Philadelphia Refuge, *AR* (1833), p. 19. SRJD, *AR* (1834),
p. 61. Theodore Lyman, Jr., *Addresses Made to the City Council of Boston*
(Boston, 1835), pp. 17–24.

29. SRJD, *AR* (1849), p. 11.

30. Curtis, *Examination of Subjects Who Are in the House of Refuge,* pp. 3, 5.

tioned the sudden decease of a religious child, and of her happy close."[31] The girls responded to this advice and to their situation generally by attempting to escape or, failing that, by disrupting the institution even to the point of trying to burn it down. This behavior in turn reinforced the refuge managers' belief that girls should not have been accepted in the first place. An official at the Philadelphia Refuge told Beaumont that the reformation of females "is a chimera which it is useless to pursue."[32]

Negro children were either excluded from the refuges or, if admitted, were treated as inferior to the white children. The superintendent of the Philadelphia Refuge rationalized his institution's exclusionist policy to Beaumont: "It would be degrading to the white children to associate them with beings given up to public scorn." In 1849 Philadelphia philanthropists eventually opened a separate House of Refuge for Colored Juvenile Delinquents; the new inmates were characterized as "the offending offspring of the poorest, most ignorant, most degraded and suffering members of our community." The New York and Boston institutions were rigidly segregated. In 1834 the Manumission Society of New York donated five thousand dollars to

31. Report of the Ladies Committee (September 8, 1825), Papers of the New York House of Refuge, Archives of Syracuse University Library. Peter Slater notes that nineteenth-century writers were especially interested in juvenile death scenes and described the act of dying as a "step toward heaven." In this way, authors avoided debating infant damnation or the consequences of innate depravity for deceased infants and children, while at the same time they could still warn children of the need to remain pious in order to be happy "even when dying." The death of children in the New York Refuge was certainly seen as a good opportunity to impress inmates with the frailty of their condition. When John Gillen died on July 18, 1830, "the boys were marched through the Hospital to see the corpse—and in the evening after they were locked up—the Matron brought the girls over to see the cold clay." See Peter G. Slater, "Views of Children and of Child Rearing During the Early National Period: A Study in the New England Intellect" (Ph.D. diss., University of California, Berkeley, 1970), pp. 294–98, and Daily Journal, Vol. II, New York Refuge MS.

32. Beaumont and Tocqueville, pp. 123–24. Later refuges and reform schools often excluded girls entirely; it was not until 1856 that the first institution strictly for female delinquents, the Massachusetts State Industrial School for Girls, was founded. On female philanthropy in the early nineteenth century see Mary B. Treudley, "The 'Benevolent Fair': A Study of Charitable Organizations Among American Women in the First Third of the Nineteenth Century," *Social Service Review* 14 (1940), 509–22, and Keith Melder, "Ladies Bountiful: Organized Women's Benevolence in Early Nineteenth Century America," *New York History* 48 (1967), 231–55.

help provide a separate dormitory to house black children. Superintendent Nathaniel Hart wrote Stephen Allen that an integrated routine
"would be injurious to our institution." British visitor Edward Abdy,
surprised and angered at the discrimination against Negro children,
commented, "It was painful to observe the studied manner in which
the white and colored children were separated and distinguished from
each other, as if moral improvement could be promoted in either
by encouraging pride and inflicting humiliation."[33]

Unconcerned with their own prejudices, refuge managers concentrated on developing institutional routines. Their general purpose was
to save children from lives of crime by inculcating them with middle-
class values—neatness, diligence, punctuality, and thrift. The term
"house of refuge" conveyed the managers' belief in the necessity of
isolating and sheltering children from the wickedness of the world
during the process of instilling these values. In this context, education
meant the learning of proper behavior, not the mastery of specific
skills.

The following typical day in the New York Refuge illustrates how
refuge managers attempted to translate their ideas into a regimen for
training children:

> At sunrise, the children are warned, by the ringing of a bell, to rise
> from their beds. Each child makes his own bed, and steps forth, on a
> signal, into the Hall. They then proceed, in perfect order, to the Wash
> Room. Thence they are marched to parade in the yard, and undergo
> an examination as to their dress and cleanliness; after which, they at-
> tend morning prayer. The morning school then commences, where
> they are occupied in summer, until 7 o'clock. A short intermission is
> allowed, when the bell rings for breakfast; after which, they proceed
> to their respective workshops, where they labor until 12 o'clock,
> when they are called from work, and one hour allowed them for
> washing and eating their dinner. At one, they again commence work,
> and continue at it until five in the afternoon, when the labor of the
> day terminates. Half an hour is allowed for washing and eating their
> supper, and at half-past five, they are conducted to the school room

33. George Wilson Pierson, *Tocqueville and Beaumont in America* (New
York: Oxford, 1938), p. 512. William Darrah Kelley, *Address Delivered at the
Colored Department of the House of Refuge, December 29, 1849* (Philadel-
phia, 1849), p. 7. Nathaniel C. Hart to Stephen Allen, December 17, 1834,
Allen MS. Edward S. Abdy, *Journal of a Residence and Tour in the United
States of North America* (London, 1835), pp. 5, 61.

where they continue at their studies until 8 o'clock. Evening Prayer is performed by the Superintendent; after which, the children are conducted to their dormitories, which they enter, and are locked up for the night, when perfect silence reigns throughout the establishment. The foregoing is the history of a single day, and will answer for every day in the year, except Sundays, with slight variations during stormy weather, and the short days in winter.[34]

Holidays were more relaxing as this extract from the superintendent's journal shows:

> January 1st, 1847. This being New Year's Day, it was devoted to amusements by the children. Mr. McKenna, our teacher . . . prepared several pieces for the children to speak and sing. We repaired to the Chapel at 11 o'clock, and were entertained for two hours with these exercises. Samuel W. Seton, Esq., was present, and added greatly to the entertainment by a well-timed address. The appropriation of the Acting Committee afforded an ample amount of good things to eat; and the day being very fine, the children seemed to enjoy their sports and amusements with great zest.
>
> In addition to the above, Alderman Seaman, who employs about one hundred boys, came over about 3 o'clock with a dinner prepared for the children,—roast turkeys, smoking hot, minced pie and cake.[35]

Refuge officials utilized various types of restraint and corporal punishment to maintain obedience to house rules. They had little conception of group reprimand; i.e., they did not force children to discipline each other under pain of sacrificing privileges for all inmates by failing to do so. The early years of the New York Refuge were especially marked by numerous conspiratorial escape attempts and inmate uprisings, but punishment like reformation proceeded on an individual basis. Superintendent Joseph Curtis, though in theory kindly disposed to children, soon put one boy in leg irons for forty-three days, and another in cloth handcuffs which the boy ate off in order to escape again. Curtis regularly whipped recalcitrant boys like Simon Bellamy ("to bend his spirit") and also punished children who wet their beds, a fairly common mishap in the refuges. The superintendent of the Boston House of Reformation reported, "I

---

34. SRJD, *AR* (1835), pp. 6–7. The routine at the Philadelphia Refuge was almost the same; see *AR* (1834), pp. 19–20.

35. SRJD, *AR* (1847), p. 23.

sometimes apply the shower bath effectually. . . . It is a severe
punishment in cold weather, and much dreaded."[36]

On a more subtle level, refuges maintained internal control by
dividing children into classes based upon their individual behavior and
by instituting trustee systems. A New York Report noted of one boy,
"Since April his conduct has been very good, he has been one of
the guard for some months and has frequently been sent to town
with the cart." Children who obeyed the rules were promoted to higher
classes, which entitled them to privileges such as extra playtime and
also supposedly hastened the day when they became eligible for indenture or release. Thus, as Michael Heale has pointed out, the spirit
of refuge reformatory concepts was as much utilitarian as moral. The
reward and punishment system appealed to the child's self-interest,
not his "better nature," the assumption being that children would
react in mechanical and predetermined ways to given stimuli both
in the institution and after release.[37]

The superintendent's strap was always ready to enforce discipline,
but the demands of the refuge work routine often imposed the necessary degree of order. Boys labored in large workshops either finishing cheap shoes or making brass nails and various types of wicker
work such as cane chairs. Contractors like Alderman Seaman paid
the refuges ten to fifteen cents a day for the labor of one boy, and
the aggregate income from refuge labor usually paid a substantial
part (from 10 to 40 percent, depending upon business conditions) of
institutional operating expenses. During the early years of the refuges,
contractors were not regarded as exploiters of child labor. Indeed,
their patronage was solicited. The depression of 1837–1838 disrupted
the New York Refuge to such a degree that the workshops operated
for less than four months. Manufacturers could not be found "even
to avail themselves of the gratuitous labor of the boys." Control
deteriorated—"a result to be expected, when children were not en-

36. Superintendent's Journal, Vol. I (1825–28), New York Refuge MS. SRJD,
AR (1825), p. 31. Boston, Common Council, *City Doc.* 18 (1841), pp. 40–41.

37. SRJD, *AR* (1825), p. 33. Michael Heale, "Humanitarianism in the Early
Republic: The Moral Reformers of New York, 1776–1825." *Journal of American Studies* 2 (1968), 161-75.

gaged in some constant employment." With the return of prosperity in 1840, chair caning and other employments were resumed.[38]

Refuges utilized the contract system not only to maintain order and to provide revenue but also, according to Philadelphia managers, "to prepare the children to earn their own livelihood, and as soon as they are sufficiently instructed to become valuable apprentices to any particular trade to bind them out, and let their labour be available first to their masters, and afterwards to themselves." This claim implies a more developed labor program than actually existed, since reformatory institutions did not provide vocational training until the last two decades of the century.[39] Louis Dwight, founder of the Boston Prison Discipline Society, observed that the workshop routine, together with Sabbath instruction and a few hours of daily school, provided the milieu in which "characters will be formed for usefulness."[40]

Apprenticeship usually meant placing children with farmers "away from their former companions and thickly spread snares of the city." More often than not, these farms were located in the East—in Pennsylvania, New Jersey, upstate New York, Cape Cod, or Connecticut. Older boys were sometimes indentured to ship captains in the whaling or merchant service on condition that their voyages last at least two years. A few children were apprenticed to skilled tradesmen in the city, and an occasional youth was retained at the refuge as an employee of the local contractor or of the institution itself. James J. Edsall, for example, became the apothecary and bookkeeper of the New York Refuge upon his release. In Philadelphia, one boy was

38. SRJD, *AR* (1838), pp. 11–12. Ibid. (1839), p. 8. Philadelphia Refuge, *AR* (1838), p. 4.

39. Philadelphia Refuge, *AR* (1828), p. 8. Enoch C. Wines and Theodore W. Dwight, *Report on the Prisons and Reformatories of the United States and Canada* (Albany, 1867), pp. 429–30. One of the questions which Wines and Dwight asked of reform school officials was: "Are they [the children] all taught a trade?" The answers were the same: "It is not an object to teach the children a trade; but they all have regular work; and are trained to habits of industry."

40. Boston Prison Discipline Society, *AR* (1827), p. 144. Dwight created this society, and until his death in 1854 it served as a platform for his advocacy of the "congregate" or Auburn system of penal organization. Dwight's publications and those of the Pennsylvania Journal of Prison Discipline (1845), a rival organization, provide a compendium of information on refuges and reform schools.

apprenticed to a former inmate who had opened his own shop. For refuge girls, maid service was the only acceptable type of indenture from the institution except for marriage. To encourage girls in the performance of household chores, John Griscom founded the short-lived Society for the Preservation of Faithful Domestic Servants (1825).[41]

Apprenticeship had, from the point of view of refuge managers, the further advantage of reinforcing institutional parental power *(parens patriae)* by permanently separating children from their siblings and natural parents. As only the institution's officials knew the whereabouts of indentured children, they could and did use discretion in answering inquiries. "If you please," requested a girl from the Philadelphia Refuge, "when you see my sisters, remind them of my love to them. . . . Theodore [her younger brother] often speaks of his father and mother, and wishes to be remembered in particular to his mother. . . ." The Journal of the New York House of Refuge bears this note on April 5, 1847:

> This was Quarterly Visiting day for the relatives and friends of the children, and the day being fair an unusually large number were on the premises. We have parted with a large number of children this spring, and many who came expecting to find children here, went away disappointed, but most of them seemed to bear it well and acted very judiciously.

Not everyone agreed with this assessment. Elijah Devoe, assistant superintendent of the New York Refuge who was fired in 1848 after a dispute with the superintendent, wrote a bitter exposé of the institution. He recalled seeing mothers "leave the house with streaming eyes" because refuge officials refused to divulge the whereabouts of their children.[42]

Various types of apprenticeship accounted for 90 percent of the

41. Minutes of Indenturing Committee (April 10, 1833), New York Refuge MS. SRJD, *AR* (1829), pp. 23–25. Philadelphia Refuge, *AR* (1841), p. 32. Griscom, *Memoir of John Griscom,* p. 163.

42. Philadelphia Refuge, *AR* (1834), p. 36. SRJD, *AR* (1848), p. 25. Elijah Devoe, *The Refuge System, or Prison Discipline Applied to Juvenile Delinquents* (New York, 1848), p. 25n. Nassau W. Senior, *Statement of the Provision for the Poor and of the Condition of the Laboring Classes in a Considerable Portion of America and Europe* (London, 1835), p. 19, contends that overseers of the poor in New York State often employed the same policy, i.e. refusing to tell adult paupers where their children had been placed.

children released each year. Death, escape, and outright release to parents or friends made up the remainder; sometimes an unmalleable or sickly child would be sent to jail or to the almshouse as the case warranted. Masters could and did return apprenticed children, sometimes with cause, as in the case of Thomas Cornelius from the New York Refuge, indentured to a Mr. Candy and "behaving ill indeed injuring his cattle and threatening worse things." "A. B. was this day returned," noted the journal of the New York House, "she has become a real bawd." On the other hand, children were returned simply because they could not work hard enough, and some girls were cashiered after being sexually abused. "Know all *men* who desire girls from the Refuge," wrote Elijah Devoe, "that the utmost care is taken in their discipline to render them *convenient* servants." Thus children continued to live under the control of the refuge even after they had left the institution and, at all times, the parental guidance of the refuge authorities was considered a privilege. In the words of New York Superintendent Nathaniel Hart, "We will be fathers to them if they obey the rules."[43]

Both the philanthropists who organized houses of refuge and other reformers who visited the new institutions deemed them successful. Stephen Allen boasted that most former inmates were "useful and honorable members of society, supporting themselves and families in comfort, some of them possessed of wealth and abundance." Dorothea Dix found the same institution "a blessing to its inmates and to society." Foreign visitors like Tocqueville and Beaumont and the Swedish educator P. A. Siljeström were equally enthusiastic. After visiting all of the refuges, Siljeström concluded that they were "uncommonly well organized, and . . . equally distinguished by the neatness and order which prevail, and by the excellent spirit which directs the endeavors to reclaim the children."[44]

43. Case 2401, Case Histories, Vol. II (1839–1841), New York Refuge MS. SRJD, *AR* (1838), p. 51. Devoe, p. 36. Curtis, quoted in Pickett, *House of Refuge*, p. 144. Sanford J. Fox, "Juvenile Justice Reform: An Historical Perspective," *Stanford Law Review* 22 (1970), 1191–92, characterizes the New York Refuge as "designed to deal with those who were still novices in antisocial conduct." Serious offenders were unwelcome.

44. SRJD, *AR* (1847), p. 9. Dix, p. 94. P. A. Siljeström, *Educational Institutions of the United States* (London, 1853), p. 281. On Tocqueville and Beaumont, see above, pp. 14, 17.

Refuge managers amplified these friendly testimonials in several ways. They informed other, presumably better behaved, children of institutional activities through the emerging medium of literature designed especially for youth. Journals such as *Juvenile Miscellany* (1826), *The Youth's Companion* (1827), *Youth's Cabinet* (1838), and *Youth's Casket* (1851) gave exalted descriptions of the physical plants and routines of the refuges and at the same time used the plight of institutionalized children to warn young readers of the consequences of crime and misbehavior. The refuge managers attempted to influence adults by printing in each annual report scores of favorable letters from farmers who had taken refuge children and from the children themselves. "James is very steady at his trade, improves very fast in school learning, attends a place of worship every Sunday, and is honest and industrious," wrote one master in a typical communication to the Philadelphia Refuge. Even more rewarding were letters from such redeemed children as the boy who left one situation for another because his first master wanted him to sell spirits. The youth testified, "I seem plucked as a brand from the burning. I am a guilty rebel, saved by grace." The boys in the Philadelphia Refuge ostensibly were equally moral. In 1854 the managers reported that they donated part of their meager earnings to missionary societies who by then were busy converting oriental peoples. We may only guess at the degrees of duress applied in such situations. Nevertheless, by saying and doing what was expected of juvenile delinquents who had been reformed, some of the refuge children became accomplices to the missionary purposes of institution founders.[45]

Internal schisms as well as outside criticisms ensured that claims of success did not go uncontested. Controversy between management and administration of the institutions centered around varying attitudes toward the problem of child discipline—attitudes not too different from the modern disputes between advocates of permissive and of disciplinarian upbringing. E. M. P. Wells and Joseph Curtis, the first superintendents of the Boston and New York refuges, were

45. John C. Crandall, "Patriotism and Humanitarian Reform in Children's Literature, 1825–1860," *American Quarterly* 21 (1969), 6–9. Philadelphia Refuge, *AR* (1836), p. 20. SRJD, *AR* (1843), pp. 36–37. Philadelphia Refuge, *AR* (1854), p. 24.

not permissive by today's standards, but they were humane men, more interested in developing each child's individual capacities and talents through programs emphasizing self-government and education than in compelling children to follow an inflexible workshop routine. Both men had been influenced by the Swiss educator Johann Pestalozzi, who emphasized individual development and self-realization as the core of the educative experience. Because workshop facilities were not at first available in the two refuges, Wells and Curtis were relatively free to follow their inclinations. Curtis instituted a trustee system letting the boys leave the refuge on errands. He allowed the better behaved boys to form a jury which recommended action on the minor infractions of the other children; he claimed, *"this liberty, this confidence,* this respect which we give to the honor of the subjects is the key to open to the benighted mind a light which shows the path to manhood and respectability." When the managers urged him to employ the whip more liberally, Curtis warned them "so long as [the children] are impressed with the idea that this institution is a prison . . . you will be disappointed in the finishing of your labors." Wells, an Episcopal minister, also instituted a jury and minimized corporal punishment. He required delinquents to grade their own conduct, which they did severely. Because there were no workshops in the Boston House of Reformation, the children spent six hours a day in school.[46]

Neither the Curtis nor the Wells regime suited the tastes of their employers. The managers of the New York Refuge, dismayed by the high escape rate and general disorder of the house, forced Curtis to resign when he refused their demand that he punish a returning escapee. Of this incident Curtis remarked, "I do not believe that the mind of a human being can be brought to that quiet and progressive state of respect for himself and others while the body is suffering punishment." Although a majority of the directors of the Boston House of Reformation supported the educational program of Wells,

46. Catherine M. Sedgwick, *Memoir of Joseph Curtis, A Model Man* (New York, 1858), pp. 65–71, 100, 102. On Wells, see Beaumont and Tocqueville, pp. 114–22, and Pickett, pp. 89–93. John M. Keagy, first superintendent of the Philadelphia Refuge, was also a Pestalozzian. See Negley K. Teeters, "The Early Days of the Philadelphia House of Refuge," *Pennsylvania History* 27 (1960), 165–87.

one dissident, Isaac Waters, claimed that Wells was no more capable of running the institution than "your horse." Waters instigated an investigation by a committee of the Common Council which attempted to demonstrate the educational deficiencies of the institution's children and the fiscal need to begin a workhouse program. Wells resigned after a number of new directors were appointed by the Council in 1834.[47]

The managers of the two institutions prevailed in their disciplinarian way. The Boston directors assured the Common Council that they had "no disposition to convert the House of Reformation into a boarding-school, to be supported at the expense of the city. They do not forget that its inmates are offenders against the good order of society, and are sent there for restraint and punishment not less than for reformation and instruction." Cadwallader Colden admonished Nathaniel C. Hart, Curtis' successor, "I know from your character that the children . . . will meet with every indulgence they can claim. If any caution on this head were necessary, it would be that they should be treated as that they may not forget that they are placed here for their misdeeds." The New York refuge managers were pleased with Hart whose own guide to child discipline, he confided to Stephen Allen, was Solomon.[48]

Pestalozzi's heritage to American children—the reduction of physical punishment in common schools—left little impression in the houses of refuge and later reform schools. Curtis and Wells were anomalies in the refuge world. In the romantic tradition, they believed that the essence of juvenile reformation lay in the cultivation of a child's essentially good qualities and sentiments. Refuge managers, on the other hand, saw children as blank tablets upon whom parents and acquaintances had already made enough unfavorable impressions to lead the children to the institution. What these youths needed, the managers argued, was an inflexible routine built around the work-

47. Sedgwick, pp. 94–106. *Report of the Standing Committee of the Common Council to Investigate the House of Reformation* (Boston, 1832). Directors of the Boston House of Reformation, *Remarks on a Report of the Standing Committee of the Common Council* (Boston, 1833).

48. Boston Common Council, *City Doc.* 6 (1834), Report of the Directors of the House of Reformation, p. 4. SRJD, *AR* (1826), p. 44. Hart to Allen (December 17, 1834), Allen MS.

shop and the schoolroom, impressing them with the importance of personal cleanliness, sobriety, frugality, and industry. Punishment would be the invariable result of rule violations. In this scheme, pious and orderly conduct by an individual child signified the success of reformatory methods; good behavior meant everything, noble thoughts little.

Elijah Devoe's inside story of "the refuge system" illumines the disputes between institution managers on the one hand and Curtis and Wells on the other. Taking into account Devoe's obvious prejudice against the management and administration of the New York Refuge, we may still believe that his pamphlet expressed feelings shared by others, and therefore some measure of truth. His characterization of the refuge's annual reports as "tautological eulogies and pompous puffs," for example, agrees with the view of William Crawford, the English prison commissioner who visited in 1834. Summarizing the methods of control used by the institution, Devoe wrote:

> Nothing short of excessive ignorance can entertain for a moment the idea that the inmates of the Refuge are contented. In summer, they are about fourteen hours under orders daily. On parade, at table, at their work, and in school, they are not allowed to converse. They rise at five o'clock in summer—are hurried into the yard—hurried into the dining-room—hurried at their work and at their studies. For every trifling commission or omission which it is deemed wrong to do or to omit to do, they are "cut" with rattan. Every day they experience a series of painful excitements. The endurance of the whip, or the loss of a meal—deprivation of play or the solitary cell. On every hand their walk is bounded; while Restriction and Constraint are their most intimate companions. Are they contented?[49]

Devoe's sympathetic accounts of refuge children—stories which reflected the loneliness and misery of their lives—showed a side of institution life seldom glimpsed in official documents. In marked contrast to other refuge officials, who saw only individual wrongdoers, Devoe noticed individual personalities and to a remarkable degree understood the problems and needs of the children. He recalled "a quaint little boy who would go about the yard with dozens of live beetles, and other bugs, thrust inside his shirt-bosom next to his skin.

49. Devoe, pp. 12, 27–28. On Crawford see Pickett, pp. 168–70.

He was somewhat solitary in his habits. . . . But he had a social, communicative spirit in his way, for he made himself friends with creeping things and held converse with them." Another boy, peering out of a grated workshop window at the bleak waterfront surrounding the refuge, said to Devoe "with naive earnestness and a delectable lisp, 'That lookths good out there, Mr. D———.' " Devoe wrote about other subjects which the managers never discussed. He told of "certain associations known to exist between large and small boys for the most degrading and health destroying vices," and the practice of publicly humiliating children who wet their beds by announcing their names in the dining hall. In replying to Devoe's question about what he disliked about the refuge, one boy probably reflected the sentiments of others when he said, "after the cat and the rattan, cold cells in winter, hot cells in summer, and bed bugs."[50]

Knowing of such treatment and conditions gives us additional understanding of the violence which periodically wracked the refuges. In 1830 an officer of the New York Refuge suffered a severe knife wound while helping to thwart a mass escape effort. On October 22, 1846, the Philadelphia Refuge reported that a boy had stabbed Samuel King, foreman in the cane shop. This inmate was sent to jail, tried, and imprisoned. Eight years later, one of his fellows burned the cane-seating factory to the ground. Small wonder then that authoress Lydia Maria Child (1802–1880) discovered many refuge children in the New York City penitentiary (Blackwell's Island).[51]

At the Boston House of Reformation, the fight between the city government and Reverend Wells was only the beginning. The disciplinary practices at this smallest of the three refuges were excessive even for those days. So damaging was it for children to be known as inmates of this institution, that magistrates at one point refused to commit them. After the passage of a state truancy law in 1850, the Boston House was filled to capacity, but with errant school children

50. Devoe, pp. 64, 65, 72, 74, 48. Stephen Allen complained annually about the "harmful effects" of keeping older boys in the refuges: SRJD, *AR* (1844), pp. 9–11.

51. John Luckey, *Life in Sing-Sing State Prison as Seen in a Twelve Years' Chaplaincy* (New York, 1860), pp. 65–66. Philadelphia Refuge, *AR* (1847), p. 5, and *AR* (1855), pp. 6, 26. Lydia Maria Child, *Letters from New York*, 3d ed. (New York, 1845), p. 204.

instead of youths who had committed felonies or the like. The Common Council attempted to close it in 1841 by transferring more tractable delinquents to the Boylston School, a city institution for dependent children. Incorrigible children were to be sent to the Boston House of Correction—that is, to jail. The directors of the House of Reformation, under the leadership of Samuel Gridley Howe, the city's most prominent philanthropist, rejected the Council's plan, reminding it of Josiah Quincy's original edict to separate and classify the dependent classes and then to treat each according to its own need. The directors summarized, "The two classes of children are different: the end to be kept in view of their treatment is different, and the whole establishment should be different."[52]

Continued life for the Boston House of Reformation meant only continued failure. Howe resigned from the board of directors and commenced an attack upon all institutions as pernicious to the welfare of children. By the 1850s, as we shall see, different types of state-operated institutions were taking over the care of delinquent children in Massachusetts, but even with a narrowed scope, the Boston House failed to function. State prison inspectors filed a report in 1863 calling it, "too much of a prison, too little an institution of instruction, too much the residence of law and punishment, too little the home of grace and culture." Although the Boston House of Reformation continued to exist, this report was, in effect, its epitaph.[53]

In the light of these disruptive events, we may ask why refuge managers continued to claim great successes for their institutions. Possibly enough children met their behavioral standards to enable them to discount both inmate uprisings and the pathetic personal histories such as those recounted by Devoe. My sample of one hundred case histories taken from a two-year period (1839–1841) in the New York Refuge indicates that 40 percent of the children either absconded

52. Michael B. Katz, *The Irony of Urban School Reform: Educational Innovation in Mid-Nineteenth Century Massachusetts* (Cambridge: Harvard University Press, 1968), p. 167. Lane, *Policing the City,* p. 62. Boston Common Council, *City Doc.* 14 (1841), pp. 18–22.

53. Boston Common Council, *Report of Committee Appointed to Investigate Alleged Abuses at the House of Reformation and House of Correction* (Boston, 1864), pp. 22–23.

from their situations or were repeatedly returned to the refuge.[54]
Perhaps refuge officials would not have viewed such figures with
alarm. They considered their refuge philanthropy a hazardous un-
dertaking in the first place. A New York report warned, "When all
the faculties of the mind have for years been accustomed to flow in a
vicious and corrupt channel, how difficult a task to arrest them in
their downward course, and cause them to flow back in an exactly
opposite direction."[55] Therefore, any cases which turned out satis-
factorily were construed to be the result of refuge care and discipline.
More important, refuge managers believed in the value of their institutions because they could not conceive of themselves as being involved
in *any* philanthropy which might fail. Imbued with the high moral
purpose of attending to the destitute and delinquent children of their
communities, they saw the "success" of the refuges as a natural con-
comitant of their initial commitment. The mere designation of some
children as delinquents and their incarceration in the refuges provided
the managers with sufficient assurance of their own rectitude no matter
how many inmates were or were not improved by the experience.

Early refuge managers must have communicated their enthusiasm
to other philanthropists, for by 1850 a number of other municipal
and state institutions for juvenile delinquents were either in the planning stage or had been opened. Ceremonies at the new institutions
invariably paid tribute to the first refuges and usually reflected the
same concern which had aroused the original philanthropists—the
need to remove children from jail and the even greater need to teach
them the value of thrift, honesty, and individual responsibility.[56]

54. Five groups of twenty cases each, selected at random throughout the two-
year period, were studied in detail. The number of children who "failed," i.e.
either absconded after behaving poorly or were returned to the refuge, was as
follows: 8 (40%); 5 (25%); 10 (50%); 6 (30%); 11 (55%). Total 40/100
or 40%.

55. SRJD, *AR* (1848), p. 15.

56. Among the institutions opened around the midcentury: House of Refuge,
New Orleans (1847); State Reform School (boys), Westborough, Massachu-
setts (1847); Western House of Refuge, Rochester, New York (1849); Colored
House of Refuge, Philadelphia (1850); House of Refuge, Cincinnati (1850);
New York Juvenile Asylum (1853); Children's Aid Society, New York (1853);
Western House of Refuge, Pittsburgh (1854); State Industrial School (girls),
Lancaster, Massachusetts (1856); Ohio Reform School, Lancaster, Ohio
(1857).

Although the proliferation of reform schools bespoke the failure of houses of refuge to prevent the growth of juvenile delinquency by reforming delinquents, it also reflected the spread of a need to find certain children and identify them as a special class of deviants called juvenile delinquents. Growth of different sorts was a marked feature of American life in the second half of the nineteenth century. War, industrialization, and immigration quickened the pace of urban life in midwest as well as seaboard cities. Children continued to be sent to jail for petty offenses, and the number of juvenile crimes and juvenile delinquents continued to increase. In 1849 New York Chief of Police George Matsell warned of "constantly increasing numbers of vagrant, idle and vicious children of both sexes . . . who are growing up in ignorance and profligacy, only destined to a life of misery, shame and crime, and ultimately to a felon's doom."[57]

This warning—indeed, this report—could easily have been written thirty years earlier by the members of the Society for the Prevention of Pauperism. The Society for the Reformation of Juvenile Delinquents, lineal descendants of the SPP, perceived the conditions that Matsell described as warrant to build a newer and larger institution on Randall's Island in the East River. There they could apply more systematically the reformatory regime which they believed had been so successful. Some public reform schools imitated the congregate organization of early refuges but other institutions initiated different types of programs to reform delinquent children.

The efforts of older institutions to cope with what they regarded as an expanding problem, the attempts of state institutions to combine traditional methods and new concepts, and the different ideas about juvenile delinquency of midcentury philanthropists—these developments defined attitudes and policies toward juvenile delinquency in the later nineteenth century.

57. Bremner, *Children and Youth in America,* I, 755.

CHAPTER 2

Preventive Agencies and Reform Schools, 1850–1890

Police Chief Matsell's 1849 report warning of the increase of juvenile delinquency in New York City found a receptive public. Citizens such as Phoebe Palmer, Lewis Pease, Charles Loring Brace, Samuel Gridley Howe, and Rufus Cook did not require much urging to begin a variety of works on behalf of juvenile delinquents. They translated their concern into action by founding a variety of philanthropic organizations. The most prominent of these—the Children's Mission to the Children of the Destitute (1849), the Five Points Mission (1850), the New York Juvenile Asylum (1851), the New York Children's Aid Society (1853)—found imitators in other cities.[1]

These philanthropists and their organizations approached the problem of juvenile delinquency from viewpoints markedly different from those of the refuge founders. Charles Loring Brace, for example, saw the explanation of both poverty and delinquency as emanating, at least in part, from degraded environmental circumstances. "People don't get a fair chance in life, and very few do anything to help them to it," he wrote to Theodore Parker. Brace never referred to children as "convicts" or "depraved young persons"—traditional refuge terms

---

1. R. Richard Wohl, "The 'Country Boy' Myth and Its Place in American Urban Culture: The Nineteenth-Century Contribution," *Perspectives in American History* 3 (1969), 108, estimates the spread of organizations similar to the New York Children's Aid Society. Wohl died in 1957. This article was edited for publication by Moses Rischin.

implying at least some degree of innate wickedness. The popular author Ned Buntline (E. Z. C. Judson) also portrayed delinquent children as victims not of their own sinfulness but of slum life. Horace Mann's refusal to purchase from the American Sunday School Union religious tracts and books emphasizing the close connection between trivial juvenile offenses and eternal damnation was but another indication of the faltering appeal of the concept of innate depravity as an explanation for juvenile delinquency.[2]

The newer philanthropists may have been skeptical of Calvinistic theories of man's fallibility, but their own religiosity cannot be questioned. Indeed, the evangelical fervor with which they undertook child-saving work is one of their defining characteristics. Charles Loring Brace wrote, "It often seems to me that if I could begin to convey to men what Christ did to me, even as He did, I would so gladly: for what is suffering or deprivation or death if one could only be sure we were raising the outcast and helpless?"[3] In a similar spirit Phoebe Palmer of the Ladies Home Missionary Society of the Methodist Episcopal Church founded the Five Points Mission, which took its name from one of the poorest sections of New York. Drawing upon the ideas of Thomas Guthrie, founder of the British "ragged schools," the Mission initially concentrated on proselytizing the poor and providing vagrant and destitute children with rudimentary common schooling. Reverend Lewis Pease, mission director, realizing the limitations of this approach, began to make food and clothing distributions and introduced contract shirt manufacturing into the gospel center during the day. To dramatize his personal witness of the problems of the poor, Pease and his wife moved their home into Five Points and opened their own mission, the Five Points House of Industry. Disdaining remoter forms of charity, Pease recognized that circumstances beyond individual control were segregating the poor into less desirable neighborhoods. The Protestant churches had re-

2. Emma Brace, ed., *The Life of Charles Loring Brace: Chiefly Told in His Own Letters* (London, 1894), p. 180. Ned Buntline (E. Z. C. Judson), *The G'Hals of New York* (New York, n.d.), p. 15. On Mann see Griffen, *Their Brothers' Keepers*, pp. 137–39.

3. *Life of Brace,* p. 179.

moved from these areas along with their affluent parishioners.[4] Brace, in his letter to Parker, spoke on this point:

> It does surprise me, as I look round in our city, to see the general aspect of men who profess to be especial ambassadors of Christ. There are not half a dozen of the whole number who have ever even traversed the poorest streets of the city. . . . They do not lead a single great enterprise of humanity; and they do help the universal American mind to become swallowed up in its formalism.

In another letter Brace concluded, "I do think that Christianity now needs a reformation, as much as it did in Luther's time."[5]

The urgency inherent in Christian mission was accentuated by the philanthropists' heightened fear of the consequences of inaction. As a young man touring Europe, Brace had visited Johann Hinrich Wichern, leader of the Inner Mission in Hamburg, Germany. Wichern impressed Brace by warning him that the urban masses would become reckless revolutionaries if their misery were not alleviated. The poor and their children thus became the "dangerous classes" about whom Brace was to worry so much in the years to come. "Talk of heathen!" he wrote to his friend Fred Kingsbury, "All the pagans of Golconda would not hold a light to the ragged, cunning, forsaken, godless, keen devilish boys of Leonard Street and the Five Points. . . . Our future voters, and President-makers, and citizens! Good Lord deliver us, and help them!"[6] More than the refuge founders, Brace and his colleagues recognized and feared the danger of letting the discontents of the lower classes go unattended.

4. Timothy L. Smith, *Revivalism and Social Reform: American Protestantism on the Eve of the Civil War* (New York: Abingdon Press, 1957), pp. 168–71. On "ragged schools" see J. J. Tobias, *Crime and Industrial Society in the 19th Century* (New York: Schocken, 1967), pp. 173, 175–76, and Wiley B. Sanders, ed., *Juvenile Offenders for a Thousand Years*, pp. 202–13. On the relationship between American Protestantism and the slums in the nineteenth century see Carroll Smith Rosenberg, *Religion and the Rise of the American City: The New York City Mission Movement, 1812–1870* (Ithaca: Cornell University Press, 1971); Aaron I. Abell, *The Urban Impact on American Protestantism, 1865–1900* (Cambridge: Harvard University Press, 1943); and Henry F. May, *Protestant Churches and Industrial America* (New York: Harper and Row, 1949).

5. *Life of Brace,* pp. 181, 178.

6. Wohl, pp. 112–14. *Life of Brace,* pp. 178–79. See also Charles Loring Brace, *The Dangerous Classes of New York and Twenty Years' Work Among Them* (New York, 1872).

Although the new philanthropists were afraid of urban lower-class disorder, their awareness of its pervasiveness made them suspicious of plans for institutions resembling the houses of refuge, which, they believed, overemphasized the period of incarceration required to teach children how to behave. In their minds, the great numbers of neglected street waifs precluded such schemes, and, equally important, they saw little indication that the institutional approach was having its desired effect. Edward Crapsey in his exposé, *The Nether Side of New York* (1872), bemoaned "the huddling of children in public reformatories" and "the old semi-penal system." Mrs. Louisa Harris, a police matron in St. Louis during the 1880s, summarized the anti-institutional feeling: "I don't like the terms 'Poorhouse,' 'House of Refuge,' 'Magdalen Asylum,' 'Slum-Missions,' nor 'Training Schools.' These all bear upon their faces reproach or criminality."[7]

Philanthropists of the new child-saving organizations were inspired by the quite traditional belief that the family, not the institution, was the best reform school. They thought that delinquency would largely disappear if their societies collected vagrant and destitute slum children and placed them out with farm families on the expanding and developing middle border. "Placing-out" describes an informal procedure whereby child-saving societies employed agents to take groups of children west by railroad. In the various towns along the way, children were given to families as each agent saw fit. No apprenticeship or binding-out agreement was involved. The New York Children's Aid Society was the primary proponent of immediate placing-out, while the New York Juvenile Asylum and the Boston Children's Aid Society maintained institutions to discipline children, usually for about six months, prior to sending them to their new homes.

Charles Loring Brace (1826–1890), founder of the New York Children's Aid Society, shaped the philanthropy to conform to his own ideas. As a student, Brace had begun to train for the ministry but

7. Crapsey, *The Nether Side of New York* (New York, 1872), p. 127. Louisa Harris, *Behind the Scenes: Or Nine Years at the Four Courts of Saint Louis* (St. Louis, 1893), pp. 22–23. These were but two of a genre of sensational books purporting to tell all about life in the large cities of the United States. Foremost among the others were James D. McCabe [Edward Winslow Martin], *The Secrets of the Great City* (Chicago and Philadelphia, 1868); McCabe, *New York by Sunlight and Gaslight* (Chicago and Philadelphia, 1882); and Helen Campbell, *Darkness and Daylight* (Hartford, Conn., 1891).

soon lost interest in the arid debates that characterized the Yale
curriculum of the 1840s. Turning to charitable work, he served as a
missionary to prisoners on Blackwell's Island [New York City] and as
an assistant to Lewis Pease in the Five Points. There, in the pinched
faces of street gamins, he discovered his life's vocation—"child-
saving."

Brace's visit to Germany in 1850–51 helped him to focus his approach. Impressed with the "good sense and good feeling" of German
middle-class family life, he began to think of juvenile delinquents as
victimized children who, for reasons of want or neglect, had been
denied this protection. The lack of care was especially noticeable and,
in Brace's view, dangerous in the slum areas where the pressures of
urban life demoralized parents and freed children of family control.
The child-saving task was, therefore, twofold: to detach street children from the urban environment and to attach them to American
farm families whose influence, Brace somewhat naively assumed,
would approximate the morality, geniality, and humanity he found
characteristic of the German family.[8]

Brace's faith in the redeeming power of family life was derived
in part from Horace Bushnell's Doctrine of Christian Nurture. At
Yale, Bushnell's lectures had thrilled Brace as nothing else did. In
Views of Christian Nurture (1847), Bushnell employed organic
analogies—the parent was "God's gardener"—to emphasize the importance of parents demonstrating not only their piety but their feelings and sensitivity in order to mold their child's character and to
extend God's grace to him or her. Brace and many other philanthropists of his day subscribed to Bushnell's ideas. They believed that
there were social causes of crime and delinquency, but they saw the
reformatory process proceeding almost entirely in individual terms.
The family, which Bushnell called "God's Reformatory," nurtured the
child to accept God through Christ and live by His teachings. The
child was neither inherently depraved nor essentially good; he was
redeemable.[9]

8. Wohl, pp. 112–13.

9. Sandford Fleming, *Children and Puritanism: The Place of Children in the
Life and Thought of the New England Churches, 1620–1847* (New Haven:
Yale University Press, 1933), pp. 203–206. Slater, "Views of Children and

When Brace began the Children's Aid Society in 1853, he made
the common missionary error of emphasizing "Boys' Sunday Prayer
Meetings"—gatherings where Protestant clergymen exhorted street
waifs to lead pious and frugal lives. Henry Ward Beecher was able
to hold their interest with "A Gospel of the Rowdies," but often
the children disbanded these meetings with the riotous cry, "Gas!
Gas!"[10] Realizing that something more concrete was needed to improve the children's welfare, Brace established newsboys' lodging
houses where homeless and vagrant youths could purchase cheaply
a bunk and a bath. He also founded a number of industrial missions
throughout the city where children, mostly "needy and ragged little
girls," received free meals and learned how to make clothes.[11]

For Brace, however, the important task in the struggle against
destitution and delinquency was "draining the city" of poor and delinquent children. He had no doubt as to where the drain should empty.
"The founders of the Children's Aid Society," he recalled, "early
saw that the best of all Asylums for the outcast child is the *farmer's
home* . . . the cultivators of the soil are in America our most solid
and intelligent class . . . their laborers or 'help,' must be members
of their families, and share in their social tone." No one believed in
the agrarian myth more fervently than Brace. He conceived of the
farming life as a great opportunity for slum children. He recounted
this speech (missing its ironic flavor) of one of his "westernized"
newsboys to fellow newsies: "Do you want to be newsboys always,
and shoe blacks, and timber merchants in a small way selling

Child Rearing During the Early National Period" (Ph.D. diss., Berkeley, 1970),
pp. 148–57. For Brace's religious views see Charles Loring Brace, *Short Ser-
mons to News Boys* (New York, 1866).

10. Quoted in Miriam Z. Langsam, *Children West: A History of the Placing-
Out System in the New York Children's Aid Society, 1853–1890* (Madison,
Wis.: University of Wisconsin Press, 1964), p. 3. The report on Beecher's
sermon was as follows: "The power of his speech was in its broad common-
sense and humor, and when, once or twice, he let himself ascend to one of
his poetic similes, the ripple of feeling passed over the eager faces as percepti-
bly, as the ruffle of still water under a puff of the south wind" (NYCAS, *AR*
(1860), pp. 39–40).

11. Brace, *The Dangerous Classes,* pp. 132–46. Brace despaired of vagrant
girls: "Except by our schools, we don't get hold of the poor girls much. It does
seem as if everything in heaven and earth was against the improvement of the
girls in our poor classes." See Wohl, p. 177.

matches? If ye do you'll stay in New York, but if you don't you'll go out West, and begin to be farmers, for the beginning of a farmer, my boys, is the making of a Congressman, and a President."[12]

Brace's placing-out idea should be considered in relation to the social and economic anxieties which plagued the New York mercantile community of his day. Many local merchants believed that they were threatened not only by the depredations of the children of the "dangerous classes," but also by the presence of hordes of aggressive young clerks seeking wealth and status through acuteness in the ways of the countinghouse. According to Allan Horlick, established businessmen feared that their clerks were absorbed in the pursuit of riches to the point of ignoring benevolent or stewardship duties which the merchants saw as necessary ingredients of social status within the community. Concerned that success was no longer being defined in traditional terms, merchants sponsored the publication of advice manuals for young men, which stressed, among other things, that novice clerks would replace, not displace, present business leaders. In the 1840s and 1850s, businessmen also required phrenology tests for prospective employees that could be used to channel or even restrict the opportunities of young clerks. Thus the work of Brace and the Children's Aid Society can be seen as complementing these conservative efforts not only by removing from the local scene children whom merchants considered bothersome, but by setting an example of charitable concern, which those who pretended to future community leadership would do well to emulate.[13]

The New York Children's Aid Society was a state-chartered though privately controlled philanthropic organization whose activities, including placing-out, were not subject to public regulation. The society received public cooperation, however, because policemen often released children to its care and municipal officials looked with favor upon the placing-out policy. The CAS did not forcibly abduct vagrant children from the Five Points, but the organization's agents were

12. *The Dangerous Classes,* pp. 225, 111-12.

13. Allan S. Horlick, "Countinghouses and Clerks: The Social Control of Young Men in New York, 1840–1860" (Ph.D. diss., University of Wisconsin, 1969), and Horlick, "Phrenology and the Social Education of Young Men," *History of Education Quarterly* 11 (1971), 23–28. On phrenology and juvenile delinquency, see below, pp. 78–79.

vigorous persuaders, and many a reluctant newsboy or match girl was sent West as a result of their zeal. Untroubled by the anguish which this procedure caused children and, in some cases at least, their parents too, Brace pursued his idea enthusiastically. "If enough families can be found to serve as reformatory institutions, is it not the best and most practical and economical method of reforming these children?" he asked rhetorically.[14]

Under the chaperonage of a clergyman or society agent the trip west was eventful. An early expedition included "a clever little black boy," the group flagbearer, who, we are told, "enjoyed his importance much, and his appearance marshalling the little host, everywhere attracted attention." The sight of the children induced "unsolicited donations from our fellow-passengers," according to Agent C. C. Tracy. The group was often given free passage by charitable railroad officials. Upon arriving in a major settlement, the business of placing-out commenced. This report from Kalamazoo, Michigan, in 1856 is representative:

> Our village has been astir for a few days. Saturday afternoon, Mr. C. C. Tracy arrived with a party of children from the Children's Aid Society in New York. . . .
> Sabbath day Mr. Tracy spoke day and evening, three times, in different church edifices to crowded and interested audiences. In the evening, the children were present in a body, and sang their "Westward Ho" song. Notice was given that applicants could find the unappropriated children at the store of Carder & Ryder, at nine o'clock Monday morning. Before the hour arrived a great crowd assembled, and in two hours *every child was disposed of,* and more were wanted.
>
> We *Wolverines* will never forget Mr. Tracy's visit. It has cost us some tears of sympathy, some dollars, and some smiles. We wish him a safe return to Gotham, and a speedy one to us with the new company of destitute children, for whom good homes are even now prepared.

The report added, somewhat ominously, "The call is mostly for girls from nine to twelve."[15]

It is difficult to estimate how well the children liked their new

14. Second Convention of Managers and Superintendents of Houses of Refuge and Schools of Reform, *Proceedings* (1859), p. 48.

15. NYCAS, *AR* (1857), pp. 30–31.

homes. The society kept only informal tabs on the former street waifs, assuming that relocation with a farm family would automatically cure their behavioral problems. Richard Wohl has pointed out that Brace believed that "a decent trust in human nature and in the wholesome effects of farm life should . . . make both parties [child and family] content."[16] The children themselves sometimes wrote letters confirming this view. One girl wrote in 1861:

> My Dear Friend: . . . To-day Mrs. W——and I were talking of what a change four years have wrought upon me; then I was in New York, a poor girl, ignorant, destitute of all common sense. To look back now, I would not for anything exchange my situation for what it was then. If I took up a book or paper, I could no more read it than if it was French, but now I can read almost as well as any of my age.

Other children, however, inquired plaintively of the whereabouts of brothers and sisters and conveyed the impression that their own lives were hard. M.T. reported, "Father and mother work like work-hands, and are very industrious, and learn their children how to work; they don't like to see idle people."[17]

Brace occasionally gave the impression that placing-out was practicable only in the United States. He once wrote, "The United States have an enormous advantage over all other countries, in the treatment of difficult questions of pauperism and reform, that they possess a practically unlimited area of arable land." Brace obviously believed in the safety valve theory which Frederick Jackson Turner later described as a powerful factor in shaping the identity of those who called themselves Americans. From this point of view, open lands in the West existed to absorb and redeem, economically, morally, and socially, the impoverished masses enduring life in the cities of the east coast.[18]

Brace was wrong to consider placing-out an exclusively American practice. In the 1860s, Miss Annie Macpherson and other English philanthropists began to place children in the Colonies, principally in Canada. "We cannot rid ourselves of our adult pauperism," said Miss

16. Wohl, p. 117.
17. NYCAS, *AR* (1862), pp. 50, 54.
18. Brace, *The Dangerous Classes,* p. 225.

Macpherson, "but we can save the children if we resolve to do so; there is a boundless field in the colonies for planting out these neglected ones." Dr. Thomas John Barnardo not only established homes for deserted and neglected street children in England, but sent "Barnardo Girls" to Canada and Australia.[19] Australia had received children sentenced to criminal transportation since the late eighteenth century, but as this fate was usually reserved for the most recalcitrant, few children collected by placing-out charities were sent there until the later nineteenth century.[20]

Placing-out was practiced elsewhere in the United States, too. In Boston, the idea found enthusiastic support. One of the most unusual placing-out agencies, the Children's Mission to the Children of the Destitute (1849), even preceded Brace's efforts.[21] Founded by Unitarian clergymen, the Mission maintained a temporary home from which children were passed on to jobs and foster homes. The home was maintained in part by the contributions of more affluent children in the Unitarian Sunday schools of Boston. The children whom the mission collected were delinquent only in the technical sense of the

19. Macpherson quoted in George C. Needham, *Street Arabs and Gutter Snipes: The Pathetic and Humorous Side of Young Vagabond Life in the Great Cities* (Boston, 1884), pp. 281–309. J. Wesley Bready, *Dr. Bernardo* (London: George Allen and Unwin, 1930). Educator Henry Barnard used both his *American Journal of Education* and a special collection of reports to inform Brace and other Americans about the origin and development of reform schools in Europe during the nineteenth century. See Henry Barnard, *Reformatory Education: Papers on Preventive, Correctional, and Reformatory Institutions and Agencies in Different Countries* (Hartford, Conn., 1857).

20. Sanders, pp. 69, 135–36. Tobias, pp. 211–14. W. Branch Johnson, *The English Prison Hulks* (London: Christopher Johnson, 1957), pp. 146–56. A. G. L. Shaw, *Convicts and the Colonies* (London: Faber and Faber, 1966), pp. 30, 160–63, 243–44, 284–86. In the 1820s, a spirited controversy over the value of criminal transportation was carried on in the United States. The New York Society for the Prevention of Pauperism opposed transportation "to any distant spot, beyond the jurisdiction of municipal authorities" as a threat to "existing moral and civil institutions." James Mease, a supporter of the Philadelphia House of Refuge, argued that the purchase of a group of islands in the South Atlantic would be a desirable place to send second-time offenders and black convicts. See SPP, *Report on the Penitentiary System in the United States*, pp. 78–79. James Mease, *On the Penitentiary and Penal Code of Philadelphia* (Philadelphia, 1828), pp. 19–20, 35–39. See also Harry Elmer Barnes, "Transportation of Criminals," in *Encyclopedia of Social Sciences*, XV, 90–93.

21. Now known as Parents' and Children's Services of Children's Mission, 329 Longwood Avenue, West Roxbury.

word. "Patrick B., 13 years . . . has been idle around the streets for months, and his parents fear that he would get into trouble . . . Richard B., 15 years—has been absent from school several months, his mother represented him to be a very disobedient boy . . . Sarah R., 10 years of age . . . found in the street begging for work" read typical entries in the mission's records.[22]

Samuel Gridley Howe (1801–1876), Boston's leading philanthropist, also shared Brace's views on juvenile delinquency. Once a director of the Boston House of Reformation, Howe had come to distrust the reformative or curative powers of all centralized institutions. He had broken down the large and congregate Perkins School for the Blind into cottage units in order to separate the sexes and better classify the students. He had in mind an even more radical curative plan for the blind "and indeed for several other classes of youth" when he wrote, "The larger a community of infirm or defective persons is, the more they act upon each other; the more salient become the particularities flowing out of their infirmity; the more they become like each other and the more unlike ordinary persons— hence the less fitted for ordinary society."[23]

Of the Boston House of Reformation Howe remembered "that some of the most satisfactory cases of reformation . . . were those effected out of the House, and in families, after the Institution had failed to do them any good." In 1854 Howe proposed unsuccessfully that the Massachusetts State Reformatory for Girls, then in its planning stage, be developed as a placement agency where, "the first business of the Superintendent would be to procure places in suitable families for the girls as fast as they should be sent to him." Families were "the *natural reform schools* existing in the Commonwealth." Like Brace, Howe doubted that most juvenile delinquents were as bad as they were made out to be. "Ah! this imaginary line between the

22. Unpublished records, Children's Mission. Sunday schools increasingly became adjuncts to middle-class churches. Members of missions, as the word implies, were meant to go elsewhere in order to convert and help—in this case, slum children.

23. Draft of undated (185?) article on the education of handicapped children, folders 1411 and 1412, Samuel Gridley Howe Papers, Houghton Library, Harvard University.

righteous and sinners!" he wrote to Horace Mann. "Of how much uncharitableness and wrong is it in origin."[24]

The Boston Children's Aid Society (1864), unlike its New York counterpart, maintained a home to discipline children before placing them out. Located on Pine Farm in suburban Newton, the home emphasized agricultural work and family living and thus attempted to simulate the environment into which most of the children would find themselves placed. But the Boston society's greatest claim to originality in dealing with delinquent children lay in the fact that it greatly enhanced a rudimentary system of juvenile probation begun in the Suffolk County Court [Boston] years earlier.

John Augustus (1785–1859) was a shoemaker who had no official position with the Boston courts. Indeed, in 1841 when he began providing bail for men convicted of drunkenness, he was made to feel officially unwelcome. In his simple, practical way Augustus kept many people out of jail. He also sympathized with the plight of child offenders. "During the year 1846," he wrote, "I became bail to the amount of about $3000, in the Police Court. . . . That year I became surety for eleven boys, who were arrested for larceny; they were young, being from nine to thirteen years old." Augustus supervised the children throughout their probation—sometimes he got them jobs or provided clothing and temporary shelter. He often paid court costs at the expiration of their sentences.[25]

After Augustus' death, his work was taken up by Rufus R. Cook, chaplain of the Suffolk County Jail. "Uncle" Cook consented to act as the agent of the Boston Children's Aid Society soon after its founding in 1864. The society's members were dissatisfied with merely visiting the jail in order to distribute religious tracts and pious advice

24. Samuel Gridley Howe, *A Letter to the Commissioners of Massachusetts for the State Reform School for Girls* (Boston, 1854), pp. 26–29. Harold Schwartz, *Samuel Gridley Howe: Social Reformer, 1801–1876* (Cambridge: Harvard University Press, 1956), p. 275.

25. John Augustus, *A Report of the Labors of John Augustus, for the Last Ten Years, in Aid of the Unfortunate* (Boston, 1852), pp. 33–35, 95–96. Augustus reported two interesting cases: one of a boy seven years old convicted of rape, and another of a boy convicted of highway robbery for stealing six cents. See also Henry W. Thurston, *Concerning Juvenile Delinquency: Progressive Changes in Our Perspective* (New York: Columbia University Press, 1942), pp. 74–77.

to incarcerated children. Cook was employed to screen out the most promising cases for further help. He put up bail for some accused children and then sent them to Pine Farm. Often he was able to persuade the judge to place other children on probation prior to their trial. Cook also led many children who were friendless or destitute to the Catholic Home which was also established in 1864.[26]

In New York City, Brace had some friends, but he had some enemies too. Robert M. Hartley (1796–1881), organizer and secretary of the New York Association for Improving the Condition of the Poor (1843), believed, like Brace, that western immigration was the best solution to the social problems of the city. One historian has written that his general advice to the poor was: "Go somewhere else."[27] Within Hartley's organization, however, a number of men felt that for the destitute and delinquent children of the city this dictum should read: "Go somewhere else, but not before we teach you how to behave." In 1849 A. R. Wetmore, Joseph B. Collins, Peter Cooper, and other members of the AICP formed a committee within that organization to plan an institution "differing in some of its features from any before projected for the benefit of the friendless, neglected, and vicious children, which abound in this city." The outcome of their planning was the New York Juvenile Asylum (NYJA), incorporated in 1851 and, like Brace's CAS, a privately controlled philanthropic organization.[28]

The Juvenile Asylum received from parents and public authority destitute children as well as those convicted of minor criminal offenses; if children of either type proved unmanageable, the institution

26. Francis E. Lane, *American Charities and the Child of the Immigrant* (New York: Paulist Press, 1932), pp. 84–86. Boston Children's Aid Society, *Report of the Executive Committee* (1865), pp. 5–8, 12–16. Thurston, pp. 77, 79.

27. Robert Bremner, *From the Depths: The Discovery of Poverty in the United States* (New York: New York University Press, 1956), pp. 35–38. The AICP, like the CAS, undertook numerous projects—model tenements, public baths, local dispensaries, etc.—to aid those impoverished people who did not take its advice to go West.

28. AICP, *AR* (1851), p. 20. The AICP continued its own work after the Juvenile Asylum was opened; see Dorothy G. Becker, "The Visitor to the New York City Poor, 1843–1920," *Social Service Review* 35 (1961), 382–96; and Roy Lubove, "The New York Association for Improving the Condition of the Poor: The Formative Years," *New-York Historical Society Quarterly* 43 (1959), 307–28.

could return them to their parents or to the court or send them to the New York House of Refuge. The asylum regarded the refuge as a "quasi-prison" for children, but the main differences between the two institutions were that a child had to spend a longer time in the refuge and that the asylum had a more comprehensive indenturing system. The organization of the two reform schools was not much different. Like the refuge, the asylum received money from public authority. The city provided an initial general disbursement to match private funds and also gave the asylum a varying share of the common school fund.[29] There was a greater emphasis upon school work in the asylum, but this extract from the institution's rules reflects the similar outlook of the two reform schools:

> The work of the boys may consist of gardening, tailoring, shoe-making, the plaiting of straw and palm, the manufacture of brass nails. . . . The girls shall be employed in cooking, washing, ironing, scouring, sewing, knitting. . . .
>
> No play or conversation shall be allowed among the children, while engaged at their work, on parade, at meals, or after they have retired to their sleeping rooms.[30]

The managers of the Juvenile Asylum were less concerned with the similarities between their institution and the New York Refuge than angered by the placing-out policy of the Children's Aid Society. Placing-out was also the asylum's main reformatory activity, but the institution's children had to complete a period of training beforehand. In 1856 George H. Allan was officially employed as the asylum's indenturing agent, although earlier, "140 children had been sent to Illinois in charge of Reverend E. Kingsbury, and were settled by him in Edgar and Vermillion counties." Four or five times each year Allan or his assistant conveyed a company of about forty children to Illinois, where they were parceled out to families whose suitability had been previously determined. The agent also visited asylum children already indentured and attempted to discipline the unruly or to comfort those who were unhappy with their situations.

---

29. Second Convention of Managers and Superintendents of Houses of Refuge and Schools of Reform, *Proceedings* (1859), pp. 38–39. NYJA, *AR* (1863), pp. 50–63.

30. NYJA, *AR* (1853), pp. 19–22.

The more informal system of placing-out inaugurated by Brace enraged the asylum managers, and they did not hesitate to let him know it. "Why sir," cried John Bryan, "the Children's Aid Society is taking a child . . . out of the streets . . . not knowing what influences have been brought to bear upon him previous to the age of four [and transplanting him] into a family where they expect all the hallowed influences of a home to surround him. . . . That is all very poetical but the facts will not bear it out." Bryan summarized the asylum's attitude with a traditional metaphor:

> The "vagabond boy" is like a blade of corn, coming up side by side with a thistle. You may transplant both together into a fertile soil, but you have the thistle still. . . . I would have you pluck out the vagabond first, and then let the boy be thus provided with "a home", and not before.[31]

From the beginning, Brace had encountered opposition to placing-out. Midwestern farmers occasionally charged that no family could be expected to reform the "criminal children" whom the CAS had "dumped" on them. Brace consistently denied these accusations, but he did so with added vigor after visiting the West himself in 1859.[32] In 1875 the CAS, after a detailed survey of western prisons and almshouses, claimed that few if any of their children got in further trouble.[33] Brace believed that the main opponents of placing-out were not irate westerners, but the "asylum interests"—either reform schools which refused his advice and services or philanthropists whose institutions trained children before placing them out. In 1864 the chaplain of the Western House of Refuge in New York refused a CAS offer

31. Second Convention, *Proceedings* (1859), p. 44.

32. NYCAS, *AR* (1858), p. 7. Langsam, p. 45. Opposition of reformatory officials to placing-out continued; see National Conference of Charities and Correction (NCCC), *Proceedings* (1879), pp. 56–62, 158–60; and Robert W. Hebbard, "Placing-Out Children: Dangers of Careless Methods," NCCC, *Proceedings* (1899), pp. 171–76.

33. NCCC, *Proceedings* (1876), pp. 135–50. A critic of this report pointed out that children often concealed the location of their original home when apprehended. A later study in Minnesota, however, supported the conclusions of the CAS. See Hastings H. Hart, "Placing-out Children in the West," NCCC, *Proceedings* (1884), pp. 143–50. For a survey and evaluation of complaints against the placing-out policies of the Boston Children's Aid Society, see Ruth W. Lawton and J. Prentice Murphy, "A Study of Results of a Child Placing Society," NCCC, *Proceedings* (1915), pp. 164–74.

to take a refuge boy west saying, "As we do not lack for good places in this vicinity, where we can continue a personal supervision of the children, it may be considered a matter of questionable expediency to send them to different states unless we are well assured as to the position."[34]

The New York Juvenile Asylum catered more explicitly to the fears of western farmers. "Shall we take these children as they are brought to us, thieves, liars, profane swearers, licentious, polluted in body and soul, and put them into your families in that condition?" asked an asylum manager. Brace denied that the CAS was "scattering poison over the country" and retorted by derogating the "institutional child" as one who "is lighted, warmed and watered by machinery . . . even his vices do not present the frank character of a thorough street-boy; he is found to lie easily, and to be very weak under temptation . . . and . . . *the longer he is in the asylum, the less likely he is to do well in outside life.*"[35]

Brace was the *enfant terrible* of the first conventions of reform school managers and officials in 1857 and 1859. When refuge superintendents claimed that their large congregate institutions were run as families, he remarked disparagingly, "Whatever . . . sympathy we may have with the poorest subjects put under our care, I hold that it is impossible for a man to feel towards them in any degree as a father feels towards his own offspring." When they exclaimed on the need to separate boys and girls within institutions, Brace replied,

I think . . . we may be a little too morbidly delicate with reference to these children. They are sometimes not so bad as they appear. . . . It will not do to separate one sex from another. . . . We must not excite passions by secluding the sexes from each other, but have . . . a healthful intercourse between the boys and the girls. The interchange of notes or communications would not be of great danger, but to shut them up, as in a nunnery, would be bad.[36]

34. New York State Agricultural and Industrial School (formerly the Western House of Refuge), Chaplain's Report (March 24, 1864), Papers of the Western House of Refuge, Syracuse University Library.

35. Brace, *The Dangerous Classes,* pp. 235–36. Second Convention of Managers and Superintendents of Houses of Refuge and Schools of Reform, *Proceedings* (1859), p. 29.

36. First Convention of Managers and Superintendents of Houses of Refuge and Schools of Reform, *Proceedings* (1857), pp. 24, 51. At these conventions,

We shall see how changing conditions after the Civil War led the CAS and the New York Refuge to make common cause: but during the first decade of the society's existence, men devoted to the institutional care of juvenile delinquents believed that Brace and his organization were trying to solve the problem of juvenile delinquency in a dangerously permissive way.

The growth of preventive agencies in the decade before the Civil War reflected a more optimistic attitude toward the problem of juvenile delinquency. Despite differences over the policy of placing-out, the men who initially guided these philanthropies believed that delinquent children were by and large poor and neglected waifs whose delinquencies would cease if their environment were changed. A crowded and poor urban environment had caused their delinquency: a spacious and modest rural environment would cure it. A foster farm family would overcome the child's behavior problems by providing ample food and clothing, moral guidance, and genuine sympathy. The work of these agencies affected the program of both the older refuges and the ever-increasing number of new state and municipal institutions for juvenile delinquents. "Child-saving" philanthropy left reform schools with the least tractable children, but it also provided them with new ideas concerning the reformation of children. Both the preventive agencies and the reform schools were soon faced with even greater problems unleashed by the forces of war, immigration, and industrialism that gripped the nation during the last half of the nineteenth century.

Beginning in the midnineteenth century, municipal and state governments began to play an increasing role in the founding and ad-

---

reform school officials digressed endlessly on inmate classification, placing-out, discipline, and other topics of administrative concern. There were no further conventions during or immediately after the Civil War, but the National Prison Congress on Penitentiary and Reformatory Discipline (1870), the National Prison Association, meeting annually beginning in 1871, and the National Conference of Charities and Correction, meeting annually beginning in 1874, gave reform school authorities ample opportunities to express their views. The NCCC met originally as a charities conference within the American Social Science Association. This connection was ended in 1879. See Alexander Johnson, comp., *A Guide to Proceedings of the National Conference of Charities and Correction, 1874–1907* (1908), pp. 156–75. This guide was published by the authority of the executive committee of the NCCC.

ministration of institutions for juvenile delinquents. That these were usually called reform schools instead of houses of refuge indicated the increased emphasis that was placed on formal schooling. Michael Katz has noted that reform school commitments for "stubbornness" often indicated the offense of truancy—a misdemeanor which little concerned founders of the early houses of refuge. The 1876 report of the Commissioner of Education lists fifty-one reform schools; of these, twenty-three were state institutions, twelve were municipal, twelve were privately incorporated, and three were combined state and municipal or state and county institutions. One congressionally supported reform school was about to open in the District of Columbia. By 1890 nearly every state outside of the South had some type of reform school for boys and often a separate institution for girls. At this time, these institutions cared for most of the delinquent children in the United States and for numerous destitute children as well.[37]

Children found their way to these schools in a bewildering variety of ways. An 1880 survey of reform schools by the U.S. Commissioner of Education illustrates the difficulty of legally defining juvenile delinquency in the nineteenth century. Six of the thirty schools required that children be convicted in court of some crime punishable by imprisonment; in seventeen other cases, conviction for an imprisonable offense was sufficient ground for commitment. Fourteen schools admitted children who had committed offenses for which the law provided no penalty—idleness or "decidedly mischievous propensities," for example. Thirteen schools took children found guilty of "determined rebellion against parental authority." Seven schools received children neglected or deserted by parents; five accepted children committed by parents without specified reasons. In every school, children had to be younger than 16 at the time of commitment; the lower age for commitment varied from school to school between 7 and 11.

37. Katz, *The Irony of Urban School Reform,* pp. 177–78. U.S. Commissioner of Education, *Report, 1876* (Washington, D.C.: Government Printing Office, 1878), pp. 868–69. For a bibliography of various writings on reform schools and the juvenile court, see Augustus Frederick Kuhlman, comp., *A Guide to Material on Crime and Criminal Justice* (New York: H. W. Wilson, 1929), pp. 547–62, 592–604. Beginning in 1880, U.S. Census reports give comprehensive summaries of the activities of many private and all public institutions for juvenile delinquents. The annual reports of the U.S. Commissioner of Education (1880 and after) are also useful.

Several schools employed alternate sentences which gave them the discretion to move "unmanageable" children to prison. Children could be confined until they attained majority (18 for girls, 21 for boys) or "until . . . reformed"—the latter a determination which was made exclusively by school officials.[38]

Some state governments initially needed private benefactors or municipal funds, or both, to supplement state appropriations for the new reform schools. The Maine State Reform School, for example, would not have materialized as soon as it did (1853) without the assistance of a group of Portland merchants whose exasperation with local delinquents led them to purchase a Cape Elizabeth farm and donate it to the state so that it could be used as a reform school. Elsewhere, citizens responded to requests for support in a manner which they deemed appropriate to their station. Former Boston Mayor Theodore Lyman gave $22,500 to enable Massachusetts to found the first state reform school for boys at Westborough (1847). The Reverend Thomas M. Clark of Hartford, Connecticut, exhorted his congregation to use God's money to help match a state grant for the construction of a reform school. "For what has God given you your wealth?" he asked. "Is it that you may pamper your body, upon which the worms have a lien which they will soon execute? . . . You know it is not." Smaller expressions of concern were also appreciated. A. O. Moore donated "a lot of books" to the State Reform Farm in Ohio and the American Bible Society gave "the welcome gift of sixty Bibles . . . through the kindness of Rev. J. S. Galloway of Springfield, Ohio, and R. F. Rowe, of New York City."[39]

Despite the initial assistance of private benevolence, state and municipal governments had to support their charitable and penal institutions largely out of their own revenues. Because of budgetary restrictions, friction was often created, as in Maine and New Hampshire,

38. U.S. Commissioner of Education, *Report, 1880* (Washington, D.C.: Government Printing Office, 1882), pp. clxxxi–ii.

39. Raymond B. Wilbur, "The Maine State Reform School: The Crisis Years" (unpublished seminar paper, University of New Hampshire, Department of History, 1972). Thomas W. Clark, "State Reform School," *The Prisoners' Friend* 5 (1852), 6–11. Ohio *Executive Documents* (1857), I, Doc. 14, "Second Annual Report of the Board of Commissioners for Reform Schools, 1857" (Columbus, 1858), p. 614.

where state legislators required that local communities partially support children whom they had committed to the state school. Under this circumstance, the "pests" of villages and towns distant from the institutions often remained at home. Private as well as public eleemosynary institutions, like early canal and railroad companies, were not bashful about requesting aid in the form of land grants from the federal government. In 1853 the managers of the St. Louis House of Refuge asked for "a sufficient quantity of the public domain to establish and support institutions calculated to prevent the growth and accumulation of pauperism and crime." Earlier, in 1819 and in 1826, Congress had supplemented state aid to the privately incorporated Connecticut and Kentucky asylums for the deaf and dumb. In 1854 Congress, responding to a memorial from Dorothea Dix, passed a bill granting twelve and a half million acres of land to help the several states to establish institutions "for the benefit of indigent insane persons." President Franklin Pierce's lengthy veto of Miss Dix's bill did not discourage the supporters of the St. Louis Refuge who petitioned Congress: "as highly as we approve a measure designed to ameliorate the condition of the indigent insane, yet, we are fully persuaded that a measure looking to the improvement and reformation of the indigent and vicious children of large cities, is one of much greater importance." Congress ignored the petition and others like it, thereby establishing a precedent of denying public land to the charitable institutions of the states and cities. Had Miss Dix's bill become law, the ability of both voluntary and public charitable and custodial institutions to support themselves would have been greatly strengthened.[40]

Despite the allocation of more time (usually half a day) to schooling, many state and municipal institutions were indistinguishable from the early refuges—large congregate institutions with strict workshop

40. New Hampshire *Laws* (1858), ch. 2087 (Concord, 1858). Maine *Revised Statutes* (1858), ch. 142 (Augusta, 1858). M. Tarver, "Juvenile Reform Schools," *The Western Journal and Civilian* 11 (1853), 186–88. *Annals* of the Congress of the United States, 15th Cong., 1st sess. (1819), p. 2513. "An Act . . . to complete the location of the grant to the Deaf and Dumb Asylum of Kentucky" (1827), ch. 8, in Richard Peters, ed., *U.S. Public Statutes at Large,* IV, 202; *Memorial of D. L. Dix . . .*, 30th Cong., 1st sess. (1848), Senate Misc. Doc. 150. *Congressional Globe,* 33d Cong., 1st sess. (1854), 1061–63. Pierce veto message in James D. Richardson, *Messages and Papers of the Presidents,* V (Washington, D.C.: Government Printing Office, 1897), pp. 247–56. See also *The Western Journal and Civilian* 11 (1852), 80–81.

routines. Massachusetts and Ohio, however, following the lead of European institutions, founded reform schools which represented significant departures from the refuge system. The Massachusetts State Industrial School for Girls (1856) and the Ohio Reform or Farm School (1857) introduced the cottage or family plan to America. This institutional organization divided children into small families of forty or fewer; each family had its own cottage and autonomous schedule. The terms *cottage system* and *family system* were often used synonymously, much to the chagrin of congregate school officials who resented the implication that their institutions were not familial. Responses of congregate schools to a question posed by the U.S. Commissioner of Education—"Is your institution operated on the cottage system?" included the following: "We have one family" and "No; but we have the family spirit." Congregate workshops were not unknown in cottage schools, but the fragmented nature of the cottage routine, combined with the enthusiastic preference for agricultural over industrial labor on the part of the founders, led to the establishment of several cottage farm schools. "Habituate him [the delinquent] to the life and labor of a farm," advised the commissioners of the Ohio Reform School, "and he will, in nearly every case, continue so to live and labor when restored to society."[41]

Just as European philanthropists had helped Charles Loring Brace conceptualize the placing-out idea, so too they initiated the development of the cottage reform school. In 1833 Johann H. Wichern, whose association with Brace we have noted, established as part of Hamburg's Inner Mission a cottage institution called the *Rauhe Haus* (Rough House). Similar institutions were established in Reutingen, where in 1836 Gustav Werner founded *Gotthilf* (God help), and in Mettray, France, where the jurist Frederic Auguste Demetz began a farm school in 1840. In 1848 the London Philanthropic Society, sponsor of one of the oldest reform schools, moved its institution from St. George's Fields to rural Redhill and reorganized on the cottage plan. English philanthropists Mary Carpenter, Joseph Sturge, and Barwicke Baker, influenced by developments in Hamburg and Met-

41. U.S. Commissioner of Education, *Report, 1888–1889,* II (Washington, D.C.: Government Printing Office, 1891), 1408. Ohio, Commissioners of the Ohio Reform School, *Report* (1856), p. 619.

tray, established reform schools which were privately controlled but received government funds under provisions in the Youthful Offenders Act (1854). Their work represented an effort to go beyond Lord Shaftsbury's sectarian "ragged schools" whose routines were built around Bible study, rudimentary education, and temporary shelter and nourishment.[42]

Mary Carpenter and her colleagues received only the more confirmed delinquents for individual care and attention. The Youthful Offenders Act, as initially passed in 1854, required that the children serve a brief time in jail prior to commitment. Miss Carpenter opposed this provision, which was intended to frighten children into obedience, but she eagerly and hopefully accepted the children who, as a result of the law, were committed to her Kingswood Reformatory (1852) and Red Lodge Girls' Reformatory (1854). She wrote: "I would enlist the will of the child in the work, and without this I do not think that any true reformation can be effected. There should be that degree of confidence shown to the children which will make them feel that they are workers together with the teachers."[43]

European cottage institutions emphasized the importance of inspired and intimate guidance for each delinquent and the need for a more aesthetic and varied institutional life. Gymnastics, swimming, and music were often integrated into the daily routine. The "elder sisters" and "elder brothers" who guided the individual cottages were supposedly chosen because they intuitively understood and sympathized with the destitute and delinquent children under their care. "Only where persons are actuated by a proper feeling of love," wrote Gustav Werner, "can children be made partakers of love, and this

---

42. Mary Carpenter, *Reformatory Schools for Children of the Perishing and Dangerous Classes and for Juvenile Offenders* (London, 1851), pp. 324–30, 339–40. David Owen, *English Philanthropy, 1660–1960* (Cambridge: Harvard University Press, 1964), pp. 145–67. Sanders, pp. 226–29. For a recent study see John P. Resch, "Anglo-American Efforts in Prison Reform, 1850–1900: The Work of Thomas Barwicke Lloyd Baker" (Ph.D. diss., The Ohio State University, 1969). Baker was more modest in his aims than Mary Carpenter and the others. Believing that reform schools could modify a child's behavior but not work a transformation of character, Baker was accordingly less enthusiastic about the cottage system.

43. Quoted in Geraldine S. Cadbury, *Young Offenders Yesterday and Today* (London: Allen and Unwin, 1938), pp. 53–61. For documents relating to the passage of the Youthful Offenders Act, see Sanders, pp. 230–40.

love may even excel a parent's love, in the formation of human character, if its wisdom be combined with holiness."[44]

In 1843 Horace Mann, one of the first American visitors to Wichern's *Rauhe Haus,* noted with satisfaction the absence of walls and other signs of penal restraint. When Mann asked Wichern how he reformed his children, the German replied, "By active occupations, music, and Christian love." Mann told his friends of Wichern's work and one of them, Samuel G. Howe, was sufficiently impressed to idealize the family plan in his letter to the Massachusetts State commissioners, who were planning an institution for delinquent girls. As we have pointed out, the commissioners did not adopt Howe's proposal, which aimed to eliminate the institution altogether, but they did attempt to emulate, perhaps too explicitly, Wichern's cottage plan. "Each house is to be a *family,* under the sole direction and control of the matron, who is the *mother* of the family," ordered the trustees in their first report. "The government and discipline are strictly parental. It is the design to give a home interest, a home feeling and attachment, to the whole family."[45]

The commissioners of the Ohio Reform School were also attracted to the cottage plan, particularly as it had been adapted at Mettray and Red Hill. In 1856 commissioner Charles Reemelin, visiting these two institutions, was impressed by their emphasis upon the reformatory value of agricultural labor. The Ohio commissioners also visited the older refuges and reformatories in the United States but on the strength of Reemelin's report recommended that the legislature locate the new state reform school upon a farm. The legislature purchased land near Lancaster, Ohio, and in the summer of 1857 the first inmates helped to build the initial cottage.[46]

Although the Ohio Reform School and other farm reform schools gave expression to the idea of rural reform envisioned by Demetz

44. Quoted in Ohio Commissioners of the Reform School, *Report* (1856), p. 632.

45. Horace Mann, *Account of the Hamburgh Redemption Institute* (n.p., 1843), pp. 3–7. On Howe see above, pp. 42–43. Massachusetts report in Bremner, *Children and Youth in America,* I, 705–706; italics in original. Theodore Parker was also an admirer of the cottage system; see his *A Sermon of the Dangerous Classes of Society* (Boston, 1847), p. 47.

46. Ohio *Executive Documents* (1857), I, 612–15.

and Wichern, Americans and Europeans expected different results from their respective institutions. The Ohio commissioners, like Charles Loring Brace, shared the popular belief that farming life offered great possibilities, not only for individual social and economic improvement, but for moral betterment as well. Aiming to establish "the *model farm* of the State," the Ohioans wanted to provide delinquents with "those . . . passports to the favors of the world—polite manners, clean habits, and a capability to adapt themselves easily to each new family." Europeans, on the other hand, viewing agricultural labor in a more traditional way, wanted their cottage reform schools to produce deferential peasants or faithful domestic servants, not self-reliant, egalitarian farmers and entrepreneurs. Wichern told Horace Mann that the routine of the *Rauhe Haus* "commends and habituates them [the delinquents] to the idea of an honorable poverty."[47]

Cottage reform schools, some located on farms but others not, spread widely in the United States. New Jersey (1864) and Indiana (1866) opened cottage schools, and some older institutions converted from congregate to cottage plan. In 1859 the Massachusetts Reform School for Boys was partially destroyed by incendiarism and rioting. In the ensuing reorganization, superintendent Joseph Allen abolished cruel punishment and introduced a modified cottage plan which dispersed the living units but retained the work shops. "Fear may restrain," he wrote, "but *love* only can reform." The House of Refuge for Western Pennsylvania (1851) and the Philadelphia House of Refuge converted more completely. The Western House removed from the town of Allegheny to a farm near Morganza in 1876, and the Philadelphia Refuge eventually moved from the city to the Glen Mills Farm in 1892. Here as elsewhere, the cottage system offered reform school officials the opportunity to segregate children residentially by employing one or a number of criteria—age, "hardness," sex, race, or state of advancement in school work.[48]

Advocates of the cottage reform school were enthusiastic over its

47. Ohio Commissioners of the Reform School, *Report* (1856), p. 619. Mann, p. 5. See above, p. 22 for the concept of John Griscom, who, like many Europeans, saw the reformed delinquent as a menial.

48. Katz, pp. 192–93. Joseph Allen, *Westboro' State Reform School Reminiscences* (Boston, 1877), p. 11. U.S. Commissioner of Education, *Report, 1887–1888* (Washington, D.C.: Government Printing Office, 1889), I, 978.

merits and criticized older institutions. Commissioners Enoch C.
Wines and Theodore W. Dwight of the Prison Association of New
York, making their comprehensive survey (1866) of conditions in
the reform schools, jails, and penitentiaries of the northern and border
states, found the Industrial School for Girls at Lancaster, Massachusetts, "first among its peers." The Boston House of Reformation, on
the other hand, they described as "more open to criticism than any
we met with elsewhere in the whole course of our visitation." Commissioners of the Ohio Reform School drew this odious comparison
between "the family and the big house system": "In the first, the
inmates are always more mannerly, more cleanly and more cheerful.
Manners, neatness, and all those so called outer qualities of men are
almost invariably neglected in the big houses. The inmates sleep, eat,
walk, dress and play slovenly." In 1867 the Ohio Board of State
Charities concluded of the Cincinnati House of Refuge "that it was
a mistake to locate an institution of this character so near a city, and
we prefer the farm and family system." Managers of the Philadelphia
Refuge thought Mary Carpenter was "favorably impressed" with their
institution, but in fact she disapproved of both the New York and
Philadelphia houses of refuge. She wrote, "There is no natural life
or freedom; young men of an age to have very large experience of
vice are associated with young boys; all arrangements are artificial;
instead of the cultivation of the land, which would prepare the youth
to seek a sphere far from the danger of large cities, the boys and
young men were being taught trades, which would confine them to
the great centres of an overcrowded population."[49]

Officials of refuges and other congregate reform schools vigorously
rebutted these charges. They resented contentions that congregate
organization corrupted innocent children by mixing them indiscriminately with older and presumably hardened offenders. "You may
divide these boys into classes, and the vicious will grow more vicious,"

49. Enoch C. Wines and Theodore W. Dwight, *Report on the Prisons and
Reformatories of the United States and Canada* (Albany, 1867), pp. 354–55.
Ohio Commissioners of the Reform School, *Report* (1856), p. 622. Ohio
Board of State Charities, *AR* (1867), pp. 13–15. On Mary Carpenter see Phila-
delphia Refuge, *AR* (1874), pp. 25–26, and NCCC, *Proceedings* (1875), p. 69.
William P. Letchworth read Miss Carpenter's paper. Charles Loring Brace
visited Mary Carpenter in 1865 and may have influenced her with his own
caustic view of the houses of refuge. See *Life of Brace,* pp. 272–73.

cried Orlando Hastings of the New York Western House of Refuge, "but when mixed with the rest, and when they see a public opinion in favor of reform, they will reflect, improve, and in the end be re-formed." Mrs. Mary E. Cobb, a later defender of congregate reform schools, denied that they were *ipso facto* "hard and unloving," and continued, "While less demonstrative and impulsive, the interest is steady and just and soon understood by the child to be used solely to its advantage."[50]

The incessant arguing between supporters of the cottage and of the congregate reform schools partially obscured the common prob-lems that war and industrialization forced upon both kinds of institu-tions. During the Civil War, the population of penitentiaries and county jails in the northern states generally declined, but the reform schools filled to overflowing. The managers of the Philadelphia Ref-uge reported that "the absence of so many fathers engaged in the defence of their country, has thrown upon our charge a very large number of children." Despite the establishment of a ship school to care for older boys (14 to 16 years), the Massachusetts Boys' Reform School at Westborough was repeatedly forced to turn away children for lack of room. Franklin B. Sanborn, Secretary of the Massachusetts Board of State Charities, while touring the state's jails in 1865 found an "increasing proportion" of young prisoners—"Among them . . . mere infants . . . such as the one I found in Plymouth House of Correction, sentenced to thirty days imprisonment—and he only six years old."[51] In New York City the number of juvenile delinquents increased far beyond the capacity of existing institutions to accommo-date them. Young men and boys played a prominent part in the draft

50. First Convention of Managers and Superintendents of Houses of Refuge and Schools of Reform, *Proceedings* (1857), p. 29. Mary E. Cobb, *The Re-sponsibility of States to Their Dependent Children* (Fall River, Mass.: 1888), p. 15.

51. Katz, pp. 177–78. Emerson D. Fite, *Social and Industrial Conditions in the North during the Civil War* (New York: Peter Smith, 1930), pp. 304–306. Philadelphia Refuge, *AR* (1864), p. 10. Massachusetts Senate *Documents,* 74 (1865), 66–67. On the ship school see M. L. Elbridge, "History of the Massa-chusetts Nautical Reform School," in Enoch C. Wines, ed., *Transactions* of the National Congress on Penitentiary and Reformatory Discipline (1870), pp. 352–53. The Nautical School trained many boys for the Merchant Marine and the Navy. Skilled labor shortages existed in both services during and immedi-ately after the war.

riots of July 1863, which threatened the survival of the city government.[52]

Reform schools made room for new inmates by releasing older boys
to military service. In August 1861, six boys were discharged from
the Western House of Refuge (New York) "to enlist in Captain
Charles Russell Lowell's Co. 3d Cavalry Regiment" and six months
later ten boys were allowed to join "Captain McMahon's Company
of the Irish Regiment." Reform school managers prided themselves
on the heroism of their youths. The Philadelphia Refuge praised "the
gallant élèves of the Institution [who] have perilled their lives in defence of their country." The New York Juvenile Asylum reported
that a "psalm singing company" composed of many former inmates
went into battle "chanting the beautiful words of the 23d Psalm. Not
a man in the company was injured though many fell around them."[53]

The young soldiers confirmed the expectations of their keepers.
One boy wrote to C. C. Macy of the New York Children's Aid
Society, "This has been a good country to me and it is my duty to do
something to defend its institutions; and I pray God, if I fall in battle,
I shall not die like a coward, but like a brave man." Another pious
private condemned his own officers for "using the most profane and
vulgar expressions a man could think of." Perhaps reflective of the
genuine feelings of some "reform school soldiers" was the plaintive
note of a New Hampshire boy: "When I was on the battlefield, I
wished myself back to your home."[54]

While refuges and reform schools were being besieged by rapidly
increasing numbers of delinquent children, economic factors were
forcing the institutions to modify their operations. War and postwar
inflation drastically shrank the purchasing power of their funds. At the
New York Refuge, for instance, per capita cost of food and provisions increased nearly 50 percent from 1862 to 1865.[55] State legislatures, faced with numerous other demands, did not or could not

52. Joel T. Headley, *The Great Riots of New York* (New York, 1877), pp.
202, 213. Bremner, *Children and Youth in America,* I, 756–57.
53. NYSA&I, MS, Superintendent's Journal, XVI. Philadelphia Refuge, *AR*
(1864), p. 7. NYJA, *AR* (1863), p. 46.
54. NYCAS, *AR* (1862), pp. 55, 51. New Hampshire State Reform School,
AR (1863), p. 33.
55. SRJD, *AR* (1865), pp. 6–7.

provide additional revenue. During the second half of the nineteenth century, governments in the northern and western states increasingly assumed responsibility for the welfare of many different types of dependents. Institutions for juvenile delinquents vied for state funds with orphanages, almshouses, insane asylums, and schools for the blind, deaf, and dumb. Faced with this competition, reform school trustees relied increasingly upon the contract system to provide needed revenue.

The contract system had been part of the reform school routine from the beginning, but it now assumed a different, perhaps more exploitative character. Manufacturers, whose piece work was once welcomed because it supposedly instilled correct habits, were viewed more skeptically because they often insisted upon controlling institution children during working hours. Philadelphia Refuge officials made this complaint to Wines and Dwight:

> Those immediately entrusted with the government of the boys are generally but illy qualified for so responsible a position. . . . If the work be well done and a responsible amount of it, they are satisfied. These seven and a half hours of labor are spent without one moral lesson taught the boys, at least so far as the workmen of the shops are concerned.

In 1874 Reverend Marcus Ames, superintendent of the girls' cottage reformatory at Lancaster, Massachusetts, resigned rather than accept the installation of workshops. At the New Jersey State Reform School at Jamesburg, farming and maintenance work gave way to shirt making in 1875, and a factory appeared among the cottages. A few years later, investigators from the state legislature found life in the institution "hard, routine and monotonous." In his comprehensive study of New Jersey institutions, James Leiby concludes, "Jamesburg was not a family, nor a reformatory, but a boys' prison."[56]

A few reform school officials continued to defend the contract system. Chaplain Bradford Peirce of the New York Refuge considered workshop labor an "indispensable" agency of reformation.[57] Over a fifteen-year period following the Civil War, contract labor

56. Wines and Dwight, p. 431. Massachusetts State Industrial School for Girls, *AR* (1875), pp. 8–9. James Leiby, *Charities and Correction in New Jersey* (New Brunswick, N.J.: Rutgers University Press, 1967), p. 82.
57. New York Assembly, *Documents* (1871), IV, Doc. 18, p. 131.

at the refuge had reduced by 20 percent the per capita cost of inmate upkeep.[58] At the same time, however, state legislative investigations were demonstrating the exploitative nature of the system. In 1871 the New York Commission on Prison Labor, headed by Enoch Wines, investigated the institution and uncovered many instances of exploitation and brutality. Refuge boys were paid thirty cents per day for doing the same work for which an outside worker received four dollars. The commissioners got this picture of shop life from former New York Refuge employees, Thomas Crowne and Valentine Feldman:

> Q. Have you ever known instructors employed by the contractors to strike the boys? A. (Crowne) I have seen them do it, though it is forbidden. I have also seen them, when a keeper was around, and they did not dare to strike, tread on the boys' bare toes (they wear no shoes in summer), so as to cause them to squirm all around. Q. What was the general character of the contractors' instructors? A. They are compelled to be very selfish. I have been told by one of the contractor's agents that I did not report my boys and get them whipped half often enough, thus not getting enough work out of them. . . . Q. Have you ever seen any of the boys abused by the contractors' employees? A. (Feldman) Often and often. They do not call it abusing a boy to give him a kick, or a blow on the head. . . . Q. Please describe the way in which they are punished. A. I have seen boys punished for not completing their tasks, so that blood ran down into their boots.

Conditions were much the same at the Philadelphia House of Refuge, where the boys were paid twenty-five cents per day and severely lashed when they failed to meet contractors' quotas. The directors of the Cleveland Refuge admitted that their chair-caning industry had driven prices "far below what should be obtained for such labor" and continued, somewhat ambivalently, "The question is not, and never should be: What can these youths earn for the institution? (though we would not lose sight of this by any means) but: What can we, their guardians, for the time being do to educate and fit them for usefulness in the world?"[59]

---

58. Robert I. Cooper, "William Rhinelander Stewart and the Expansion of Public Welfare Services in New York State, 1882–1929" (Ph.D. diss., City University of New York, 1969), p. 255.

59. New York Assembly, *Documents* (1871), IV, Doc. 18, pp. 125, 163, 164, 168, 181. Pennsylvania House of Representatives, *Documents* (1876), "Evi-

The contract labor controversy was sharpened by the vigorous protests of workingmen who had objected to the competition of both penitentiary and reform school labor since the 1830s. The New York State Workingmen's Assembly petitioned the legislature to stop further appropriations for the New York Refuge because "we find a contractor making to the amount of $183,800 clear profit on the earnings of the inmates confined there." Although this petition was unsuccessful, nautical reform schools in Massachusetts, New York, and California expired in the 1870s, in part because adult seamen protested that they could not find work during the depressions of that decade.[60]

From the institutional point of view, protests of workingmen had the more serious result of demythologizing the workshop routine. No longer was it believable for reform school officials to portray the ritual as primarily a beneficial aid in inculcating industrious habits or shaping children for "usefulness." The violence and exploitation characteristic of reform school workshops gave the lie to this allegation. The havoc may have been no greater than that which occasionally wracked the early houses of refuge, but the association of conflict and the contract system in the minds of victims and outside labor interests made it now seem intolerable. And indeed, rioting, incendiarism, and even murder did characterize institutional life. In 1859 Daniel Credan and five of his friends put the torch to the Massachusetts Reform School. On May 17, 1872, Justus Dunn stabbed to death Saul Calvert, an overseer in the North Shop of the New York Refuge. "In March last (1877)," reported Superintendent Loring Lathrop of Massachusetts girls' reform school, "House No. 3, an old

---

dence Taken by the Committee of the House of Representatives to Investigate the Management of House of Refuge," pp. 12–13, 225. Cleveland, Ohio, Directors of the Workhouse and House of Refuge and Correction, *AR* (1876), pp. 17–18. For a summary of state investigations of prison labor see U.S. Commissioner of Labor, *AR* (1886), pp. 287–368.

60. New York Senate, *Documents* (1871), IV, Doc. 55, p. 1. Massachusetts *Public Documents* (1871), III, Doc. 19, p. 18. George P. Jacoby, *Catholic Child Care in New York* (Washington, D.C.: Catholic University of America Press, 1941), p. 44. Frances Cahn and Valeska Baroj, *Welfare Activities of Federal, State and Local Governments in California, 1850–1934* (Berkeley: University of California Press, 1936), pp. 49–50. The California ship school *Jamestown* was financed in part by the federal government and abandoned largely because of its maintenance expense.

building . . . replete with interesting associations, was burned to the ground, having been set on fire by two of our inmates." William Murphy, an inmate of the second division at the [New York] Western House of Refuge, perhaps spoke for many other school boys when, threatening a guard with a knife, he told him, "You god-damned son of a bitch, I will drive this into you if you do not leave me alone."[61]

During the later nineteenth century, institutions began to lose control of their children without as well as within the institutions' walls. Indenture to farmers and craftsmen declined steadily after 1850, and the number of outright discharges increased commensurately. "The destruction of the system of apprenticeship renders it very difficult to obtain suitable places where the inmates can be placed to learn suitable trades," complained the managers of the Philadelphia Refuge, adding, "and many of them are not inclined to become agriculturalists." In desperation the refuges turned to their philosophical rivals, the preventive agencies, and requested their help in placing boys far from the eastern cities. As early as 1858, the New York Refuge asked Reverend W. C. Van Meter of the Howard Mission to locate farmers who needed help and whose farms were inaccessible to the expanding railroad system which served runaway apprentices all too easily.[62] Charles Loring Brace no doubt took pride in the fact that he could continue to berate "congregated reformatories" while at the same time help the New York Refuge place its children on western farms. Despite the efforts of Brace and his colleagues, rural placing-out declined steadily during the 1880s—not by chance the decade of a substantial decline in the agricultural labor market. There is a final irony. Newsboys' Lodging House of the NYCAS—last stopping place for children heading west—became the source and inspiration for a

61. Massachusetts State Reform School at Westborough, *AR* (1859), pp. 3–4. SRJD, *AR* (1872), pp. 45–47. Massachusetts State Industrial School for Girls at Lancaster, *AR* (1878), p. 16. NYSA&I, MS, Superintendent's Journal, XVIII (March 23, 1873). In 1871, the year before the killing at the New York Refuge, Chaplain Bradford K. Peirce wrote: "The inmates of the Refuge, after an absence of a few years visit their old home with the enthusiasm of returning children, and fall upon the arms of their teachers often with the warmth of a long-absent youth coming into the presence of a beloved mother"; see Peirce, "New-York House of Refuge," *Appleton's Journal* 5 (1871), 301–308.

62. Philadelphia Refuge, *AR* (1874), p. 9. SRJD, *AR* (1858), p. 8.

young author named Horatio Alger. Alger's novels invariably describe the rise to wealth of poor but honest boys who come from rural areas or small towns to the city in order to succeed.[63]

The proponents of placing-out and defenders of the reform school system differed over ways to care for delinquents, but philanthropists of both persuasions were staunch Protestants (many were ministers) who on occasion used their position to proselytize the children under their care. The New York Refuge, commented one observer, was "in its faith and practice, eminently Protestant." And "good rural homes" were, as James Leiby notes, "mostly Protestant, of course."[64]

Catholic opposition to the religious policies of Protestant-dominated institutions increased sharply in the 1840s when the number of destitute and delinquent children in the seaboard cities also increased with the immigration of thousands of Irish Catholic peasants fleeing famine in their native land. "Boston is a dreadful place for making Protestants of people," a priest in Halifax advised an Irish mother, "and you must be careful, especially of the children, or they will get them from you." A group of New York Catholics complained, "All . . . institutions organized for the protection of destitute children are Protestant, having Protestant directors, Protestant superintendents, Protestant teachers, Protestant worship, and Protestant instruction and training." A New Jersey legislator argued that Catholics "would not submit to having their children sent to an institution [Jamesburg] where the love of their religion was likely to be crushed out."[65]

The New York City missions and institutions worked hard to convert Catholic children, whom Bradford Peirce referred to as "worse than heathen." Charles Loring Brace insisted that some of his best friends were Catholic and praised them lavishly for their humanism and missionary spirit. Unfortunately, Francis Xavier and Ignatius Loyola were not alive to receive his commendation, and contemporary Catholics heard him only when he denounced "the spiritual lifeless-

---

63. Charles Loring Brace, "What Is the Best Method for the Care of Poor and Vicious Children?" *Journal of Social Science* 11 (1880), 93–98. SRJD, *AR* (1879), p. 27. On Alger see Wohl, pp. 121–39.

64. Jacoby, p. 42. Leiby, pp. 82–83.

65. Quoted in Lane, p. 47. New York Catholic Protectory, *AR* (1865), p. 61. Legislator quoted in Leiby, p. 83.

ness of Romanism." Brace sadly concluded, "A Protestant has great difficulty in coming into connection with the Romanist poor."[66]

Some Catholics who were not so poor made efforts to aid the destitute and delinquent children of their faith. In 1842 the Brothers of the Holy Cross opened a Manual Labor School at Notre Dame, South Bend, Indiana, and shortly thereafter, the Sisters of the same order established a home for girls in Bertrand, Michigan. The Home of the Angel Guardian was founded in Boston (1851), and by 1860 the Holy Cross order had opened two more schools in Baltimore and New Orleans. In 1863 the largest single effort to aid Catholic children was begun by Archbishop John Hughes of New York and a number of wealthy laymen who incorporated the Society for the Protection of Destitute Roman Catholic Children of the City of New York. Much like the Society for the Reformation of Juvenile Delinquents, this Catholic group managed its own institution, the New York Catholic Protectory (NYCP).[67]

The leading spokesman for the protectory was its first president, Levi Silliman Ives (1797–1867) who, before his conversion in 1852, had been the Episcopal bishop of North Carolina. Ives was particularly incensed by the activities of child-placing agencies that, he contended, purposefully separated children from their parents and, more important, from the religion of their parents. "What charity commenced," he said, "fanaticism has grossly perverted; or what we had supposed charity, turns out to be only sectarian zeal."[68] Ives led

---

66. Jacoby, pp. 80–83. Bradford Peirce, *A Half Century with Juvenile Delinquents* (New York, 1869), p. 60 and *passim*. Brace, *Dangerous Classes,* pp. 155–56. See also Langsam, pp. 45–56.

67. Aaron I. Abell, *American Catholicism and Social Action: A Search for Social Justice, 1865–1950* (South Bend, Ind.: University of Notre Dame Press, 1963), pp. 18–23. Hughes was more intimately connected with another but similar dispute—the common-schools controversy of the 1840s. Catholics were embittered by their failure to gain public funds for their own schools and by the anti-Catholicism of common school officials and textbooks. See Lawrence Kehoe, ed., *Complete Works of Most Reverend John Hughes,* 2 vols. (New York, 1866), I, 41–283; and Vincent P. Lannie, *Public Money and Parochial Education: Bishop Hughes, Governor Seward and the New York School Controversy* (Cleveland: Press of Case Western Reserve University, 1968).

68. Levi Silliman Ives, "The Protection of Destitute Catholic Children," in NYCP, *AR* (1864), p. 72. See also John O'Grady, *Levi Silliman Ives, Pioneer Leader in Catholic Charities* (New York: Kenedy, 1933), pp. 57–61.

a successful drive to gain state funds for his institution over the objections of Protestant opponents who argued that church-state relationships had been violated. He satirically phrased the argument of his opponents: "We want both your money and your children; but if you will persist in holding on to your children, we must at least have your money: keep your children, but pay your taxes to us!"[69]

In operational terms, the New York Catholic Protectory resembled more than it contrasted with Protestant-led institutions. The Catholic Protectory and the New York Refuge, with monstrously Victorian administration buildings and chair-caning shops, were very much alike. Both institutions assumed that their special mission entitled them to state money. Levi Silliman Ives believed that outcast children, the plague of Augustan Rome, could be the progenitors of a modern catastrophe too if they were left untended. Indeed, little besides religion separated the Catholic and Protestant philanthropists, but in an age of sectarianism and bigotry, this difference was enough.

The economic, religious, and disciplinary problems which continued to plague reform schools and other institutions led governments in some states to seek administrative solutions by scrutinizing institutional operations in a systematic way. To implement this examination, the governments organized boards of state charity. Massachusetts led the way, establishing a board in 1863; by 1882 eight northern states and North Carolina had followed suit. Board members were unpaid in order to discourage spoilsmen and to attract, according to one enthusiast, "gentlemen of public spirit and sufficient leisure."[70]

The chief duty of these gentlemen was to inspect, report on, and recommend improvements for reform schools, asylums, and almshouses. Their principal power, in most states, was their right to remove children and insane persons from county and local almshouses and to transfer them to separate and special institutions or to make other provisions for them. State legislatures were not required to act on board reports—and often didn't. Nevertheless, state and state-supported institutions now had reason to fear for vitally needed

69. NYCP, *AR* (1865). For an example of state financial aid to the protectory see New York *Laws* (1866), ch. 647 (Albany, 1867), pp. 27–28.

70. George I. Chace, "The Proper Functions of Boards of State Charities and Corrections," in NCCC *Proceedings* (1882), p. 26.

appropriations unless they heeded the board's remedial suggestions. Institutional officers generally followed board recommendations, perhaps because they could no longer rely upon their own annual reports to justify or even cover up institutional conditions.[71]

The investigative efforts of state boards were often supplemented by inspections of private voluntary associations such as the New York State Charities Aid Association (1872). Both state boards and philanthropic societies attracted prominent citizens to their cause. In 1869 Frederick H. Wines (1838–1912), son of penologist Enoch C. Wines, was appointed first secretary of the Illinois board. Franklin B. Sanborn (1831–1917), secretary of the Massachusetts board, established a widely copied system of inspection and reporting. Hastings H. Hart (1851–1932) served as first secretary of the Minnesota board in 1883 and in 1909 was appointed director of the child-helping department of the Russell Sage Foundation. Louisa Lee Schuyler (1837–1926), a principal organizer of the New York State Charities Aid Association, had been active in the Children's Aid Society as well as the U.S. Sanitary Commission, a federation of voluntary associations which helped government agencies care for Union soldiers and sailors during the Civil War. Later she led a campaign to remove insane persons from almshouses. In 1876 Josephine Shaw Lowell (1843–1905), who had been active in the Freedman's Aid Association during the war, became the first woman member of the New York State Board of Charities. The leading figure of the New York board was its president, William Pryor Letchworth (1823–1890). A prosperous Quaker businessman, Letchworth began devoting the major portion of his time to philanthropic projects after the Civil War. In 1869 he was appointed to the New York State board and seven years later became its president.

Although members of the state boards visited all types of institutions, they were, as we have noted, primarily concerned with the deplorable conditions they discovered in county poorhouses and, in particular, with the plight of many children who were incarcerated

71. Jeffrey R. Brackett, *Supervision and Education in Charity* (New York, 1903). State boards were authorized to inspect private institutions like the New York Refuge and the New York Catholic Protectory because both places received state financial aid.

there. Wines reported scenes of "nakedness, filth, starvation, vice, and utter wretchedness, which a very slight exercise of common sense and of humanity might have entirely prevented." Letchworth also noted flagrant cases of child abuse and torture, and he soon mobilized concerned citizens and public officials to focus their efforts on a "child-saving" campaign to remove children from almshouses and to place them in orphanages, foster homes, and reform schools.[72]

This drive was generally successful. Indeed, it was the pride of organized charitable endeavor. A committee of the National Conference of Charities and Correction concluded in 1893 that the widespread creation of private and public orphan asylums and the removal of children from almshouses "resulted in releasing hundreds of thousands of infant members of society from the pauperizing influences of the poorhouse as well as the demoralizing influences of degenerate parents." The number of children in almshouses in New York declined sharply in the last quarter of the nineteenth century, and the number of children in newly established state and county orphan asylums increased commensurately. In New York, the "Children's Law of 1875" proved to be more of an obstacle than an aid in the transfer. The legislation, which provided for the removal of dependent children from county poorhouses and for their placement in institutions "governed or controlled by officers or persons of the same religious faith as the parents of such child, as far as practicable," set off bitter debate and caused some almshouses to resist efforts to transfer their children to Catholic asylums.[73]

Gerald Grob has noted a certain irony in the proliferation of children's institutions. One of the main reasons that state boards had been established was to coordinate and regulate existing institutions with the eventual aim of reducing or perhaps even eliminating state expenditures for pauperism. On the other hand, the very organization of the boards as well as the main result of their activities—that is,

72. Wines quoted in Bremner, *From the Depths,* pp. 49–50. Thomas M. Bennett, "William Pryor Letchworth and His Work in Child Saving" (M.A. thesis, The Ohio State University, 1967). See also C. D. Randall, "Report of the Committee on Child-Saving Work," NCCC *Proceedings* (1893), pp. 131–39.

73. "History of the State Boards," NCCC *Proceedings* (1893), p. 37. Cooper, pp. 62–63, 261. New York *Laws* (1875), ch. 173 (Albany, 1876). Jacoby, *Catholic Child Care in New York,* pp. 49–50.

the proliferation of public institutions, especially orphan asylums—increased rather than decreased state welfare activities. Perhaps the organizers of the state boards expected that their emphasis on providing institutions for children would ultimately lead to a reduced welfare and custodial role for the state. Rhode Island philanthropist George Chace wrote, "Such homes and schools, although requiring at the start a considerable outlay, would in a single generation . . . far more than repay their cost, in the diminished expense for jails, prisons, and workhouses."[74]

Influenced by an investigative spirit, founders of the state boards provided the basis for a modern methodological approach to the study of crime, poverty, and delinquency. They did not eschew traditional moral pronouncements on these subjects, but their emphasis upon inductive methods of investigations gave them greater understanding of the causal complexity behind impoverished living conditions and criminal behavior and of the need to organize remedial treatment systematically and differentially. Implicit in this approach was the need for an expert. Chace wrote:

> Legislators, prison inspectors, trustees of reform schools and other similar boards of management, have neither the opportunity, nor the leisure for a thorough investigation of the deep and dark problems of social science, and yet without the results of such investigation they are not prepared for the intelligent and proper discharge of their several duties. It is the special function of Boards of State Charities and Corrections to furnish this needed information and guidance.[75]

Differentiation certainly characterized the efforts of state boards to deal with the "deep and dark problems" of juvenile delinquency. In the 1880s, state boards became convinced that removal was only half the battle. To take children from the "poisoned moral atmosphere" of the almshouse and then to dump them indiscriminately in reform schools and other institutions solved one problem but created another. "Absolute separatism should be maintained between the innocent and the guilty and between the pure and morally depraved, by means of separate institutions," wrote William Letchworth. He continued, "the

74. Gerald N. Grob, *The State and the Mentally Ill* (Chapel Hill: University of North Carolina Press, 1966), pp. 180–81. Chace, p. 22.

75. Chace, p. 20.

ultimate good of society would be realized by correcting the bad and preserving the good character of the good." Josephine Shaw Lowell advised Letchworth, "Keep bad boys in the House of Refuge . . . homeless and truant boys should be sent to entirely other and distinct institutions, when it is necessary to send them to institutions at all."[76]

Letchworth proposed that state governments operate separate institutions for four classes of children whom he defined as felons, minor offenders, truants, and the merely homeless. Letchworth urged that job training replace contract labor, and in order to effect further behavioral classifications among juvenile delinquents, he favored the cottage system within each institution. He also endorsed the system of family visitation established by the Massachusetts Board of State Charities in 1869. Under this plan, an agent of the state board took charge of delinquents before they appeared in court and often secured their probation or release on condition of their future good behavior.[77] Under Letchworth's guidance the first comprehensive vocational education program began in 1885 at the Western House of Refuge, Rochester, New York; many reform schools, however, continued to use the contract system even in the early decades of the twentieth century.[78]

76. William P. Letchworth, "Classification and Training of Children, Innocent and Incorrigible," in NCCC *Proceedings* (1883), p. 16. Bennett, pp. 20, 34. William R. Stewart, *The Philanthropic Work of Josephine Shaw Lowell* (New York: Macmillan, 1911), p. 248. Truant children, she wrote to her cousin, Elizabeth Gardiner Evans (Mrs. Glendower Evans), were "an entirely distinct class from dependent and criminal children"; see Josephine Shaw Lowell to Elizabeth Glendower Evans (March 21, 1892), folder 69, Papers of Elizabeth Gardiner Evans, Schlesinger Library, Radcliffe College. Mrs. Evans (1856–1937) was a prominent Boston philanthropist and reformer.

77. William P. Letchworth, "Children of the State," *Lend a Hand* 1 (1886), 576–81. On family visitation see Massachusetts *Acts and Resolves* (1869), ch. 483 (Boston, 1869), pp. 762–64; Gardiner Tufts, "Family Visitation of the Wards of the State as Practised in Massachusetts," in Enoch C. Wines, ed., *Transactions* of National Congress on Penitentiary and Reformatory Discipline (1871), pp. 360–69.

78. William P. Letchworth, *Technologic Training in Reform Schools* (Buffalo, 1884), pp. 34–37. New York *Laws* (1884), ch. 46 (Albany, 1884), pp. 44–47. C. A. Gower, "Industrial Training in Juvenile Reformatories," NCCC *Proceedings* (1888), pp. 229–34. The Centennial Exposition exhibit of the Imperial Technical School of Moscow greatly stimulated American interest in programs of vocational education; see C. M. Woodward, *The Manual Training School* (Boston, 1887), and Charles Alpheus Bennett, *History of*

Boards of state charities emphasized saving innocent children, not protecting juvenile delinquents. William Letchworth and Josephine Shaw Lowell spent their early careers trying to rescue children from almshouses. They also criticized the failure of authorities to discriminate between those children sent to orphanages and those to reform schools. Lowell and Letchworth were anxious to clear as many children as possible of the stigma of delinquency. Their aversion toward the New York House of Refuge explains in part the 50 percent reduction of the population in that institution during the period, 1880–90. Nevertheless, they believed that the children who behaved so badly that they ended in the refuge generally deserved the rough treatment that they received there. And as we shall see, the reform schools continued to have problems.

Beginning in the 1870s and as another part of the development of comprehensive welfare and penological programs, state governments established reformatories for young men (16 to 25 or 30 years old) who were first-time offenders. This development, which further restricted that category of children known as juvenile delinquents, had been in the making for some time. In the 1840s, Stephen Allen of the New York Refuge had demanded a separate institution for older juvenile offenders. In 1851 *The Pennsylvania Journal of Prison Discipline* called for an institution to provide for "a large class of grown-up boys, and the very worst in the community." Advances of European penologists during the middle decades of the century made reformatories for young men a reality. In 1840 Captain Alexander Maconochie was appointed superintendent of Norfolk Island, the British penal colony in Australia. There he attempted to replace the traditional flat sentence with a task sentence based upon a convict's industry and behavior both as an individual and as a member of an inmate work group. Though unable to eliminate the fixed sentence himself, Maconochie's work did offer the possibility of a more flexible penal system both in Australia and England. Sir Walter Crofton combined the idea of the task sentence with the ticket-of-leave plan (an early form of parole which freed inmates on a conditional basis),

---

Manual and Industrial Education up to 1870 (Peoria, Ill.: Manual Arts Press, 1917). A survey of the subject is Berenice Fisher, *Industrial Education: American Ideals and Institutions* (Madison: University of Wisconsin Press, 1967).

and the two combined became known as the Irish system. Education and vocational training shaped the routine of English and Irish reformatories. According to the French judge Bonneville de Marsangy, the principle of conditional liberation around which the new penology was built was "nothing more nor less than the extension to adult convicts of a principle applied with such great success to juvenile offenders."[79]

American penal reformers soon applied the European innovations even if they did not always acknowledge them. The New York State Reformatory at Elmira was incorporated in 1869 and opened in 1877 under the superintendency of Zebulon R. Brockway, formerly superintendent of the Detroit House of Correction. Enoch Wines and Theodore Dwight, then in the twilight of their careers with the Prison Association of New York, were influential in gaining legislative support for this institution, as was Gaylord B. Hubbell, Warden of Sing Sing Prison and a supporter of Crofton's system of intermediate prisons. In 1877 a determined group of women led by Ellen Cheney Johnson (1829–1899), another veteran of the U.S. Sanitary Commission, persuaded Massachusetts legislators to found a reformatory for girls "too old to be sent to Lancaster." Franklin Sanborn helped to establish the Massachusetts Reformatory for Men (1884), and in 1893 Josephine Shaw Lowell roused New Yorkers to found a reformatory for women convicted of misdemeanors, chiefly those involving sex offenses.[80]

---

79. *Pennsylvania Journal of Prison Discipline* 4 (1851), 187. John Vincent Barry, *Alexander Maconochie of Norfolk Island* (Melbourne: Oxford University Press, 1958) pp. 69–79. Marsangy quoted in Frederick H. Wines, *Punishment and Reformation* (New York: Thomas Crowell, 1918), p. 225n. In 1862 the ticket of leave was being utilized by the municipal reform school in Chicago. Superintendent George W. Perkins reported: "These tickets are renewed each month if the boy is doing well, and the fact of having to return the ticket every month and get a new one does much to regulate the conduct of the boys who receive them" (Sanders, pp. 396–97).

80. Eugenia C. Lekkerkerker, *Reformatories for Women in the United States* (The Hague: J. B. Wolters, 1931), pp. 89–98. Blake McKelvey, *The History of American Prisons* (Chicago: University of Chicago Press, 1936), pp. 137–43. For the influence of Elmira upon the establishment of the Huntington Reformatory in Pennsylvania, see Harry Elmer Barnes, *The Evolution of Penology in Pennsylvania* (Indianapolis: Bobbs-Merrill, 1927), pp. 399–402. For a summary of the European contributions to the reformatory movement see Max Grünhut, *Penal Reform* (Oxford: Oxford University Press, 1948), pp. 89–94.

Penologists of the time debated whether or not the reformatory movement was built upon principles which had already been applied to juvenile delinquents. E. M. P. Wells and Joseph Curtis had employed a mark system in the Boston House of Reformation and the New York Refuge respectively. Good behavior had resulted in special favors within the institution and the possibility of early indenture, a form of parole. Like his father, Frederick Wines saw the connection:

> Somewhat unconsciously, perhaps, the methods adopted resembled those which had been long in use in institutions for the reformation of juvenile offenders. Indeed, it could not be otherwise, since men are but children of a larger growth, and the methods which succeed at a youthful age ought, with necessary modification, to succeed, though probably not to the same degree, with older men.

Zebulon R. Brockway, never one to hide his light under a bushel, thought otherwise. Writing to penologist Louis A. Robinson, he "denied explicitly that he in any way drew on the institutions for juvenile delinquents for suggestions as to principles and procedure." In his autobiography, *Fifty Years of Prison Service,* Brockway claims to have discovered independently the indeterminate sentence and other innovations of European penal reformers.[81]

Whatever the merits of this dispute, the growth of the reformatory did relieve some institutions for juvenile delinquents of their older and often more troublesome inmates. In the light of other problems facing those institutions that were attempting to reform children, such a development could not have been unwelcome.

This discussion of attitudes and policies toward juvenile delinquency has largely centered upon the preventive efforts of philanthropies and institutions, founded mostly in eastern and midwestern cities and states. Juvenile delinquents themselves did not acknowledge this framework, however, and throughout the nineteenth century they

81. Frederick Wines, pp. 207–208. Enoch C. Wines, *The State of Prisons and of Child Saving Institutions in the Civilized World* (Cambridge, Mass., 1880), pp. 151–52, 625–28. Louis N. Robinson, *Penology in the United States* (Philadelphia: John C. Winston, 1923), pp. 121–22; Zebulon R. Brockway, *Fifty Years of Prison Service* (New York: Charities Publication Committee, 1912), pp. 133–35. David M. Schneider, *The History of Public Welfare in New York State, 1609–1866* (Chicago: University of Chicago Press, 1938), pp. 317–25. On Wells and Curtis see above, pp. 24–27.

disrupted the peace of locales far removed from refuges and conventions for reform school managers. Francis Lieber, translator of Tocqueville and Beaumont's study of the American prison system and a professor at South Carolina College from 1835 to 1852, recorded the case of a well-bred Charleston boy who was expelled from college for dueling, later shot his antagonist, studied law, served a prison term for the shooting, and then was elected to the state legislature—all before he was twenty-two years old. Jack Kenny Williams, historian of the South Carolina prison system, noted other cases of white youths convicted of forgery, vandalism, theft, and passing counterfeit money. These boys were usually pardoned if they were "of respectable parents." On the frontier, an editor in Houston, Texas, recorded a "quarrel between two little boys, the oldest of whom was scarcely ten years; and, strange to say, one of them actually drew a small pocket pistol and shot at his opponent, fortunately, without doing injury."[82]

As we have noted, westerners often blamed eastern philanthropists, particularly Charles Loring Brace, for whatever juvenile delinquency occurred in their states. Reform schools in western states were not founded, however, just to receive placed-out children who had run away from their rural homes or committed other delinquencies. The new institutions were established because settlers and early leaders of western states, often former residents of older states, were impelled by the same positive ideas concerning juvenile incarceration which inspired the founders of houses of refuge and early reform schools. The warden of the Iowa State Penitentiary echoed a familiar sentiment: "The State ought, by all means, to provide a suitable house of correction for the reception of these juvenile offenders where they would not come in contact with old criminals but receive a different schooling from what we can give them here." J. G. Riheldaffer, first superintendent of the Minnesota State Reform School (1867), em-

82. Thomas S. Perry, ed., *The Life and Letters of Francis Lieber* (Boston, 1882), p. 126. Jack Kenny Williams, *Vogues in Villainy: Crime and Retribution in Ante-Bellum South Carolina* (Columbia: University of South Carolina Press, 1959), pp. 18–20; and Williams, "White Lawbreakers in Ante-Bellum South Carolina," *Journal of Southern History* 21 (1955), 360–73. Editor quoted in Kenneth W. Wheeler, *To Wear a City's Crown: The Beginnings of Urban Growth in Texas, 1836–1865* (Cambridge: Harvard University Press, 1968), pp. 54–55.

phasized the more positive theme of education. Denigrating reformatory concepts which stressed "the mere duty of *safely keeping*
the boys and . . . employing them at *remunerative* labor," Riheldaffer attempted to implement a routine centered in the classroom instead
of the workshop. Truants were especially likely candidates for the
Minnesota school.[83]

Western reform schools benefited from shortcomings of some
eastern institutions by locating in the country and organizing the
institutional routine around farm work. In general, the contract system and sectarian preaching were prohibited, and schooling occupied
a greater proportion of the children's time (usually half a day) than
had heretofore been the case. In 1872 an Iowa report advised, "The
first step is to convince the boy that you are his *friend*. That whatever
you require him to do is for his *benefit*. This cannot be accomplished
by harsh treatment."[84] But reform school authorities were always reminded of the shortcomings of their institutions. Iowa officials laid
one year's high number of escapes to boys who were "averse to farm
labor," and not given opportunities to learn mechanical trades. A
Kansas report posed the alternatives in starker terms:

> Our boys cannot and will not all become farmers. Many must enter
> professions, adopt trades, or take their chances in the overcrowded
> ranks of the unskilled multitude and be confronted with the ever-
> present temptations which harass a dependent and unsettled condi-
> tion of life.[85]

By the 1890s, most western reform schools had introduced rudimentary programs of vocational education as well as military drill
and organization. By so doing, they came to resemble the older,
eastern institutions and were thus bound in a common destiny.

In the South, no special provisions were made for young lawbreakers until the end of the nineteenth century. Before the Civil War,
the South was an agricultural society based upon Negro slave labor.

83. Iowa Legislative Documents, II, *Report of the Warden of the Iowa State
Penitentiary* (1866), p. 6. Minnesota Executive Documents, *Report of the
Minnesota State Reform School* (1869), p. 288; emphasis in original. On the
controversy over placing-out, see above, pp. 44–48.

84. Iowa Legislative Documents, III, *Report of the Board of Trustees of the
Iowa State Reform School* (1872), p. 7; emphasis in original.

85. Iowa Legislative Documents, II, *Report of the Iowa State Reform School*
(1870), p. 15. Kansas Public Documents, II, *Report of the Board of Trustees
of State Charitable Institutions* (1888), p. 7.

Plantation discipline took care of the disobedient Negro child, and few if any southerners dreamed of considering him as a juvenile delinquent in need of special care. We have already indicated a high degree of tolerance for the activities of white children which probably would be classified as juvenile delinquency in other sections of the country. Edgar Knight notes that the manual labor schools of the antebellum South, which were established to teach the sons of white artisans trade and farming skills, were often disrupted when students broke agricultural implements and abused livestock. Louisiana provided some exception to the region's general indifference toward organized treatment of juvenile delinquency when, in 1822, the state legislature appointed Edward Livingston, former mayor of New York, to revise the state penal code. The Livingston Code (1824) included provisions for a school of reform that resembled the first houses of refuge. Although the code was not adopted in Louisiana, it was widely discussed in Europe and the northern states and exercised an influence on various efforts to reform criminal law. In 1847 New Orleans opened a house of refuge, but this institution did little more than separate children from older offenders.[86]

The Civil War destroyed, among other things, the growing penitentiary system in the southern states. Many prisons were completely ruined and others were converted to factories that made war supplies. The war also ended legal slavery, and as a result whites faced the challenge of providing for thousands of destitute freedmen, some of whom inevitably committed crimes. These "crimes" were often based upon trumped-up charges such as the vaguely worded vagrancy statutes in state Black Codes. Convicted Negroes were occasionally sent to jail, but the great majority were leased out on contract to railroad companies and manufacturers, where they were treated miserably.[87]

86. Edgar W. Knight, *A Documentary History of Education in the South Before 1860,* 5 vols. (Chapel Hill: University of North Carolina Press, 1949–53), IV, 62–148. Edward Livingston, *A System of Penal Law for the State of Louisiana* (Philadelphia, 1833), pp. 714–22. William B. Hatcher, *Edward Livingston* (Baton Rouge: Louisiana State University Press, 1940), pp. 245–88. Hilda Jane Zimmermann, "Penal Systems and Penal Reforms in the South since the Civil War" (Ph.D. diss., University of North Carolina, 1947), p. 95.

87. Zimmermann, pp. 50–51. Blake McKelvey, "A Half Century of Southern Penal Exploitation," *Social Forces* 13 (1934), 112–23. Negroes made up the overwhelming bulk of convict population during this period; see Vernon I.

Some of these convicts were children. Laura M. Towne (1835–1901), the abolitionist who devoted her life to the freedmen of the Sea Islands, related the case of a Negro boy in the South Carolina penitentiary who "prays night and day that God will let him die. The irons have cut into his wrists. The beds are rotten straw, full of vermin." In 1872 Robert Day (age 12, height, 4'9", complexion black, hair and eyes black, scar from dog-bite on calf of right leg) was serving life sentence for murder in the Mississippi State Prison. James Harrington (age 13, height, 5'1", complexion black, hair and eyes black) was serving ten years for "burglary with intent to rape."[88]

Because of the conditions of penal life and the unwillingness or inability of southern state legislatures to found reform schools, authorities were both reluctant to send children to jail and quick to pardon them by executive clemency. In 1870 North Carolina county jails reported only thirteen children under 16 years of age out of a total prison population of 372. Throughout the nineteenth century, state legislatures also attempted to prevent delinquency by sustaining apprenticeship laws that placed poor, orphaned, and illegitimate children under the care and supervision of individual householders— a mode of social control that had been largely abandoned in other parts of the country. Regarding clemency proceedings, author George Washington Cable reported that twenty-five children under sixteen years of age were pardoned from terms in the Huntsville, Texas, penitentiary in 1880. A Georgia pardon read: "Wade Hampton. Convicted of burglary. October term, 1893, Fulton County; sentence, five years. At time of his conviction was a mere child, and since confinement has lost a leg."[89]

Little else was done for juvenile delinquents, black or white, until

---

Wharton, *The Negro in Mississippi, 1865–1890* (Chapel Hill: University of North Carolina Press, 1947), pp. 234–43, and George B. Tindall, *South Carolina Negroes, 1877–1900* (Columbia: University of South Carolina Press, 1952), pp. 260–76.

88. Rupert Sargeant Holland, ed., *Letters and Diary of Laura M. Towne* (Cambridge, Mass.: Riverside Press, 1912), p. 302. Mississippi House of Representatives, *Journal* (1873), pp. 573, 580.

89. Sanders, pp. 410–13. George Washington Cable, *The Silent South* (New York, 1885), pp. 155–56. Georgia House of Representatives, *Journal* (1895), p. 82.

the Populist uprisings near the end of the century. Some children continued to suffer in jail, in convict camps, and on the county road gangs and prison farms which gradually replaced the lease system in the 1890s. In 1869 North Carolina established a state board of charities that graphically described the plight of children in the state penitentiary, but the legislature ignored its remedial recommendations.[90]

The number and variety of reform schools for juvenile delinquents multiplied during the later nineteenth century, but so too did the severity of institutional problems. Child-saving philanthropies also developed rapidly during this period, but they avoided reform school problems by limiting institutional features and by emphasizing the placing-out system. By the 1880s, the latter approach appeared to be in the ascendancy. A. O. Wright of the Wisconsin Board of State Charities summarized the feeling:

> If I were to classify the order of places, best or worst, in which people may be placed, especially children or young people, I say first of all, a good home; second best, a small institution rightly managed under proper persons, meaning by a small institution, one or two hundred inmates or less; thirdly, a large institution; fourth, a bad home.[91]

In the years to follow, concerned citizens emphasized pessimistic or optimistic explanations of delinquency as these accorded with their individual attitudes. Philanthropists who were encouraged by the success of preventive efforts instigated further reforms designed to remove delinquents from the processes of criminal law altogether. Pioneers in the natural and physical sciences provided new ideas about human behavior which gave interested citizens a different combination of perspectives for analyzing juvenile delinquency.

90. Zimmermann, pp. 113–14, 117–18. Sanders, pp. 414–16.
91. NCCC *Proceedings* (1881), p. 305.

CHAPTER 3

Scientific Explanations
of Delinquency, 1880–1910

THE IMPORTANCE OF scientific study of children in general and of juvenile delinquency in particular is usually associated with the impact of Darwinian ideas on the new and developing professions in the social and natural sciences. This view is not incorrect, but it does obscure other factors that should be kept in mind. First, concurrent scientific theories, relating to delinquent children and originating in criminology and physiology, derived their causal explanations from the empirical method more than from the evolutionary hypothesis. Also, the magnitude of the concept of evolution beguiles the scholar to cite it as evidence of the intellectual bases of those men and women who employed it to explain juvenile delinquency; in fact, their ideas often originated from traditions existing prior to the advent of organized scientific disciplines. And finally, the tendency to focus on developments flowing from Darwin's work submerges earlier interpretations of delinquency which also purported to be scientific.

During the 1830s and 1840s, phrenology, to cite a case in point, was considered a science. Phrenologists claimed to be able to analyze character and behavior by studying the shape and protuberances of individual skulls. As John D. Davies has pointed out, these practitioners viewed the lawbreaker merely as a person "whose mental organs had not developed properly." The famous Scottish phrenologist George Combe (1788–1858) toured America from 1838 to 1840 giving optimistic lectures on the possibility of reforming young criminals by stimulating through education the uses of such propensities as concentrativeness ("It renders permanent, emotions and ideas in the mind") and adhesiveness ("Attachment: friendship and society result from it").[1] Visiting the Boston House of Reformation in 1838, Combe examined the heads of some children and reported "the moral and intellectual organs favorably developed in proportion to the animal organs." Although Combe was unsuccessful in an appeal for better educational programs in prisons and refuges, he won the admiration of Samuel Gridley Howe, who saw in phrenology confirmation of his belief in the infinite educability and improvability of the human race.[2]

Like Howe, Charles Loring Brace supported an optimistic view of juvenile reformability with scientific (though not phrenological) jargon. Although Brace is mainly associated with a moralistic and agrarian solution to the problem, his account of a young girl's "fall" also included hereditarian speculation:

> The "gemmules" or latent tendencies, or forces or cells of her immediate ancestors were in her system, and working in her blood, providing irresistible effects on her brain, nerves and mental emotions, and finally, not being met early enough by other moral, mental and physical influences, they have modified her organization until her will is scarcely able to control them and she gives herself up to them.[3]

Brace believed that even the worst children had virtuous gemmules

1. John D. Davies, *Phrenology: Fad and Science* (New Haven: Yale University Press, 1955), p. 80; George Combe, *Notes on the United States of America During a Phrenological Visit in 1838–9–40,* 5 vols. (Philadelphia, 1841), I, xx–xxiii. The areas of concentrativeness and adhesiveness were located near the base of the skull; see George Combe, *Essays on Phrenology* (Philadelphia, 1822). A recent work is David A. De Guistino, "Phrenology in Britain, 1815–1855: A Study of George Combe and His Circle" (Ph.D. diss., University of Wisconsin, 1969).

2. Combe, *Notes on the United States of America,* I, 113, 86–87. Not everyone shared the optimism of Howe and Combe. In 1840 James Silk Buckingham toured the New York Refuge and reported, "the worst collection of countenances we had ever seen . . . the phrenologist and physiognomist would both have found abundant proofs of the general truths of their theories, that the shape of the cranium and the expression of the features are often faithful indexes of the minds within." See James Silk Buckingham, *America: Historical, Statistic and Descriptive,* 3 vols. (London, 1841), I, 130.

3. Charles Loring Brace, *Dangerous Classes,* pp. 43–44. Gemmule is the diminutive for gemma, a bioligical term for a bud.

and that if parents would allow him to place their children with farm families, these virtuous buds would rise to the surface and serve as antidotes to the poison in their blood. He was enthralled by Darwin's *Origin of Species* (1859), reading it thirteen times and concluding that "the law of natural selection applies to all the moral history of mankind, as well as to the physical. Evil must die ultimately as the weaker element, in the struggle with good." On the other hand, Brace denounced Herbert Spencer's social Darwinism because it denied the existence of God as a cause or a factor in human existence. He wrote to his friend George Howard, "Would not mankind take chloroform if they had no future but Spencer's? No individual continuance, no God, no superior powers, only evolution working towards a benevolent society here, and perfection on earth."[4]

Brace's reliance upon Darwin was selective, but so was that of scholars who, quite unlike Brace, wished to frame comprehensive social philosophies based upon the application of the concept of evolution to mankind. Herbert Spencer's philosophy, which came to be called Social Darwinism, employed two of Darwin's principal concepts, the struggle for existence and the survival of the fittest—the latter phrase was Spencer's—to explain the development of human society. Ernst Haeckel similarly adopted Darwin's theory of recapitulation to the maturation process of individual human beings. According to Haeckel, man was supposed, in the relatively brief period of his maturation, to live through the entire course of paleontological evolution.

Darwinian ideas shaped the emerging disciplines of child and educational psychology. In 1877 Darwin published a biography of his infant son which emphasized the importance he attached to the study of child development. In the United States, William James and G. Stanley Hall integrated the evolutionary point of view into psychology, where it overshadowed the formalist laboratory psychology of Wilhelm Wundt and the German School. James and his foremost student Edward L. Thorndike went beyond Darwin and Spencer to argue that the individual's mind was not only molded by environment but that it reacted upon environment in a creative manner. The American psychologists believed that man in concert with his fellows could both

4. Emma Brace, ed., *The Life of Charles Loring Brace*, pp. 300–302, 365. Brace knew Darwin and corresponded with him.

know the world and change it, but that in order to do so he would have to be educated to use his talents purposefully and efficiently in the struggle for a just and humane civilization. John Dewey synthesized this view with a theory of education which made the school an agent of human social change instead of a dispenser of immutable and received truths. Dewey's definition of education was "that reconstruction of experience which adds to the meaning of experience, and which increases ability to direct the course of subsequent experience."[5]

James, Thorndike, and Dewey did not trifle with categories of children. They had no particular interest in juvenile delinquency, although their work influenced pioneer child psychiatrists Adolf Meyer, Lightner Witmer, and William Healy whose ideas we shall discuss later in context with the juvenile court movement. The scientist who did develop an evolutionary explanation of juvenile delinquency was Granville Stanley Hall (1846–1924), a German-trained psychologist who founded in 1882 the first laboratory of experimental psychology at Johns Hopkins University. Six years later, he was appointed first president of Clark University, where, for the next thirty years, he organized and developed the child study movement. Hall's study of the origins of and changes in youthful behavior laid the basis for the modern belief that childhood, youth, and adolescence are separate stages of life with their own values, often different from or hostile to values of the adult world.[6]

G. Stanley Hall's concept of adolescence, which shaped his views

5. John Dewey, *The School and Society* (Chicago, 1899), pp. 89–90. Thomas M. Canfield, "Psychologists at War: The History of American Psychology and the First World War" (Ph.D. diss., University of Texas, 1969), discusses the increasing variety of the science as it developed in the United States. On the relationship between education and evolutionary theory, see Lawrence A. Cremin, *The Transformation of the School* (New York: Knopf, 1961), pp. 93–126. See also Paul F. Boller, *American Thought in Transition: The Impact of Evolutionary Naturalism, 1865–1900* (Chicago: Rand McNally, 1969); and Thomas C. Cochran, *The Inner Revolution* (New York: Harper and Row, 1964).

6. For an interesting summary of Hall's concept of adolescence and the maturation process, see John and Virginia Demos, "Adolescence in Historical Perspective," *Journal of Marriage and the Family* 31 (November 1969). See also Dorothy Ross, "G. Stanley Hall, 1844–1895: Aspects of Science and Culture in the Nineteenth Century" (Ph.D. diss., Columbia University, 1965); and Dorothy Ross, *G. Stanley Hall: The Psychologist as Prophet* (Chicago: University of Chicago Press, 1972).

on juvenile delinquency, was based upon his application of Haeckel's recapitulation doctrine to mental evolution. Thus Hall believed that the years of childhood were psychologically and physiologically years of savagery, "when the very worst and best impulses in the human soul struggle against each other for its possession." He regarded the beginning of adolescence as a period of "storm and stress"—a passing phase to be followed at maturity by the emergence of a new and civilized self. Hall took an indulgent view of juvenile delinquency. "The youth who go wrong are," he wrote, "in the vast majority of cases, victims of circumstances or of immaturity, and deserving of both pity and hope." Hall denounced "ignorant and cruel public opinion" that condemned "all those who have once been detected on the wrong side of the invisible and arbitrary line of rectitude."[7]

Hall's students were quick to develop this theme. After interviewing a number of prominent men and totaling up their youthful pranks and delinquencies, Edgar J. Swift concluded in 1901 that a period of semicriminality was not only right but necessary for healthy boys. Going beyond individual delinquencies, J. Adams Puffer in 1912 described gang delinquency as an "ancient virtue of savagery" and assured the gang boy's worried parents, "as his ganginess fades with later adolescence, much of his native barbarity will go with it. Till that time comes the wise adult will not attribute to thorough going depravity what is only a temporary stage in the boy's psychic evolution."[8]

Even Jane Addams was influenced by the recapitulation theory. Pondering a title for her 1909 survey of the problems of urban

7. G. Stanley Hall, *Youth: Its Education, Regimen and Hygiene* (New York: D. Appleton, 1906), pp. 135, 136, 140. For Hall's original statement on recapitulation see his "The Moral and Religious Training of Children," *Princeton Review* (January 1882), pp. 26–48. See also the introduction of Charles E. Strickland and Charles Burgess to a compendium of Hall's writings, *Health, Growth and Heredity* (New York: Columbia University Teachers College, 1965), esp. pp. 6–11, 19–22. Hall's ideas about delinquency are available in more detail in his *Adolescence,* 2 vols. (New York: D. Appleton, 1905), I, 334–410.

8. Edgar J. Swift, "Some Criminal Tendencies of Boyhood: A Study in Adolescence," *Pedagogical Seminary* 8 (March 1901), 63–91. J. Adams Puffer, *The Boy and His Gang* (Cambridge, Mass.: Houghton Mifflin, 1912), pp. 24, 85. See also William B. Forbush, *The Boy Problem* (Boston: Pilgrim Press, 1902), pp. 23, 41.

children, she discarded *Juvenile Delinquency and Public Morality* and settled instead on *The Spirit of Youth and the City Streets.* She believed that juvenile delinquents were often promising young people whose natural, if primitive, pursuit of joy had been frustrated by an urban environment organized for commercial pursuits but not for creative recreation. Children broke laws "in their blundering efforts to find adventure and in response to the age-old impulse of self expression."[9]

This optimistic view, which derived as much or more from Jane Addams' faith in humanity as from her knowledge of social Darwinism, failed to satisfy other scholars and scientists. They wanted to know why some "promising young people" were sent to reformatories while others were not. William Forbush, a prolific writer on boyhood, offered the explanation that some children suffered "psychic arrests" during their recapitulation of the savage stages of evolution. For example, a continued dispensation to steal indicated the persistence of the predatory instinct that characterized the animal kingdom. If psychic arrests became permanent, criminal conviction was only a matter of time.[10]

The concept of psychic arrest, like the theory of recapitulation itself, was essentially speculative and not subject to the process of empirical verification which characterized the scientific method. Recognizing this shortcoming, G. Stanley Hall and other pedagogues incorporated into their study of children some of the techniques of observation and verification which were being used in the sciences of criminal anthropology and physiology. Inevitably, some of the ideas of these disciplines were also included. Late nineteenth-century criminology was dominated by Cesare Lombroso (1835–1909), an Italian professor of legal medicine. His *L'Uomo delinquente* (1876) contended that the habitual criminal constituted an abnormal anthro-

---

9. Edward C. Marsh to Jane Addams (February 23, 1909) and Jane Addams to Edward C. Marsh (February 27, 1909), Reel 2, Addams Papers, Schlesinger Library, Radcliffe College. Jane Addams, *The Spirit of Youth and the City Streets* (New York: Macmillan, 1909), pp. 6, 69. Jane Addams contrasted with earlier child-savers like Charles Loring Brace in that she believed that children not merely were redeemable but, because they were naturally good, could redeem society.

10. Forbush, *The Boy Problem,* pp. 38–41.

pological type clearly distinguished by characteristic stigmata that were anatomic, physiological, psychological, and social. He explained the origin of this type by the theory of atavism—the criminal was a reversion to the more primitive, presocietal type of species. Lombroso studied hundreds of criminals, systematically recording the anatomical and physiological measurements of each, in his search for a criminal type. His findings met opposition from French criminologists and sociologists, most notably Gabriel Tarde (1834–1904). Tarde distrusted rigid systems of explanation and criticized Lombroso for ignoring the social bases of crime in favor of a physical-structural theory of causation. Like Lombroso, however, Tarde appreciated the importance of gathering in a systematic way facts and statistics out of which conclusions were shaped. Both men, for example, drew upon the work of Adolphe Quetelet (1796–1874) in anthropometry (the science of body measurements). Quetelet, a Belgian astronomer and statistician, believed in "nature fixed types," and, after measuring many people, he conceived of a new man, the physically average man: he regarded variations from this type as defective human beings and as such prone to crime and disease.

Those Americans interested in child study used and combined both Italian and French criminology.[11] Some scholars sought only a better understanding of the physical changes of child development, but others attempted to establish a causal link between the results of their measurements and various kinds of juvenile misbehavior. The

11. For an annotated bibliography of physical child study, see Bird T. Baldwin, "The Physical Growth of Children from Birth to Maturity," *University of Iowa Studies in Child Welfare* 1 (1920–21), 320–402. Lombroso was popularized in England and America during the 1890s. See Robert Fletcher, "The New School of Criminal Anthropology," *American Anthropologist* 4 (1891), 201–36; James Weir, "Criminal Anthropology," *Medical Record* 45 (January 13, 1894), 42–45; Havelock Ellis, *The Criminal* (New York: Charles Scribner's Sons, 1900); Frances Kellor, *Experimental Sociology* (New York: Macmillan, 1901), and "Criminal Sociology," *Arena* 23 (1900), 301–307; and Charles Richmond Henderson, *Introduction to the Study of the Dependent, Defective and Delinquent Classes* (Boston: Heath, 1901), pp. 215–36. Lombroso's own work was published later. See Cesare Lombroso, *The Female Offender* (New York: Appleton, 1903); and Lombroso, *Crime: Its Causes and Remedies* (Boston: Little, Brown, 1912). The central influence of European criminology in America is analyzed in Arthur E. Fink, *Causes of Crime* (Philadelphia: University of Pennsylvania Press, 1938), pp. 108–33. See also Marvin E. Wolfgang, "Cesare Lombroso," in Hermann Mannheim, ed., *Pioneers in Criminology* (London: Stevens & Son, 1960), pp. 168–227.

American pioneer in juvenile anthropometry was Harvard physiologist Henry Pickering Bowditch (1840–1911). His principal experiment extensively measured Boston school children over a twenty-year period beginning in 1872. Anthropologist Franz Boas (1858–1942) coordinated for the 1893 World's Fair Exhibit a series of similar measurements in Oakland, Toronto, St. Louis, Milwaukee, and Worcester, Massachusetts. Both Bowditch and Boas concluded, among other things, that American and Canadian children were taller and heavier than children of foreign-born parents. Unlike many of their colleagues, however, they did not make pejorative judgments about the smaller and lighter subjects of their study. William Townsend Porter, for example, claimed in his study of St. Louis school children that there was a physical basis for the precociousness of some youths. Dull children, he concluded, were lighter and precocious children heavier than the average child. Porter and others associated mediocrity of mind with mediocrity of physique. Henry G. Beyer claimed that "successful children are larger than unsuccessful."[12]

To these scientists and pedagogues, juvenile delinquents exemplified physically "unsuccessful" children. Applying Lombrosian criminology to the measurement of reform school youths, they seemed bent upon finding a physical basis to explain the misdemeanors of these children. George E. Dawson, another Hall student, compared Worcester public school children with delinquents from the Lyman School for Boys and the State Industrial School for Girls at Lancaster, Massachusetts. He concluded that the delinquent children were not only less intelligent, smaller and lighter than the school children but also that they had "more physical anomalies than are found among normal persons . . . deformed palates . . . smaller heads, broader heads, and broader faces, the type being, in general,

12. Henry P. Bowditch, "The Growth of Children in Massachusetts," in Massachusetts State Board of Health, *AR* (1877), pp. 307–309. Franz Boas, *The Growth of Toronto School Children* (Washington, D. C., 1898). William Townsend Porter, "The Physical Basis of Precocity and Dullness," *Transactions* of the Academy of Science of St. Louis 6 (1893), 161–81. Porter, "The Growth of St. Louis Children," *Publications* of the American Statistical Association 4 (1894–95), 28–34. Henry G. Beyer, "Relation Between Physique and Mental Work," *American Physical Education Review* 5 (1900), 149–60. See also W. S. Christopher, "Measurements of Chicago School Children," *Journal of the American Medical Association* 25 (October 19, 1895), 683–87.

that of lower races or of the infantile period of our own race." Eugene
S. Talbot, a Chicago dentist, conducted anthropometrical measurements upon youths in two state reformatories, Pontiac, Illinois, and
Elmira, New York, and found "their physical stigmata (head, face,
jaws, teeth, etc.) twice as numerous as those in non-criminal individuals."[13]

The most vigorous and persistent American proponent of applying
Lombrosian criminology to the study of children was Arthur Mac-
Donald (1856–1936), an employee of the U.S. Bureau of Education.
MacDonald had studied psychology under Hall at Johns Hopkins
and then visited Europe to study and collect the works of Lombroso,
Ferri, and other criminologists. In 1897 he contributed excerpts from
their writing to the Bureau's *Annual Report* and also reprinted the
conclusions of Porter and Dawson. Soon thereafter, MacDonald began
to make his own anthropometrical and "psycho-physical" measurements of school children of the District of Columbia. Among other
things, he measured their heads to obtain their individual cephalic
index. He also tested the strength of their grasp and their sensitivity
to temperature and touch by employing his own instruments such
as the "Aesthesiometer." MacDonald then attempted to correlate
these measurements with his own arbitrarily conceived definitions of
"bright," "dull," "average," or "unruly" children. Among his conclusions were the following:

> *Shape of head.*— . . . a large proportion of boys are broad-
> headed rather than long-headed. Long-headedness, or dolichocephaly,
> seems to be an unfavorable sign, for the bright show the smallest per-
> centage, the average next and the dull the largest percentage; the un-
> ruly boys have a large percentage of long heads.
> *Sensibility to heat.*—The bright boys are the most sensitive to heat;
> but there is no further parallelism between sensitiveness to heat and
> mental ability, for the average boys are less sensitive than the dull
> boys.

The Bureau of Education tolerated these experiments until 1902,
when the appropriation under which MacDonald had conducted his

---

13. George E. Dawson, "A Study in Youthful Degeneracy," *Pedagogical
Seminary* 4 (1896), 247–48. Eugene S. Talbot, "A Study of the Stigmata of
Degeneracy Among American Criminal Youth," *Journal of the American
Medical Association* 30 (1898), 849–56.

experiments was omitted with the note, "As children come to be known and marked out in the school or in the community as possessing the bodily signs of degeneracy in such permanent form as the shape of the skull, or ears, or mouth, it would operate seriously to discourage them from efforts to form good habits."[14]

Undaunted, MacDonald began a congressional lobbying campaign to establish a criminological laboratory (with Arthur MacDonald as presumed director) in the Department of the Interior. He emphasized that this laboratory would be "a development of work already begun by the Federal Government."[15] He found supporters both inside and outside Congress. Republican Senators George F. Hoar, Boies Penrose, and Matthew Quay, reporting favorably on MacDonald's scheme, said, "It would be desirable to find what physical and mental traits are common to unruly school children and children in reformatories."[16] The American Medical Association and scholars such as Richard T. Ely and Havelock Ellis also endorsed his work.[17]

MacDonald's congressional contacts enabled him to get a number of his works published as legislative documents at government expense. In a work published in 1908 he declared, "The time has come when

14. U.S. Department of the Interior, *Report of the Commissioner of Education, 1897–1898* 2 (Washington, D. C.: Government Printing Office, 1899). U.S. Congress, Arthur MacDonald, *Man and Abnormal Man,* 58th Cong., 3d sess., Senate Doc. 187 (Washington, D. C.: Government Printing Office, 1905), pp. 26–27. Estimates of appropriations quoted in U.S. Congress, Arthur MacDonald, *Laboratory for the Study of the Criminal, Pauper and Defective Classes,* 60th Cong., 2d sess., House Report 2087 (Washington, D. C.: Government Printing office, 1909), p. 2.

15. MacDonald, *Laboratory,* p. 2. He was certainly not a Spencerian. "Every child has the right to a proper bringing up," he declared. "If it has no parents or its parents can not give it the rearing it has a right to the community or State should do it." See U.S. Congress, Arthur MacDonald, *Juvenile Crime and Reformation,* 60th Cong., 1st sess., Senate Doc. 532 (Washington, D. C.: Government Printing Office, 1908), p. 51.

16. U.S. Congress, Arthur MacDonald, *A Plan for the Study of Man,* 57th Cong., 1st sess., Senate Doc. 400 (Washington, D. C.: Government Printing Office, 1902), p. 7.

17. U.S. Congress, Arthur MacDonald, *Statistics of Crime, Suicide, and Insanity, etc.,* 58th Cong., special sess., Senate Doc. 12 (Washington, D. C.: Government Printing Office, 1903), pp. 551–54. Other endorsements came from The American Laryngological Society, the American Electro-Therapeutic Society, The Old Colony Association of Universalists of Massachusetts, and The Silver Bow County Medical Association of Butte, Montana.

it is important to study a child with as much exactness as we investigate the chemical elements of a stone or measure the mountains of the moon." To assist scholars wishing to engage in this precise task, MacDonald offered his description of "children who seem to be vicious by nature":

> There is a certain animality in the face, the eyes are without expression, the forehead is low or depressed, the jaws are very large, the edges of the ears are rough, the ears extend out prominently from the head. . . . Such children may be too large or too small for their age or they may appear older or younger than they are. Some do not look you straight in the face, but have a stealthy, oblique, or variable glance.[18]

At different times, MacDonald proposed that Congress establish his laboratory in the Department of Justice, the Department of Commerce and Labor, and, in 1909, independent of any department at all. This latter proposal received a favorable report from the House Committee on the Judiciary, but a biting minority dissent prevented the bill from coming to a vote. In essence, the congressmen who were opposed to MacDonald's proposal confirmed the earlier report of the Bureau of Education:

> We have no hesitation in our opinion that a bureaucratic inquisition into these matters by officers of the government would be resented even in a reformatory, and would be utterly out of place in hospitals, schools, and charitable institutions. The results would be by no means as trustworthy as those obtained by physicians, clergymen, and philanthropists in the ordinary walks of life; that an attempt to distinguish physical defects as criminal is dangerous in any hands.

Although MacDonald's congressional supporters continued to introduce similar legislation for fifteen more years, this 1909 report delivered the *coup de grâce* to his plans for a laboratory.[19]

18. MacDonald, *Juvenile Crime and Reformation*, pp. 44–45, 296.

19. MacDonald, *Laboratory*, p. 4. The minority report was signed by Republican Representatives John J. Jenkins, Richard W. Parker, Charles Q. Tirrell, and H. S. Caulfield. MacDonald's own interests strayed from the study of juvenile delinquency, but not from anthropometry. During the late 1920s, Senator Royal S. Copeland attempted unsuccessfully to have him appointed "an official examiner of Congressional brain weights." In 1933 MacDonald studied the relative brain weights of senators and representatives and, because senators had a higher average weight, he concluded, "It takes more brains to

The effort to apply Lombrosian criminology to the study of juvenile delinquents suffered at the hands of its most zealous advocates. One physician, Thomas Travis, even went beyond MacDonald. Travis claimed that the best remedy for delinquency was to operate upon children in order to change the shape of their crania, jaws, and palates. Presumably their behavior would alter directly with their appearance. Travis concluded, "For those who are not amenable to reformation there is only on realm left, and that is extirpation."[20]

Contentions such as these did not go unanswered by more careful students of criminal anthropology, particularly Franz Boas. In two volumes—*Immigration and Crime* and *Changes in Bodily Form of Descendants of Immigrants*—of a huge federal investigation of immigration (1911), Boas attacked "craniology" with statistics of his own. He admitted that immigrant children were committed to reform schools in excess of their representation in the juvenile population, but he denied that their commitment was related to either their racial type or their physical structure. Emphasizing the healthful and regenerative effects of the American environment upon immigrant children, he concluded that they were taller and heavier than their parents. Boas documented changes in the cephalic indexes of children, believing that distinctive types of head shape such as dolichocephaly (long-headedness) and brachycephaly (wide-headedness) tended to disappear over generations. Ever the optimist, Boas believed that as long heads grew shorter and short heads longer, an assimilated American child, healthy and well behaved, was sure to evolve.[21]

Other investigations supplemented Boas' findings that delinquency

---

get into the Senate than into the House." Before his death in 1936, MacDonald wrote on another subject of interest to him: "The Scientific Political Training of Calvin Coolidge," as noted in his obituary in the New York *Times* (October 18, 1936).

20. Thomas Travis, *The Young Malefactor* (New York: Thomas Y. Crowell, 1908), pp. 209–11.

21. Thomas F. Gossett, *Race: The History of an Idea in America* (Dallas: Southern Methodist University Press, 1963), p. 421. For Boas' report see U.S. Congress, *Reports of the Immigration Commission* 36, 61st Cong., 3d sess., Senate Doc. 750 (Washington, D.C.: Government Printing Office, 1911), pp. 8, 261–64, and Vol. 38, 61st Cong., 2d sess., Senate Doc. 208 (Washington, D. C.: Government Printing Office, 1911). See also John Higham, *Strangers in the Land* (New York: Atheneum, 1965), p. 125.

derived from environmental problems, not individual structural abnormalities. In an 1898 study of children admitted to the New York
Juvenile Asylum, anthropologist Aleš Hrdlička noted their abnormally
high rate of malnutrition and physical neglect. He attributed the
children's delinquency "not so much to their constitution as to the
social circumstances and environment to which they were subjected."
He added, "Misbehaved children are not characterized as a class by
any considerable physical inferiority, or by any great proportion of
physical abnormalities." Edward F. Waite, a judge of the juvenile
court in Minneapolis, asserted that much of the delinquency of
children appearing before his court resulted more from children ag-
gravated by remediable defects such as infected tonsils, poor eye-
sight, and bad teeth than from any structurally criminal types acting
in conformity with their shapes.[22]

Despite the findings and disclaimers of Boas and Hrdlička, criminal
anthropology, with its emphasis upon structural deficiency, debated
the problem of juvenile delinquency from an essentially defensive
and pessimistic point of view. During the late nineteenth and early
twentieth centuries this mood was reinforced by the rising popularity
of hereditarian explanations for crime, vice, pauperism, and other
social ills. In 1875 Richard Louis Dugdale (1841–1883), a visitor
for the Prison Association of New York, wrote *"The Jukes": A Study
in Crime, Pauperism, Disease and Heredity* as the result of his intensive study of the consanguinity of many inmates in one county jail
in New York. Two years later he expanded this work to include
case histories of 251 convicts in the Sing Sing and Auburn State
Prisons, noting in this study many prisoners who had formerly been
refuge and reformatory boys.[23]

Although Dugdale was careful to record the histories of virtuous
members of the Juke family and to point out the importance of en-

22. NYJA, *AR* (1898), p. 73. Edward F. Waite, "The Physical Bases of Crime:
From the Standpoint of the Judge of a Juvenile Court," *Bulletin* of the American Academy of Medicine 14 (1913), 388–95. See also J. P. Munroe, "The
Problem of Defectives and Delinquents," *Journal of Pedagogy* 20 (1910),
160–75; John H. Witter, "The Physical Basis of Crime from the Standpoint
of the Probation Officer," *Bulletin* of the American Academy of Medicine 15
(1914), 102–104; and Fink, *Causes of Crime*, pp. 108–33.

23. Richard Louis Dugdale, *"The Jukes": A Study in Crime, Pauperism,
Disease and Heredity* (New York, 1877), pp. 98–100.

vironment in modifying individual behavior, other observers were more alarmist. Samuel Gridley Howe, writing in the second annual report of the Massachusetts Board of State Charities (1864), blamed the state's high number of paupers and delinquents on "inherited organic imperfection—vitiated constitution, or *poor stock*." In 1879 Josephine Shaw Lowell advocated the establishment of a (New York) state reformatory for women to incarcerate sexually delinquent, vagrant girls and thus, in her words, "prevent the transmission of moral insanity." "What right have we today to allow men and women who are diseased and vicious to reproduce their kind, and bring into the world beings whose existence must be one long misery to themselves and others?" she asked. Oscar C. McCulloch, an Indianapolis minister, sensationalized hereditarian study and shocked delegates at the 1888 NCCC convention by emphasizing the notoriety of a family whom he called "The Tribe of Ishmael".[24]

We have noted that before the 1890s, hereditarian theories of crime and delinquency derived more from social prejudices than from organized bodies of scientific knowledge. Dugdale's work was ignored for years, as were Gregor Mendel's discoveries in the 1860s which laid the basis for the science of genetics. Howe spoke as a Brahmin besieged by poor European migrants, not as a scientist inquiring methodically into the ancestry of individual paupers and criminals. Also, as Mark Haller and Arthur Fink have shown, many penologists and medical authorities resisted the implications of hereditarian ideas and continued to believe that criminals could be reformed by Christian persuasion and by improvement of social conditions. Frederick H. Wines acknowledged that heredity might be one cause of crime, but he also stressed the social and cosmic sources of crime and the interrelationship of all causes of dependency and delinquency. In 1884 alienist John P. Gray, refuting the rigidly hereditarian attitude toward crime, cited numerous cases of parents who had delinquent children and of adult criminals with well-behaved offspring. Zebulon R. Brockway, an enthusiastic hereditarian, won little support from his

24. Howe, quoted in Katz, *The Irony of Early School Reform*, p. 181. Josephine Shaw Lowell, "One Means of Preventing Pauperism," in Stewart, *The Philanthropic Work of Josephine Shaw Lowell*, p. 97. Oscar C. McCulloch, "The Tribe of Ishmael—A Study of Social Degradation," NCCC *Proceedings* (1888), pp. 154–59.

colleagues in the National Prison Association when he suggested that half of the men and women in prisons were incorrigible by reason of defective parentage.[25]

The organization and development of eugenics, the science of improving human breeds, during the first two decades of the twentieth century, gave hereditarian explanations of crime and delinquency the authoritative gloss which they had previously lacked. Whether drawing upon Mendelian theory or not, eugenics seemed to offer proof that mating transmitted from generation to generation characteristics which obeyed their own fixed laws without regard to the external life of the organism. Sir Francis Galton, a cousin of Darwin, coined the word eugenics and developed it as a science. To him, eugenics meant advancing the human race by encouraging the propagation of its better elements while at the same time restricting the breeding of criminals, paupers, idiots, and insane persons. Eugenicists, however, often became preoccupied with the latter groups as evidenced by their extensive debates over various ways—restrictive marriage laws, incarceration of the morally delinquent, different methods of asexualization—to stop procreation of people whom they classified as dependent and delinquent. Galton preached his gospel to biologists and scientists, many of whom saw, in John Higham's words, "a way of converting their scientific interest into a program of social salvation— a program based wholly on manipulation of the supposedly omnipotent forces of heredity."[26]

A number of scholars have noted the special appeal of eugenics among members of the nativist middle and upper classes. Those citizens who were particularly affected by eugenic ideas lived in eastern cities where immigration from southern and eastern Europe seemed to threaten their social and economic security. "From Italy, Hungary and other countries of the south of Europe, a filthy stream

25. Mark H. Haller, *Eugenics: Hereditarian Attitudes in American Thought* (New Brunswick, N.J.: Rutgers University Press, 1964), pp. 36–39, 49. Fink, *Causes of Crime,* pp. 151–78. John P. Gray, "Heredity," *American Journal of Insanity* 41 (1884), 1–21.

26. Stanley P. Davies, *The Mentally Retarded in Society* (New York: Columbia University Press, 1959), pp. 33, 49–70. Albert Deutsch, *The Mentally Ill in America* (New York: Columbia University Press, 1949), pp. 366–78. Higham, *Strangers in the Land,* p. 150.

pours into and mingles itself with the purer waters of our communities," wrote Dr. Enoch V. Stoddard, Commissioner of the New York State Board of Charities. The leading American eugenicist was Charles Benedict Davenport (1860–1944), a Puritan New Englander who was worried about the supposed "dying out" of the aristocratic breed. In 1903 Davenport helped to organize the American Breeders' Association, which gave practical advice about eugenics to plant and animal breeders. Four years later this organization was enlarged to include a eugenics division whose activities were soon dominated by Preston F. Hall and Robert DeCourcey Ward of the Immigration Restriction League. Simultaneously, Davenport established a genetics research center at Cold Spring Harbor, Long Island, New York. In 1910 he persuaded Mrs. E. H. Harriman to finance an adjoining Eugenics Record Office which prepared an index of the American population and advised individuals and local groups on eugenical problems.[27]

One result of Davenport's activity was the revival of studies similar to *The Jukes* but claiming to be more scientific and objective. Arthur H. Estabrook, a colleague of Davenport's, verified Dugdale's original notes and brought the study of the family up to date with his own study, *The Jukes in 1915*. Estabrook concluded that all of the Jukes who were criminals were also feebleminded. Henry H. Goddard, psychologist at the Vineland (New Jersey) Training School for the Feebleminded, studied two branches of the Kallikak (Greek for good/bad) family. He contended that the criminality and feeblemindedness of one side were hereditary and therefore likely to be transmitted to future generations. Davenport, in his own work, *Heredity in Relation to Eugenics* (1911), was more positive; he claimed that two mentally defective parents would produce only mentally defective offspring. Frank W. Blackmar, a sociologist at the University of Kansas, described the crimes and immorality of a "tribal

27. New York State Board of Charities, *AR* (1897), I, 599. See also Barbara M. Solomon, *Ancestors and Immigrants: A Changing New England Tradition* (Cambridge: Harvard University Press, 1956); Higham, *Strangers in the Land*, pp. 150–53; and Haller, *Eugenics*, pp. 40–57. For an excellent study of the eugenics movement in one state, Wisconsin, see Rudolph J. Vecoli, "Sterilization: A Progressive Measure?" *Wisconsin Magazine of History* 43 (1960), 190–202. Like Higham, Vecoli points out the reformist appeal of eugenics, with its emphasis on state action and race improvement through education.

group" whom he called "The Smoky Pilgrims." He concluded by demanding that the tribal home be broken up and that the older children be sent to the state reform school.[28]

Physicians and officials of state schools for feebleminded children, discouraged by the difficulties of their task, welcomed the eugenic message and created out of it a new type of child whom they labeled "moral imbecile" or "defective delinquent."[29] Isaac N. Kerlin, Superintendent of the Pennsylvania Training School for Feebleminded Children at Elwyn, called attention to "a group of cases quite distinct in their symptoms of derangement, and requiring forms of discipline quite unusual as compared with those applicable to the children ordinarily recognized as idiotic." He listed as their characteristic behavior "thieving, generally without acquisitiveness; a blind and headlong impulse toward arson; delight in cruelty . . . delight in the sight of blood; habitual willfulness and defiance." Kerlin suggested not only that these children were of "faulty stock" but also that they accounted for most of the delinquents whom reform schools and refuges failed to improve. Martin W. Barr, chief physician at Elwyn, supported this view:

> It is needless to speak of reformatories. These may reshape a deformed nature, perhaps recover what has been lost, but never yet have they recreated what never existed; and with this element they

28. Eugenic studies include Arthur H. Estabrook, *The Jukes in 1915* (Washington, D.C.: Carnegie Institution, 1916); Henry H. Goddard, *The Kallikak Family* (New York: Macmillan, 1912); Charles B. Davenport, *Heredity in Relation to Eugenics* (New York: Henry Holt, 1911); F. W. Blackmar, "The Smoky Pilgrims," *American Journal of Sociology* 2 (1897), 485–500; Florence Danielson and Charles B. Davenport, *The Hill Folk* (Cold Spring Harbor, N.Y.: Eugenics Record Office, 1912); and Elizabeth S. Kite, "The Pineys," *Survey* 31 (October 4, 1913), 7–13, 38–40. It is ironic that these eugenicists, who were so afraid of being overwhelmed by degenerate immigrants, should justify their demand for immigrant restriction with studies which purported to demonstrate the heredity of crime, pauperism, and feeblemindedness in old American families. An important exception, the story of the Zero family from Europe, is described in Gertrude Davenport, "Hereditary Crime," *American Journal of Sociology* 13 (1907), 402–409.

29. Norman Dain, *Concepts of Insanity in the United States, 1789–1865* (New Brunswick, N.J.: Rutgers University Press, 1964), pp. 204–10, notes the rise of pessimism about the curability of mentally ill persons after 1850. Crowded conditions in asylums, combined with psychiatrists' inability to understand the problems of an increasingly poor, immigrant clientele, defeated attempts at moral treatment and reduced the probability of achieving cures.

may dig deep and patiently, yet never find the moral soil in which good principles may take root and grow. It is not there, and never has been.

Barr and his colleagues proposed to solve this problem by "permanent sequestration" in special institutions where "asexualization should be the law . . . not only assuring to the individual release in large measure from exaggerated impulses and desires, but also the safety of society in event of a possible escape."[30]

Special institutions for defective delinquents were expensive and, at first, were established in only a few states. In 1894 New York opened the Rome State Custodial Asylum for helpless and unteachable idiots. The efforts of Dr. Walter E. Fernald of the Massachusetts School for Idiotic and Feebleminded Youth led that state to authorize separate provision for defective delinquents in 1911, but Massachusetts did not provide the necessary funds until 1922. A year earlier New York had opened a special institution for male defective delinquents at Napanoch.[31]

Laws in some states allowed physicians charged with the care of defective delinquents in state asylums to perform various types of sterilizing operations. Indiana passed the first sterilization statute in 1907, requiring sterilization for "confirmed criminals, idiots, imbeciles

30. Isaac N. Kerlin, "The Moral Imbecile," NCCC *Proceedings* (1890), pp. 244–45, 248–49. Martin W. Barr, "The Unrecognized Irresponsible," *Proceedings* of the Third National Conference on the Education of Truant, Backward, Dependent and Delinquent Children (NCET, 1906), pp. 7, 10. The literature on this subject is considerable. See for instance, Martin W. Barr, "The How, the Why, and the Wherefore of the Training of Feebleminded Children," *Journal of Psycho-Asthenics* 4 (1899), 204–12; Alfred Wilmarth, "The Rights of the Public in Dealing with the Defective Classes," *Journal of the American Medical Association* 31 (1898), 1276–78; J. H. McCassy, "How to Limit the Over-Production of Defectives and Criminals," *Journal of the American Medical Association* 31 (1898), 1345–47; George A. Auden, "Feeblemindedness and Juvenile Crime," *Journal of Criminal Law and Criminology* 2 (1911), 228–38; Clara Harrison Town, "Mental Types of Juvenile Delinquents Considered in Relation to Treatment," *Journal of Criminal Law and Criminology* 4 (1913), 83–89; Hastings H. Hart, "The Extinction of the Defective Delinquent: A Working Program," *Proceedings* of the American Prison Association (1912), pp. 207–17.

31. Stanley P. Davies, *Social Control of the Mentally Deficient* (New York: Thomas Y. Crowell, 1930), pp. 132–45. This book was originally published as *Social Control of the Feebleminded* (New York: Columbia University Press, 1923).

and rapists." By 1936 twenty-five states had eugenic sterilization laws, and, although they were all eventually declared unconstitutional, *Eugenical News* reported in 1946 that 45,127 sterilizations had been performed under extant laws in thirty states. The most common operations were the vasectomy (section of the seminal ducts in the male) and the salpingectomy (section of the fallopian tubes in the female). Only Oregon permitted castration.

Some physicians were so eager to perform these operations that they did not wait for state sanction. Dr. Hoyt F. Pilcher, Superintendent of the Kansas State Home for the Feeble-Minded, castrated eleven allegedly feebleminded youths in the home. Dr. Henry C. Sharp, physician at the Indiana state reformatory, sterilized several hundred inmates in 1905, two years before state law legalized the practice. His action so thrilled the National Christian League for the Promotion of Purity that it resolved to advocate "a more healthful, effective and merciful treatment by efficient surgeons, for special criminals and degenerate children."[32]

Other reformatory officials sympathized with Pilcher and Sharp even if they could not imitate them. When Goddard's Training School asked twenty-seven superintendents to provide the approximate number of defective delinquents in their institutions, the estimates averaged nearly fifteen percent for each school. The Preston School of Industry, Ione, California, complained that because state homes for the feebleminded were full, "a great many foolish boys are sent to this institution that ought not to be sent here." An Iowa reform school official agreed: "Boys of weak mentality often make it very difficult to maintain the standard of discipline. . . . I regard them as a very undesirable class of inmates in an institution such as ours."[33]

32. Martin Barr and Mary Ellen Lease, the Populist orator and, in 1895, president of the Kansas State Board of Charities, hailed Pilcher as a heroic pathfinder. There were apparently some Kansans whom Mrs. Lease did not want raising corn, hell, or anything else. See Martin W. Barr, "President's Annual Address," *Journal of Psycho-Asthenics* 2 (1897), 1–13; and Kansas Board of Trustees of the State Charitable Institutions, *Ninth Biennial Report* (1892–1894), pp. 86–87. On Sharp see Haller, *Eugenics,* pp. 49–50, 131–32, 136, and National Christian League for the Promotion of Purity, *Annual Meeting* (1909), pp. 4–5.

33. "Estimated Number of Feeble Minded Persons in State Reformatories and Industrial Schools," *The Training School Bulletin* 9 (1912), 8–10.

Eugenic theories gained important support from the origination and widespread application of intelligence tests designed to measure in quantifiable terms the mental abilities of children and, later, of adults. Developed originally by the French psychologists Alfred Binet (1857–1911) and Theophile Simon (1873–1961), these tests were a series of problems, graded in difficulty and requiring for their solution little else but pencil, paper, pictures, and a few common objects. In 1904 Binet tested Paris school children and used the results to devise a rough scale aimed at diagnosing feebleminded or subnormal pupils. Before he died, Binet, in collaboration with other specialists, twice revised his scale, including within it the concept of mental age which further refined measurement of the academic achievements of school children.[34]

In the United States, Henry H. Goddard of the Vineland Training School became the leading apostle of Binet tests, first applying them in 1906 to the feebleminded children in his institution. To Goddard, the tests were the ultimate weapon in confirming the common belief that persistent wrongdoers must be mentally defective. In 1911 he claimed, "Now we may say with perfect assurance that the Binet tests of intelligence are entirely satisfactory and can be relied upon to pick out the mental defective at least up to the age of twelve years." Goddard hoped to use the public schools as "clearing houses" for defective delinquents. After testing had identified these children, he claimed, "they can then be cared for as condition leads. . . . When we have learned to discriminate and recognize the ability of each child and place upon him such burdens and responsibilities only as he is able to bear, then we shall have largely solved the problem of delinquency."[35]

Because Binet tests were inexpensive and easy to administer, they were widely used, not only by public and private schools but also by

34. For selections and an analysis of Binet's and Simon's work, see William Kessen, *The Child* (New York: Wiley, 1967), pp. 188–208.

35. Henry H. Goddard, "The Treatment of the Mental Defective Who Is Also Delinquent," NCCC *Proceedings* (1911), pp. 64–65. Frederick Kuhlmann and Lewis M. Terman pioneered revisions of Binet tests in the United States. Kuhlmann, however, designed tests to discover feeblemindedness while Terman attempted to find the upper limits of human mentality. See A. A. Robeck, *History of American Psychology* (New York: Collier, 1964), pp. 456–63.

juvenile courts, reform schools, institutions for defective and dependent children, and, eventually, by the U.S. Army. Designed primarily to detect mental incapacity, they enthusiastically confirmed their purpose. During World War I, for instance, Army recruits were tested, and their poor showing contributed to the popular fear that the United States was being inundated by a rapidly propagating population of idiots and morons.[36]

Juvenile delinquents fared little better with Binet tests. Studies of boys in the Texas Reform School (Gatesville) and the Whittier State School (California) found most of them far below the average mental age for their respective chronological ages.[37] A psychologist testing children who passed through Judge Ben Lindsey's juvenile court complained, "Instead of sterilizing or segregating these people, we are still buying them Bibles."[38] Henry Goddard and his colleagues tested one hundred children in the juvenile court of Newark, New Jersey, and fifty-six girls on probation from an anonymous reform school. In the first study they found only one normal child (that is, whose chronological age corresponded to his mental age) and, in the latter, only four girls who were not feebleminded. "Mabel B————, 16 years old physically; 10 years old mentally. Taken by her mother from a laundry where she and another girl had been spending the night with two Chinamen. . . . Nina N————, 15½ years old physically; 9.3 years old mentally. . . . This girl absolutely incorrigible, steals, associates with commonest type of men, even yelling to them from House of Detention, absolutely immoral," read typical entries in the examination of girls detained by the Newark Juvenile Court. Like

36. On the early history of Binet tests in the United States, see J. E. Wallace Wallin, *Problems of Subnormality* (New York: World Book Company, 1917); James B. Miner, *Deficiency and Delinquency* (Baltimore: Warwick and York, 1920); Gardner Murphy, *Historical Introduction to Modern Psychology* (New York: Harcourt, Brace, 1949), pp. 354–57; and Canfield, "Psychologists at War."

37. Truman Lee Kelley, *Mental Aspects of Delinquency* (Austin: University of Texas Press, 1917). J. Harold Williams, *The Intelligence of the Delinquent Boy* (Whittier State School: Whittier, California, 1919). J. Harold Williams, "Intelligence and Delinquency," *Journal of Criminal Law and Criminology* 6 (1916), 696–705.

38. C. S. Bluemel, "Binet Tests and Two Hundred Juvenile Delinquents," *The Training School Bulletin* 11 (1915), 193.

Josephine Shaw Lowell of an earlier day, Goddard demanded permanent institutionalization for such girls, thus assuring "that this race should end with them; they shall never become the mothers of children who are like themselves."[39]

Even before World War I, it was evident that the fatalistic conclusions of these psychologists and test administrators had failed to satisfy other, more sophisticated students. An early critic raised the possibility, well proven today, "that the differences in the classification are primarily due to subjective differences in the examiners and not to objective differences in the groups examined." Two eminent psychologists, Robert M. Yerkes and James W. Bridges, were even more emphatic: "Indeed, we feel bound to say that the Binet scale has proved worse than useless in a very large number of cases."[40] Advocates of intelligence tests such as psychologist James B. Miner cautioned against extremist interpretations of their results. "Nobody has suggested isolating all persistent delinquents," he claimed.[41]

Psychometric studies of juvenile delinquents in institutions declined after World War I, as did the percentage of feebleminded children

39. Mrs. E. Garfield Gifford and Henry H. Goddard, "Defective Children in the Juvenile Court," *The Training School Bulletin* 13 (1917), 132–35. Henry H. Goddard and Helen F. Hill, "Delinquent Girls Tested by the Binet Scale," *The Training School Bulletin* 8 (1911), 50–56. See also John Slawson, *The Delinquent Boy* (Boston: Richard G. Badger, 1926); and Davies, *Social Control of the Mentally Deficient*, pp. 90–91. Robert P. Daniel, *A Psychological Study of Delinquent and Non-Delinquent Boys* (New York: Columbia University Press, 1932) describes the results of Binet tests given to Negro boys in the Virginia Manual Labor School; he makes no mention of environmental factors, which undoubtedly conditioned their performance.

40. Wallin, *Problems of Subnormality*, p. 120. Robert M. Yerkes and James W. Bridges, *A Point Scale for Measuring Mental Ability* (Baltimore: Warwick and York, 1915), p. 94. As President of the American Psychological Association in 1917, Yerkes (1876–1956) was commissioned a Major in the U.S. Army to mobilize psychologists for various war activities. Though their efforts were known primarily through the intelligence testing of 1,700,000 men and officers, many scientists, including Yerkes, were active in the National Research Council, which was established to deal with numerous problems—motivation, propaganda, rehabilitation—engendered by national participation in a global war. See Roback, *History of American Psychology,* pp. 449–55, and Canfield, "Psychologists at War."

41. Miner, *Deficiency and Delinquency*, p. 250. Miner and others were influenced by Charles Goring's *The English Convict* (London: Wyman & Sons, 1913), which claimed on the basis of case studies that only a few children of criminals inherited a predisposition to crime.

supposedly discovered in each test. In 24 separate studies, 1910–1914, an average of 45 percent of the children were termed feeble-minded; in 65 studies during the period 1915–1919, this average dropped to 32 percent and, in 56 tests, 1920–1928, it declined to 17 percent.[42]

G. Stanley Hall's evolutionary psychology, Lombrosian criminology, eugenics—these sciences led the study of juvenile delinquency into a cul-de-sac. Scholars who employed them reached generally negative conclusions about the possibilities of reforming delinquent children. Even the refutation of extreme determinism by Boas and others did not lead to organized programs. Lombroso's positivism shifted the focus of criminological study from crime to the individual criminal or delinquent, but this new concern was hardly compassionate; that is, the individual criminal found little in this approach to give him hope. For while scientific studies of criminals and delinquents were based upon empirical observation and measurement, their pessimistic conclusions tended to categorize the subjects as unfit for philanthropic concern. In 1888 J. J. Blaisdell, a Beloit College professor, voiced this feeling when he asked how it was possible to help the hereditary criminal if he belonged to "a peculiar species, out of the reach of the influences and controlled by the reverse of the principles of the rest of men?"[43]

Instances have been noted of scientific theories being applied to juvenile delinquents, but these tend to dramatize the ideas, rather than to explain changes and developments in institutional care and preventive philanthropy. Some scientific concepts permeated institutional life but many did not. Harry Sharp's sterilization of Indiana delinquents was the exception, not the rule. Dr. Kenosha Sessions, Superintendent of the Indiana School for Girls, perhaps more representative of attitudes toward hereditarian and anthropological theories of delinquency, made this observation:

> I believe our business in life is to overcome our inheritance. I don't
> believe it is necessary for any one to succumb to his inheritance,

42. E. H. Sutherland, "Mental Deficiency and Crime," in Kimball Young, ed., *Social Attitudes* (New York: Henry Holt, 1931), p. 359. See also Walter C. Reckless and Mapheus Smith, *Juvenile Delinquency* (New York: McGraw-Hill, 1932), pp. 103–108.

43. Blaisdell quoted in Vecoli, "Sterilization: A Progressive Measure?" p. 62.

whether it is mental, physical or moral defect. We have to learn how to teach these boys and girls to overcome these moral inheritances which interfere with their being good law-abiding citizens.[44]

The difficulty remained learning "how to teach" morality—the supposed foundation of social and individual lawfulness. Organized care of juvenile delinquents continued to be challenged by crises and changes most of which originated quite apart from the constructs of scientists and pedagogues. Similarly, proposed solutions to institutional problems were often derived from nonscientific ideas and attitudes.

44. NCET *Proceedings* (1916), pp. 52–53.

CHAPTER 4

Crises and Changes in Institutional Care, 1880–1910

D EVELOPMENTS IN the institutional care of juvenile delinquents reflected to a degree scientific ideas about juvenile delinquency. The empirical approach showed in the increased scope, precision, and systematization of inmate records. The traditional social questions concerning the children and their parents (did they drink? did they use tobacco? profane language?) continued to interest reform school authorities, but a different type of inquiry was also being made. What was the estimated annual income of the child's father? Of the family unit? Did the mother work? What sort of housing, if any, did the child live in?—the questions were becoming more bureaucratic and thorough. Efforts to trace the child's ancestry became more systematic perhaps because of the influence of scientific studies. Individual case histories began to include each child's height, weight, other bodily measurements, dental care, and health history.

Reform school physicians and superintendents emphasized the importance of physically conditioning incarcerated children. Hamilton D. Wey, physician at the Elmira Reformatory, instituted a program of calisthenics, turkish baths, and cold showers for young men "greatly in arrears physically." Wey continued, "It is not sufficient to train them in habits of industry, with attention to mental and moral needs; but of paramount importance is the systematic culture of the body; that is, exercise and training most suitable for individual requirements, systematized and carried out under the supervision of a competent teacher." Mrs. Glendower Evans, reporting on the introduction of the Swedish or Ling system of gymnastics at the Lyman School (Massachusetts Reform School for Boys), claimed that it was "admirably adapted to developing obedience, promptness and self-control." Mrs. Evans concluded that "such exercises, valuable to every one, are especially so to those, who, as in the case with many criminals, have ill developed nervous centres." The superintendent of the Indiana Reform School added this comment on the boys whom he sought to revive physically:

> They are invariably in bad condition physically from improper nourishment, cigarettes, masturbation, irregular lives, and a bad inheritance. They are not the laughing, mirthful, mischievous, curly haired boys that some well meaning persons would have the public believe.[1]

Moralistic attitudes, as we have noted, coexisted easily with scientific explanations.

Former military men took over the administration of some reform schools and introduced army drill into the daily routine as another means of building up "underdeveloped" delinquents. Colonel E. C. Barber assumed charge of the New York House of Refuge in the 1890s and Colonel C. B. Adams became superintendent of the Boys' Industrial School at Lancaster, Ohio, formerly the Ohio Reform Farm. Colonel Adams summarized the benefits of military drill for the delinquent boys:

> There are no better exercises known for developing the chest, hardening the muscle and giving the boy an erect figure and soldierly bearing, than the seventeen setting-up exercises of the United States Drill Regulations. His training in self-control and respect for authority begins. He is taught that prompt, unquestioning obedience is a fundamental military principle. . . . He must always stand erect, look his officer in the eye, and never forget his "sirs."

"His will has become subordinate to the will of another," concluded Colonel Adams of the properly trained reform school boy. F. H.

1. Wey quoted in *Proceedings* of the National Prison Association (1888), p. 189. Mrs. Glendower Evans, "Statement from the Trustees of the State Primary and Reform Schools of Massachusetts," in *History of Child Saving in the United States* (Boston: National Conference of Charities and Correction, 1893), p. 239. Guy C. Hanna, "Vocational Training in Boys' Correctional Institutions," NCET *Proceedings* (1916), p. 2.

Nibecker of the Philadelphia House of Refuge found military drill and calisthenics valuable in teaching "that highly moral obligation of obedience to a superior authority without question, and that other social virtue in which the individual is sunk in the whole and shines as part of the whole." Lucy M. Sickels, superintendent of the Michigan Industrial Home for Girls boasted that her girls could do fourteen of the seventeen setting-up exercises in the U.S. Drill Manual.[2]

These new routines were designed as much to reinforce the authoritarian type of control for which reform schools had been traditionally noted as they were to improve the physical condition of the inmates. With the slow but steady decline of the contract system of labor, reform school officials were eager to find alternative ways to occupy the time of their inmates. As we have discussed, William P. Letchworth pioneered a breakthrough in this area by securing [New York] state approval in 1885 to introduce a program of industrial training at the Western House of Refuge, Rochester. "What we want," said one reformatory official, "is that preparation on the part of our inmates for some handicraft which will enable them . . . to care for themselves when released from the institution—the teaching of a trade for the trade's sake." Printing and carpentering were the two principal trades introduced. Some institutions introduced sloyd, a Swedish system of general manual training designed to familarize students with use of hand tools in wood carving and joining.[3]

Wherever they were instituted, programs of vocational education entailed the purchase of expensive machinery and the hiring of supervisory workers who had to be paid market wages. These expenses,

2. C. B. Adams, "The Advantages of Military Training to Delinquent Youth," NCET *Proceedings* (1904), pp. 40–41. F. H. Nibecker, "Education of Juvenile Delinquents," *Annals* of the American Academy 23 (1904), 75–84. Lucy M. Sickels, "Military Drill as Practiced at the Michigan Industrial Home for Girls," NCET *Proceedings* (1904), pp. 36–38. In *Centuries of Childhood,* pp. 267–68, Philippe Ariès emphasizes the development of military modes in the schools of France in the eighteenth century and England in the nineteenth. The ideal soldier was pictured as a tough, virile adolescent and "pedagogues henceforth attributed a moral value to uniform and discipline."

3. On Letchworth, see above, pp. 68–69. For an account of the sloyd system in operation, see Gustaf Larsson, "Sloyd as an Educational Means of Developing Delinquent Minds," NCET *Proceedings* (1904), pp. 4–8. On the continuity of the contract system, see, for example, Kentucky Legislature, *Documents* (1906–07), pp. 4–5.

which were gladly assumed by municipal governments on behalf of local high schools, often proved beyond reform school budgets, that is, unpurchasable for the money which state governments allotted to the institution. As a result, the number of reform schools organized on the less expensive cottage plan with an agricultural routine actually increased during the late nineteenth century. Few superintendents could afford to be as candid as one superintendent who rejected agricultural work in favor of vocational education because, as he put it, "Most of our boys come from cities and will surely return to their former homes after leaving us." Even the Western House of Refuge, home of the first vocational education program, removed from Rochester to the country in 1902 although retaining industrial training in some cottages.[4]

The economic and social problems of the reform schools did not evaporate in the country air. Farming equipment was also becoming complex and expensive. Few schools could stay abreast of agricultural technology, and even those that did could only train a small—and because of the labor-saving features of most machinery, an increasingly smaller—proportion of their youths in the techniques of farm management. The superintendent of the Indiana Reform School complained, "It is really a shame that there are some who are yet to be convinced that a miracle of character is being wrought when an officer takes forty, fifty, or a hundred boys out into the field to crack clods. Modern farming is not done that way." What apparently was being wrought on the farm was a fair amount of deviant sexual activity, perhaps even including buggery with the livestock population. The same superintendent's protest suggests a variety of pastimes:

The farm furnishes unlimited opportunities for boys in large numbers to get together for immoral purposes. Every management must face

4. C. A. Gower, "Industrial Training in Juvenile Reformatories," NCCC *Proceedings* (1888), pp. 229–34. A comprehensive survey of industrial education outside the reform school is given in U.S. Commissioner of Labor, *Annual Report, Industrial Education* (Washington, D.C.: Government Printing Office, 1893). Robert Wiebe's comment on the changing character of American education during the nineteenth century seems appropriate: "Once public education had kept company with abolition, temperance and humane treatment for the insane; by the 1880s its more usual companions were industrial productivity and tax policy." See Wiebe, "The Social Function of Public Education," *American Quarterly* 21 (1969), 153.

this terrible and unspeakable crime. No institution can do anything for its inmates where this degrading practice flourishes. Older boys corrupt younger ones and the crime spreads throughout the institution. Unnatural flirtations are carried on that nauseate and disgust.[5]

Nevertheless, by 1900 programs of industrial and manual training were closely enough associated with reform school routines to convince some pedagogues, principally David Snedden (1868–1951) of the Teachers College at Columbia University, that reform schools offered better education than public schools. Snedden's attraction to reform schools was understandable; he conceptualized education as a means to discipline children to standards of social efficiency rather than a way to transmit cultural heritage. He blamed public schools for having "failed largely to cooperate with and learn from juvenile reform schools" and urged them to correct their errors by classifying students on the basis of behavior and by introducing vocational education programs.[6]

Snedden's ideas failed to attract much support among pedagogues or teachers in the public schools. Anxious to establish themselves as professionals who served the needs of the more or less well behaved children, educators shunned identification with the reform school. Cubberley's history, *Public Education in the United States,* dismisses reformatories as "not usually thought of as being part of the state educational system."[7]

Beginning around 1900, public school systems established parental or truant schools to handle erratic pupils and thus began to absorb children whom reform schools might have previously claimed as proper subjects. The Chicago Parental School (1902) would not accept boys "charged with delinquency or boys who have been in penal institutions" but it depended upon the juvenile court to order

5. Hanna, "Vocational Training in Boys' Correctional Institutions," p. 3.

6. David Snedden, *Administrative and Educational Work of the American Juvenile Reform School* (New York: Columbia University Press, 1907). Snedden, "The Public School and Juvenile Delinquency," *Educational Review* 33 (1907), 374–85. Albert Shaw, "Learning by Doing at Hampton," *Review of Reviews* 21 (1900), 419. An informative monograph on Snedden is Walter H. Drost, *David Snedden and Education for Social Efficiency* (Madison: University of Wisconsin Press, 1967); see esp. p. 74.

7. Ellwood P. Cubberley, *Public Education in the United States* (Boston: Houghton Mifflin, 1934), pp. 354–55.

commitment and the sheriff's office to deliver boys to the school. The school was residential, organized on the cottage plan, and emphasized manual training and military drill. Superintendent Peter Mortenson summarized, "This is not a penal institution although in effect it is intended to deter those inclined to truancy and incorrigibility."[8]

In 1904 reform school officials, reacting to this competition among other things, established the National Conference on the Education of Truant, Backward, Dependent and Delinquent Children. Much like the charity organization societies and social work groups, whose crystallizing role in the professionalization process Roy Lubove has described, the National Conference helped reform school officials define and defend their functions in a world which was growing increasingly skeptical of their claims. The conference also provided them with a lobby to promote their claims for a share of the "child-saving" business.[9]

The anxiety of reform school officials did not materialize in a vacuum. Reformatory institutions were becoming increasingly known, in the words of one superintendent, as "not the first aid to the injured but . . . the forlorn hope, the *dernier resort*." Cruel punishment was not uncommon. At the Illinois Reformatory (Pontiac) a boy named Hamlin was hung by chains on a wall for nearly three days. He was then alternately beaten and given the "water cure" until he died with his back broken in three places.[10] Girls' reform schools were also bad.

8. U.S. Bureau of Education, *AR* (1899–1900), pp. 85–220. Peter A. Mortenson, "The Chicago Parental School" in Sophonisba P. Breckinridge, ed., *The Child in the City* (Chicago: Chicago School of Civics and Philanthropy, 1912), pp. 156–66.

9. Roy Lubove, *The Professional Altruist: The Emergence of Social Work as a Career, 1880–1930* (Cambridge: Harvard University Press, 1965), pp. 22–54. The confusion of reform school officials toward their own professional roles— were they penologists or social workers?—was illustrated by the organizational schizophrenia of the NCET. In 1922 the NCET changed its title to the National Conference of Juvenile Agencies (NCJA) and affiliated with the American Prison Association. In 1936 one segment of the NCJA left the American Prison Association to become the National Association of Training Schools (NATS) affiliating with the National Conference of Social Work. In 1954 the NCJA and the NATS merged; the new group was called the National Association of Training Schools and Juvenile Agencies.

10. H. W. Charles, "The Problem of the Reform School," *Proceedings* of the Conference for Child Research and Welfare, I (1910), 86. Clarissa Olds

The female section of the Western House of Refuge was literally in chaos for the entire year of 1887. A suspicious fire in February disorganized the cottages and set the stage for spicier happenings. On April 21 the matron complained, "The open, or associate dormitory plan is the most diabolical system yet devised for the demoralization of girls! In spite of the attention of a watch woman who gives her whole attention to one dormitory the black and the white girls elude her and get together in bed." Tension remained high the following day: "Maggie T———— is a thorn in the flesh of every lady whom she may be under, and especially her school teachers. Nothing but annihilation could give her her desserts." Similar incidents occurred throughout the year. On New Year's Eve is the note: "The last day of the old sad sad year. . . . Disorder and indolence, defiance of rules and of authority is the rule."[11]

Josiah Flint Willard (1869–1907), nephew of temperance leader Frances E. Willard, ridiculed reform schools from the inmates' point of view. In 1886, he was committed to the Pennsylvania Western House of Refuge for horsestealing. Later, under the pen name of Josiah Flynt, Willard wrote fictional and nonfictional accounts of his experience. In the novel *Ruderick Clowd,* the protagonist, a new inmate at a cottage farm school, wonders "Why don't they have walls here? . . . It's a prison, ain't it?" An "old hand" replies:

> Course it is, an' they lie when they say it ain't. They call it a home. They want us to think we ain't shut up, but we are an' they know it. A home is a place what you can go in an' out of, but I'd like to see you try that here. They'd wallop the life out o' you.

Walloping was so pervasive here that the children believed that punishment was the work of a supernatural force whom they called the

Keeler, *American Bastilles* (Washington, D.C.: The Carnahan Press, 1910), pp. 8–9. This incident took place in 1907. The water cure consisted of blasting the prisoner with ice cold water from a thick hose. A variety of this treatment once used in a Georgia convict camp was to shoot water into the nostrils of the prisoner, forcing blood from both his ears and nose. Ben Lindsey reported that he witnessed the water cure applied to boys in the state reform school of Colorado during the 1890s, the decade before he opened his famous juvenile court. See Benjamin B. Lindsey and Rube Borough, *The Dangerous Life* (New York: Horace Liveright, 1931), p. 162.

11. NYSA&I, MS, Matron's Daily Journal, April 20, 21, and December 31, 1887.

"Juju." At night they sought to appease this angry God with special prayers. Ruderick reported the prayer of one small boy:

> "Oh, Juju!" he began in place of the customary "Now I lay me down to sleep," "I'm goin' to be good to-morrow, awful good. Stay away to-morrow, Juju. Jimmie is goin' to be good too, so don't lick him either. We both love you, Juju—when you stay away. If you've got to lick somebody this week lick the Superintendent. Jimmie an' I wish you'd lick the of'sers, too. Don't forget that Jimmie an' me are goin' to be good to-morrow—Amen!"[12]

In his autobiography, Flynt satirized the cottage system at the Pennsylvania school:

> The place was arranged on the cottage plan—the boys of a certain *size* being toed off to a certain cottage. For instance, I was placed with lads much younger and far more inexperienced than I was simply because I was their height. It struck me at the time . . . that this was a very peculiar way of classifying prisoners, particularly boys.

Bored by the institution's routine and harassed by constant beatings, he escaped to a nearby farmhouse, where he made a successful plea for old clothes and shoes. "I'll only go to the devil in that school," he told the farmer. "It did me no good."[13]

Parents of delinquent children often shared the youths' dim view of institutional life. Parental letters to Colonel Adams at the Ohio Boys' Industrial School show little interest or belief in the institution's reformatory program. Getting the child out was all that mattered. Shortly before Christmas, 1905, Emma A. Depride wrote to Colonel Adams:

> Will you please to let me know how Richard is a getting along is he well. Please in the name of God will you bea so kind as to let me know just how long he will half to stay and is there no way that you will let him come home and healp me for he is all on earth that I have to depend on.

Mary L. Gaskill of Columbus begged: "Won't you *please* send

---

12. Josiah Flynt, *The Rise of Ruderick Clowd* (New York: Dodd, Mead, 1903), pp. 71–72, 77.

13. Josiah Flynt, *My Life* (New York: The Outing Company, 1908), pp. 87, 97. In *Notes of an Itinerant Policeman* (Boston: L. C. Page, 1900), pp. 85–91, Willard claimed that many children who were incarcerated in local jails were awaiting trial and then commitment to reform schools.

Georgie home *this week*. His papa is not feeling so well and I want to take him to see him Sunday and I am getting so very worried I can scarcely endure the situation myself." According to Colonel Adams's notations, both boys had too many demerits, and the requests were denied.[14]

State boards of charity, the administrative agency usually charged with regulation of reform schools, attempted to eliminate the more egregious abuses in the institutions. Under the leadership of William Letchworth, the New York board persuaded the state legislature to abolish the contract system (1884), to commit no children under twelve years of age (1891), to provide freedom of worship for all inmates (1892), and to define reform school punishment in a noncorporal way (1893). William Rhinelander Stewart, commissioner of the board, played a key role in getting much of this legislation enacted over the strong opposition of officials in the New York Refuge.[15]

The legislation which prohibited courts from sending children under twelve to reform schools was specially significant because it had the effect of placing many of these children in the hands of private child-saving organizations—in New York, the Children's Aid Society, the Juvenile Asylum, the Catholic Protectory, and the Society for the Prevention of Cruelty to Children (often called the Gerry Society after founder Elbridge Gerry). At the same time, these and similar organizations were required to submit to the same state board regulation that reform schools had experienced for years. In 1895 the New York Board of State Charities received legislative sanction to govern the licensing and inspecting of all child-saving agencies. The philanthropies protested that they should be free to place out children without state regulation; only the Gerry Society, however, was successful in gaining immunity from the legislation. Charles Loring Brace died in 1890; he would have surely been offended had he lived to see the

14. Emma A. Depride to C. B. Adams (December 16, 1905), and Mary L. Gaskill to C. B. Adams (November 22, 1905), Superintendent's Correspondence (1905–12), Papers of the Ohio Boys' Industrial School, Ohio Historical Society, Columbus, Ohio.

15. William P. Letchworth, "The History of Child Saving Work in the State of New York," in *History of Child Saving in the United States,* pp. 154–203.

purposes and policies of his society being subjected to scrutiny and regulation by the state.[16]

One reason that child-saving philanthropies objected to state regulation was their traditional aversion toward being lumped in one category with the reform schools. The continued strife within reform schools sharpened philanthropic criticism and motivated private societies to make further plans in order to keep children from being incarcerated there. The National Conference of Charities and Correction increasingly became the forum for attacks upon established institutions for juvenile delinquents. In 1891 Homer Folks, secretary of the Children's Aid Society of Pennsylvania, set the tone of criticism for the next decade by listing five major failures of the reform school:

1. The temptation it offers to parents and guardians to throw off their most sacred responsibilities . . .
2. The contaminating influence of association . . .
3. The enduring stigma . . . of having been committed . . .
4. . . . renders impossible the study and treatment of each child as an individual
5. The great dissimilarity between life in an institution and life outside.

Folks's opposition to the reform school was significant. A rising figure in the world of philanthropy, he was one of the first to question the principle of indoor relief—the efficacy of institutionalizing all persons whom state or local officials termed dependent or delinquent. During the Progressive Era, Folks would take the lead in advocating various reforms—widows' pensions, mothers' aid, and juvenile court and

16. Robert I. Cooper, "William Rhinelander Stewart" (Ph.D. diss., City University of New York, 1969), pp. 83–89. For a summary of efforts to place out delinquent children, see W. H. Slingerland, *Child Placing in Families* (New York: Russell Sage Foundation, 1919). The New York State Board later became an accomplice to the purposes of the institutions it was designed to regulate. New York Mayor John Purroy Mitchel and his commissioner of welfare John Adams Kingsbury instigated investigations of certain municipally supported but privately controlled orphan homes which were run for profit. They uncovered many instances of flagrant child abuse, which could only have existed because of a symbiotic relationship between the state board and the institutions. See Arnold Rosenberg, "Social Work and Politics: John Adams Kingsbury and the struggle for Social Justice in New York City, 1914–1918" (Ph.D. diss., New York University, 1968).

probation legislation—all of which were designed to provide for children and families outside of institutional settings.[17]

Reform school officials naturally denied that their institutions fostered dependency or crushed individuality. They claimed further, and familiarly, that the rigid routines and prison-like appearance of their schools were necessary only because they were forced to receive incorrigible youths who had to be carefully separated from society's relatively innocent children. Still, officials may have recognized the truth of some of the charges because they began to apply cosmetic touches to institutional nomenclature. At the insistence of William Rhinelander Stewart, New York reform schools, for example, changed the names of guards to "guardians" while inmates became "pupils."[18]

In the late nineteenth century, charity and children's aid organizations took the lead in offering alternative plans to juvenile incarceration. In 1881 Joseph G. Rosengarten of the Philadelphia Charity Organization Society proposed that the society minimize its traditional crusade against "the mischief of indiscriminate almsgiving" and concentrate instead upon gathering information about reform school inmates. In addition, he urged that the COS maintain a home either to help them find employment upon release or to place them in good families. In 1890 the Children's Aid Society of Pennsylvania, with the cooperation of local criminal courts, went a step further by offering to receive delinquent children who otherwise would have been committed to reform school. The experiment was not undertaken without misgiving. "We have sometimes left our wards in their home with fear and trembling, and returned half expecting the next mail to announce their evildoing and disappearance," Homer Folks recalled. "But we have been happily surprised as weeks passed by and all the reports were hopeful." Unlike the New York CAS under Charles Loring Brace's leadership, the Pennsylvania group carefully checked

---

17. Homer Folks, "The Care of Delinquent Children," NCCC *Proceedings* (1891), pp. 137–39. Walter I. Trattner, *Homer Folks: Pioneer in Social Welfare* (New York: Columbia University Press, 1968), pp. 114–19.

18. On the defensiveness of reform schools, see California, Whittier State School, *Biennial Report of Trustees* (1892–94), pp. 8–9; Iowa Legislative Documents, VI, *First Biennial Report of the Board of Control of State Institutions* (1900), pp. 174–75; NCCC *Proceedings* (1902), pp. 439–44; and Cooper, "William Rhinelander Stewart," pp. 95-129.

families applying for children in order to avoid charges that the youths were being exploited or abandoned. An approved family received a $2.00 weekly allowance to school, clothe, and provide for their child. The New York Society for the Prevention of Cruelty to Children established a similar program after influencing passage of state legislation which enabled it to receive children from court in order to place them out.[19]

Their shared aversion to reform schools did not prevent child-saving philanthropies from continuing their internecine struggles over the best way to reform delinquent children. The issue—and the combatants—were familiar. Should the children be sent out on probation immediately? Or should they be required to spend a period of time in an institution where, in the words of Elisha Carpenter of the New York Juvenile Asylum, "They must undergo to some extent a change in their ideas, tastes, and habits." Carpenter continued:

> To effect such a change is the object of a reformatory institution. Time is required, for it is a matter of growth and development under right instructions and influences. A brief period of a few months will not suffice. Observation and experience have convinced me that a period of about two years is requisite to effect a change and growth in the right direction.

Miss C. H. Pemberton of the Pennsylvania CAS replied directly to Carpenter:

> The Children's Aid Society of Pennsylvania asserts that the juvenile offender is not so much in need of *reform* as he is of *care,* and that no child is a proper subject for reform if it is possible to meet his needs by taking care of him. We have found it entirely possible to *take care* of the juvenile offender, and it is an easy task to find a very large number of good persons in rural communities ready to assist in taking care of him, provided we are willing to share with them the burden of his support and the responsibility of his future.[20]

---

19. Joseph G. Rosengarten, "Penal and Reformatory Institutions," *Papers* of the Philadelphia Social Science Association (1881), pp. 15–16. Folks, "The Care of Delinquent Children," pp. 140–44. New York *Laws* (1884), ch. 46 (Albany, 1884), pp. 44–47.

20. Wiley B. Sanders, *Juvenile Offenders for a Thousand Years,* pp. 440, 443. State boards also experienced difficulty on this issue. The New York board had a running feud with the Gerry Society because the society kept children for lengthy periods prior to probation.

During the last quarter of the nineteenth century, a few states supported the liberal attitude of the Children's Aid Society by passing probation laws designed to keep children out of reform schools and other institutions. Usually, as in the case of New York and California, these laws depended upon private charitable societies to receive delinquents and to supervise their probation. Massachusetts, however, continued to increase the size of its state visiting agency, which was established in 1869 to serve as a parole and probation office for the delinquents of that state. After 1900 the experience of this agency proved helpful to other states who were faced with demands for probation plans in the wake of the juvenile court movement.[21]

At the same time that promoters of placing-out and probation were attempting to reform delinquents without incarcerating them, other men and women were developing more elaborate programs for industrial schools which customarily had offered only temporary food and shelter. For the most part privately organized, the new industrial schools now attempted to provide residential care for dependent and semidelinquent children. Advocates of the schools made the traditional reformatory claims of success, not the least of which was that the institutions were free from the opprobrium attached to the name "reform school." Neglected girls were still considered the most appropriate subjects for industrial schools. Hastings Hart of the Russell Sage Foundation described the type:

> The girl is not vicious, she does not want to do anything wrong, but she is in a critical and dangerous situation. She is giddy, headstrong, easily influenced. She needs to be kept safe for a year or two, until she comes to herself, and in the meantime she ought to receive such training as will either enable her to support herself or will make her a more efficient housewife and mother.

In 1879 Illinois authorized private societies to establish industrial schools for girls and, shortly thereafter, a group of women opened a home in Evanston, Illinois. Similar schools were begun in Philadelphia, Baltimore, and New York.[22]

Industrial schools may have helped some children, because reform

---

21. California *Statutes* (1883), ch. 91 (Sacramento, 1883), pp. 377–78. See also Ohio, *General and Local Acts* (1892), ch. 89 (Columbus, 1892), p. 161. On the Massachusetts system see above, pp. 69–70.

22. Hastings H. Hart, *Preventive Treatment of Neglected Children* (New York: Russell Sage, 1910), pp. 70–72. Illinois *Laws,* 1879 (Springfield, 1879), pp.

schools began to call themselves industrial schools or, when that name also became suspect, training schools. All types of female industrial schools sought to disassociate themselves from reform schools by rejecting pregnant girls or girls with serious behavioral problems. The Ohio State Reform and Industrial School (1869) regularly dismissed girls "who are not regarded as suitable inmates." In 1877 Katie Cook was ordered dismissed "if her mother emigrates to the West" and Adella Brackett "because of her diseased condition, general depravity and the lack of facilities for caring for such cases."[23]

New private reformatories and schools contributed some understanding to the care of delinquents, but they too avoided incorrigible children. William Marshall Fitts Round (1845–1906), a New York prison reformer, carefully supervised adoption of the cottage plan at the Burnham Industrial Farm, a private reformatory established in 1887.[24] Believing, not without cause, that the original cottage system of Mettray and Hamburg had not received a fair trial in the United States, Round was determined that boys selected for the Burnham School would receive close personal supervision and live in family units, "not more than fifteen or twenty under one roof." He was also determined, as he wrote to former President Rutherford B. Hayes, "to save unruly, but not criminal boys." The school would not receive boys charged with anything more serious than vagrancy, and some boys were received directly from parents or guardians.[25]

The growth of private military schools around the turn of the century suggests that continuing decline in the effectiveness of family

---

309–13. This home was eventually taken over by the Illinois Children's Home and Aid Society. On the early industrial schools and missions of the New York Children's Aid Society, see above, p. 37.

23. Trustees meetings (November 17, 1871, August 16, 1872, September 4, 1877, November 5, 1877), Papers of the Ohio State Reform and Industrial School for Girls, Ohio Historical Society, Columbus, Ohio.

24. Frederick Burnham, a wealthy New York lawyer, bought a former Shaker community in upstate New York for his own use. At his wife's insistence, he donated this farm to a private nonprofit group incorporated to reform "street Arabs" of New York City. In 1896 the name of the reformatory was changed to the Berkshire Industrial Farm.

25. W. M. F. Round to Rutherford B. Hayes (December 1, 1887), Rutherford B. Hayes Papers, Hayes Library, Fremont, Ohio. Round to Hayes (September 24, 1889), Hayes MS. Hayes had an active interest in prison reform and in 1883 was president of the National Prison Association.

government was extending to the upper and middle classes. These institutions provided affluent parents with their own reform schools— places for boys whose presence at home was not wanted, often because of behavioral problems. The Culver Military Academy, founded in 1894, promoted itself as a preventer of a certain kind of delinquency by warning parents of the danger of sending their boys to college untamed: "There, with his mind unawakened and his moral nature undisciplined, he has fallen an easy victim to vicious companions or to the evil influences to which he must needs be exposed." Typical military school boys, according to Methodist clergyman James Monroe Buckley, were "somewhat sluggish, little inclined to study, and are to some extent under the influence of other boys." Some of them undoubtedly would have been called delinquent had they been poor or orphaned. But they were usually neither and hence their behavior was not labeled "delinquent."[26]

A more significant approach to the study of juvenile delinquency was made by William R. "Daddy" George (1866–1936), founder of the George Junior Republic. George was born near Ithaca, New York, but as a young man moved to New York City, where he prospered temporarily in the jewelry-box business. He spent his odd hours wandering in the Five Points and other rough districts where he became fascinated by the activities of local gangs of boys. From among these youths, George recruited his own "Law and Order Gang," which wreaked havoc upon illicit crap games and policy shops.

George was an enthusiast of the Fresh Air movement, begun in 1877 by the *New York Herald* to give poor urban children a two week summer vacation in a rural setting. In 1890 he opened a fresh air camp for Manhattan street children in Freeville, New York, not far from his boyhood home. After a few years, George became convinced that the children were taking his charity for granted and that summer outings, far from helping them, conditioned them to a

26. *Catalogue* of the Culver Military Academy (Culver, Ind., 1897), pp. 26–27. James Monroe Buckley, "About Sending Boys to Boarding School," in *Catalogue* of the Bordentown Military Institute, Bordentown, New Jersey, 1893–94 (Philadelphia, 1894), p. 31. Southern military academies were established in the midnineteenth century; unlike northern military schools, they specifically trained their graduates for military careers.

life of dependency. To promote self-reliance, he began to require that everything be paid for by labor and that the children elect their own representatives to pass and to administer laws of the camp. Youthful judges and policemen tried and punished violators of these laws, although "Daddy" George retained a veto power over actions of both judicial and legislative branches of government.[27]

In 1895 the George Junior Republic was incorporated and began to operate on a year-round basis, accepting both dependent and delinquent children mostly from New York City. "Daddy" George recalled the effect of his reformatory methods upon the first "citizens" of the Republic:

> Theoretical instruction or classroom lecture to teach the values of laws and property rights to them was simply infantile. In their daily life of practical experience they did the real thing. No idle play was their court of justice operated by their judge, attorneys and jurors; their jail and its warden; their police force with its physically fit "cops"; their town meeting where they enacted their own laws; their president who made these laws enforceable by his signature; their bank; their store; their employment at trades for which they received payment based on the value of the labor they performed. In plain words it was conditions and not theories that daily confronted them.[28]

The concept of self-government was not unknown in reform schools. E. M. P. Wells and Joseph Curtis had initiated such experiments in early days of the Boston House of Reformation and the New York House of Refuge. What made the Junior Republic different was the great emphasis which George placed upon teaching children to accumulate their own wealth. Instead of the usual inmate register noting crime committed, habits of parents, length of commitment, etc., the Republic accounted for individuals by their economic standing within the institution. The table indicates the worth of some citizens in 1898.[29]

27. Jack M. Holl, *Juvenile Reform in the Progressive Era: William R. George and the Junior Republic Movement* (Ithaca: Cornell University Press, 1971), analyzes in detail the history and significance of the Republic; on the "Law and Order Gang" and George's early career, see pp. 35–85.

28. Undated (1925?) radio speech by William R. George, Box 47 of the George Junior Republic Papers, Ohlin Library, Cornell University.

29. On Wells and Curtis, see above, pp. 24–27. George himself strenuously resisted the idea that the Republic was a reform school. See Holl, *Juvenile Reform in the Progressive Era*, p. 226n.

Wealth of Citizens in the George Junior Republic

NAME	OCCUPATION	AGE	IN JUNIOR REPUBLIC	WEALTH IN CASH	BANK ACCOUNT	LOANED	PERSONAL PROPERTY	INDEBT-EDNESS	TOTAL WEALTH
Anderson, Arthur	Publishing House	13	2½ years	$.60	No	$1.60	$15.00	No	$17.20
Jackson, Gilbert	Hotel Keeper	14	2½ years	No	$16.00	$13.25	$2.50	None	$31.75
Meade, Ella	Dining Room	16	1 year	None	None	None	None	$.40	Behind

Record Book of Citizens, Box 2, Papers of the George Junior Republic, Olin Library, Cornell University.

Those children who failed economically or who disobeyed the rules of the Republic were harshly treated. Laziness or foolish expenditures led to the pawnshop and the pauper's hotel—just like real life, according to "Daddy" George. Lawbreakers were tried and, if found guilty, sent to the Republic jail, where they donned striped suits and worked on the rockpile under the watchful eye of an armed citizen. The Republic "yell" epitomized its spirit:

> Cssss! Boom! Hear ye this!
> Down with the boss; down with the tramp;
> Down with the pauper; down with the scamp;
> Up with the freeman; up with the wise;
> Up with the thrifty; on to the prize;
> Who are we? why, we are
> Citizens of the George Junior Republic!

For George, as for John Dewey, schools and institutions were embryonic communities which, given inspired leadership, should not serve as refuges from the workaday world but should act as molders and reflectors of the social and economic values of the larger society.[30]

The George Junior Republic inspired growth of republic reform schools throughout the country as well as the adoption of self-

30. William I. Hull, "The George Junior Republic," *Annals* of the American Academy 10 (1897), 85. Holl, *Juvenile Reform in the Progressive Era,* pp. 173–222. Pictures of the Republic jail show children in leg irons, doing the humiliating "Sing Sing Shuffle" (head down, arm on the preceding prisoner) on their way to work. Even Sing Sing had abandoned this practice by the 1890s.

government as a reformatory method in existing institutions. Philanthropic citizens of Washington, D.C., and Baltimore combined to establish the National Junior Republic in 1899. The Pennsylvania George Junior Republic (1909), a replica of the parent Republic, was founded in the conviction "that delinquent youth could be saved socially by wisely directed self-training in civic responsibility." The Toledo Newsboys' Association was governed like the Republic.[31]

In 1896 and again in 1913, the New York State Board of Charities investigated the George Junior Republic and charged that it failed to meet state standards for children's institutions. Specific accusations centered upon unsatisfactory sanitary conditions, the relatively free intermingling of the sexes, and the labor system which the board regarded as exploitative rather than reformatory. Like Charles Loring Brace, "Daddy" George conflicted readily, perhaps even enthusiastically, with established authority. In these instances George and his supporters successfully refuted the state's charges although the din of battle probably made prospective imitators of the Republic idea wary about embracing it too uncritically. State institutions were even cautious about adopting inmate self-government, which was only one part of George's experiment. In 1901 the Lyman School for Boys abandoned a brief experiment in delegated power. One reform school superintendent asked, "Shall the dependent children, generally the offspring of shiftlessness and lawlessness, be left to the leadership of self-chosen members of their own fraternity, or shall the training of future citizens be given to God-fearing, sober-minded, law-abiding men and women of years and experience enough to lead their helpless, and often wayward, charges along safe paths to true manhood and womanhood?"[32]

Some reform school officials thought that the two methods were not mutually exclusive. In 1912 Calvin Derrick, a former superintendent at the George Junior Republic, instituted modified civil government at the Preston School of Industry, Ione, California. Although he was

31. Folder 800, Republic MS. John E. Gunckel, *Boyville* (Toledo, Ohio: Toledo Newsboys' Association 1905), *passim*. See also Earle D. Bruner, *A Laboratory Study in Democracy* (New York: Doubleday, 1927), pp. 2–6.

32. *Charities* 6 (1901), 467–69. On the investigations of the Republic see the *Annual Reports* of the New York State Board of Charities (1896 and 1913) and Holl, *Juvenile Reform in the Progressive Era*, pp. 121–26, 296–310.

critical of George's judicial system, believing that the Republic children were "concerned chiefly with prosecuting one another," Derrick
believed that delinquents could be reformed within institutions only
if they developed a sense of participation in their own destiny. "These
boys do not understand our civilization, or at least they do not fit into
it," he wrote. "Self-government starting with the boy's view enables
him to work out a civil and social order of his own, which he approves
and understands. . . . His comfort, happiness and progress depend
upon his social relations; his social relations depend upon his free
choice of conduct in the field of self-government." Thomas Mott
Osborne (1859–1926), prison reformer and President of the George
Junior Republic Association, introduced limited self-government into
Auburn and Sing Sing State Prisons in New York. Institutional au-
thoritarianism, he believed, only prepared men for future institutions.
As warden of Sing Sing, 1914–1916, he applied the principles of
Auburn's Mutual Welfare League which enabled prisoners to control
portions of their own leisure time.[33]

In many instances, however, reform school self-government de-
generated into but another tool of administrative control. Elected
representatives, often called boy captains, gained their position by
physically terrorizing other children into conformity with institutional
dictates or by spying on fellow inmates in exchange for minor personal
privileges awarded by the staff, or both. Josiah Flynt's recollection
of inmate organization at the Pennsylvania Western House of Refuge
gives an indication of the mode of control which institutions utilized.

> Speaking generally, the boys were divided into two sets or rings—
> the "stand patters" and the "softies." The former were the boys of
> spirit and adventure, the principal winners in their classes as well as
> on the playground; the latter were the tale-bearers, the mouthy ones
> —"lungers" was also a good name for them—who split on the "stand
> patters" when "lunging it" promised to gain favors for them. What-
> ever else I did or did not do while in the school, I fought very shy
> of all officers who tried to get me to "peach" on my companions. This

33. Derrick quoted in Stuart Queen, *The Passing of the County Jail* (Menasha,
Wis.: George Banta, 1920), p. 121. Thomas Mott Osborne, *Society and
Prisons* (New Haven: Yale University Press, 1916), pp. 139–64. See also
California, Board of Charities and Corrections, *Sixth Biennial Report* (1912–
1914), pp. 73–75. On the troubled relationships between Osborne, Derrick,
and George, see Holl, *Juvenile Reform in the Progressive Era*, pp. 129–72.

may not have been a virtue, but it secured good standing for me among the boys of spiritual enterprise, and I think that any boy wanting agreeable companionship in such a place would naturally turn to the "stand patters." Of course, my selection of cronies was watched by the officers and made a mental note of to be used later on, either for or against my record, as it suited the purposes of the observing overseer.[34]

The growth of a reform school system in southern states near the turn of the century did not signal the origin of a new type of institution for delinquents, although it did reflect features unique to that section of the country. Populist governors like James K. Vardaman of Mississippi and Jeff Davis of Arkansas warred against the convict lease system by establishing self-sustaining prison farms over the opposition of labor contractors and plantation owners. At first, reform schools were built for whites only, although Davis proposed a school "where white boys might be taught some useful occupation and the negro boys compelled to work and support the institution while it is being done. This would prove a blessing, not only to the white boy, but to the negro boy as well."[35]

Many black Americans felt that their own privately maintained reform schools would be a greater blessing. In Virginia, John Henry Smyth (1844–1908), Minister to Liberia under President Hayes and editor of the Richmond *Reformer,* led the crusade to remove delinquent Negro boys from jail. "There is no middle ground, no house of refuge, correction, or reformatory for the black boy or girl who, from defective and from no training, has taken the first step downward," he said, "and, as a consequence, crime is accelerated and increased by

---

34. Flynt, *My Life,* p. 90. For a later account of a boy captain system, similarly perverted, see Willard Motley, *Knock on Any Door* (New York: Appleton-Century, 1947), pp. 27–78.

35. Arkansas House of Representatives, *Journal* (1905), p. 31. On Vardaman see William F. Holmes, "James K. Vardaman and Prison Reform in Mississippi," *Journal of Mississippi History* 27 (1965), 229–48. Paul B. Foreman and Julien R. Tatum, "A Short History of Mississippi's State Penal System," *Mississippi Law Journal* 10 (1938), 262–67. Two surveys of development in the southern penal system during this period are Alexander J. McKelway, "The Need of Reformatories and the Juvenile Court System in the South," *Proceedings* of the American Prison Association (1908), pp. 55–64; and Jane Zimmermann, "The Penal Reform Movement in the South during the Progressive Era," *Journal of Southern History* 17 (1931), 462–92.

law." In 1897 Smyth helped to establish the Virginia Manual Labor School, a private institution financed in part by railroad magnate Collis P. Huntington. Smyth believed that delinquency among black children resulted from parents encouraging their young to pursue unattainable goals:

> Too many Negro children are guarded from soiling their hands and developing their muscles with necessary and useful toil. . . . This encouragement of laziness can have but one outcome—the living in the sweat of others' faces than their own. . . . To the extent that a child's mind becomes familiar with higher conditions and mind-work, to that degree does physical exertion in the way of mere muscle-work become distasteful, and as a result the child becomes less efficient as a mere bread-winner by the sweat of his brow.[36]

Brow sweat became the order of the day at the Virginia school and similar institutions such as the Alabama "reformatory for Negro boys," established in 1910 by the State Federation of Colored Women's Clubs. Booker T. Washington's influence was reflected in the agricultural and vocational routines aimed at preparing children for lives as menials. John Henry Smyth boasted, "that for tractableness and responsiveness to kindly influences, delinquent Negro children show themselves of legitimate kinship to that race among whom, as the classic writer tells us, 'the gods delighted to disport themselves—the gentle Ethiopians.' " Southern state governments occasionally aided efforts of Negro reformatories, but their legislative action was piecemeal. Negro children continued to serve jail sentences and to suffer, directly or indirectly, from the effects of vigilante justice.[37]

36. NCCC *Proceedings* (1898), p. 472. John Henry Smyth, "Negro Criminality," *The Southern Workman and Farm Record* 29 (1900), 625–31. See also John Henry Smyth, "Moral and Christian Influences of Reformatories," NCCC *Proceedings* (1899), pp. 319–26; and William E. Benson, "Prevention of Crime Among Colored Children," NCCC *Proceedings* (1904), pp. 257–68.

37. Smyth, "Negro Criminality," p. 631. On government aid see Alabama *Laws* (1911), ch. 336 (Montgomery, 1911), pp. 677–81; and L. McCrae, "Birmingham's Probation Plan for the Little Negro," *Charities* 19 (1908), pp. 1729–30. On the continuation of the practice of sending black children to jail, see Foreman and Tatum, "A Short History of Mississippi's State Penal System," pp. 262–67. For further information on delinquency and Negro children, see Monroe N. Work, *A Bibliography of the Negro in Africa and America* (New York: H. W. Wilson, 1928); and Elizabeth W. Miller and Mary L. Fisher, eds., *The Negro in America*, 2d ed. (Cambridge: Harvard University Press, 1970).

Penal theory lay close beneath the surface of many innovations and changes in institutional care for delinquent children in the late nineteenth century. The imaginative proposals of Homer Folks and "Daddy" George were neither widely nor faithfully emulated. The reform school system came to be increasingly distrusted as a way of reforming children. America was rapidly becoming a modern urban society—a society which needed a new frame of reference to examine old and new social problems. The juvenile court offered the possibility of change.insofar as juvenile delinquents were concerned.

CHAPTER 5

The Juvenile Court, 1899–1940

B Y THE LATE NINETEENTH CENTURY, little remained of the enthusiasm and hope which had produced the asylum, the penitentiary, and the reform school. Internal as well as external attacks upon reform schools were indicative of a larger collapse of faith in the healing powers of the edificial world. By remembering the dimensions of this deterioration of confidence, we can more clearly comprehend the significance of the juvenile court. It is especially important to understand the legal consequences of the inability of reform schools to cope with the relatively few children who did come under their charge. State legislatures and courts had justified the custodial power of reform schools on the grounds of the supposed ability of the institutions to exercise the parental power of the state. *Parens patriae* gave refuge and reform school authorities the best of two worlds: it separated delinquent children from their natural parents, and it circumvented the rigor of the criminal law by allowing courts to commit children, under loosely worded statutes, to specially created "schools" instead of jails.

Such a rationalization was acceptable as long as reform schools performed their functions circumspectly. In the late nineteenth century, however, the increasingly violent and exploitative nature of reform schools raised questions about their ability to serve in the capacity of *parens patriae*. If reform schools did not improve—indeed, if they abused delinquent children—how then could they justify their parental role? How could they avoid being labeled prisons? How could they pretend that the scope of their custodial power extended to vagrant and semidelinquent children as well as to youths convicted of felonies?

Soon after the Civil War, some legal decisions interpreting *parens patriae* began to reflect increasing distrust of the intentions and performance of reform schools and, conversely, new appreciation for natural parents. In 1870 the Illinois Supreme Court reversed the vagrancy sentence of Daniel O'Connell to the Chicago Reform School on the grounds that he had not committed a crime and had been imprisoned without due process of law. "Why should minors be imprisoned for misfortune?" asked the Court. "Destitution of proper parental care, ignorance, idleness and vice, are misfortunes, not crimes. . . . This boy is deprived of a father's care; bereft of home influences; has no freedom of action; is committed for an uncertain time; is branded as a prisoner; made subject to the will of others, and thus feels that he is a slave." Fifteen years later, the New Hampshire Supreme Court, in a similar case, made this characterization of the state's reform school:

> We cannot ignore the fact that in the public estimation the school has always been regarded as a quasi penal institution, and the detention of its inmates or scholars as involuntary and constrained. The great purpose of the institution was the separation of youthful offenders from hardened criminals of mature years, in the hope of their ultimate reformation and of their becoming useful citizens. But the fact cannot be overlooked, that the detention of the inmates is regarded to some extent in the nature of a punishment, with more or less of disgrace attached on that account. If the order committing a minor to the school is not a sentence but the substitute for a sentence . . . what is a substitute for a sentence but a sentence in and of itself?

In 1897 an appellate court freed Jonie Becknell from the Whittier State School in California on the grounds that he had been committed solely on the basis of a grand jury hearing and "cannot be imprisoned as a criminal without a trial by jury."[1]

It is true, of course, that other decisions supported the state's traditional exercise of parental power. The case of a Chinese youth named Ah Peen, "minor child, of the age of sixteen, leading an idle and dis-

---

1. *The People* v. *Turner,* 55 Illinois 280 (1870). *State* v. *Ray,* 63 New Hampshire 405 (1886). *Ex parte* Becknell, 51 Pacific Reporter 692 (California, 1897). See also *Angelo* v. *The People,* 96 Illinois 209 (1880).

solute life," is representative. Ah Peen's commitment to an industrial school without a jury trial was justifiable exercise of *parens patriae,* said the California Supreme Court, and therefore not subject to the safeguards of criminal law. The decision concluded, "The purpose in view is not punishment for offenses done, but reformation and training of the child to habits of industry, with a view to his future usefulness when he shall have been reclaimed to society." In this and similar cases, state courts relied upon the Crouse decision (4 Wharton 9, Pennsylvania 1837) discussed in the first chapter.[2]

Nevertheless, the animus against reform schools was strong and, as we have noted, philanthropic groups and state agencies in Massachusetts, New York, and Pennsylvania had begun to seek ways of reforming juvenile delinquents without incarcerating them. In this context, it is ironic that the first formally designated juvenile court should originate in Illinois, a state without its own reform schools for either boys or girls. Most discussions of the Chicago court ignore this fact in favor of a broadly based explanation linking the advent of the institution with the chaotic urbanization process which Chicago was then experiencing. A recent study emphasizes the city's large number of poor immigrants, whose children often "faced the double difficulties of city life and a strange culture." Cultural conflicts between generations often deepened to the point that the child of Polish or Irish or Slovak immigrants was "forced . . . into delinquency."[3]

The significance of this explanation should not be discounted. Surely, Jane Addams and a generation of settlement house reformers acted in light of their belief in the deleterious effects of urban life on immigrant children. And, as we shall discuss in Chapter 6, the researches of William I. Thomas and other University of Chicago sociologists who investigated different immigrant groups in the city were informed by the assumption that the children of the urban poor

2. *Ex parte* Ah Peen, 51 California 280 (1876). For similar cases see *in re* Ferrier, 103 Illinois 367 (1882) and *Prescott* v. *The State,* 19 Ohio 184 (1870); *Milwaukee Industrial School* v. *The Supervisors of Milwaukee County,* 40 Wisconsin 328 (1876); and *Rule* v. *Geddes,* 23 App. D.C. 31 (1904). On the Crouse case see above, pp. 13–14.

3. Joseph M. Hawes, "Society Versus Its Children: Nineteenth Century America's Response to the Challenge of Juvenile Delinquency" (Ph.D. diss., University of Texas, 1969), pp. 317–19. See also Ray Ginger, *Altgeld's America* (Chicago: Quadrangle Books, 1965).

were particularly vulnerable to juvenile delinquency. These sociologists saw delinquency as one of the social pathologies of city life. Nevertheless, the origin of the juvenile court may be more clearly understood by studying the peculiarly deficient structure of "child-saving" philanthropy in Chicago than by canvassing the social misery which obtained in the city of that day. In the words of Carl Kelsey of the Illinois Children's Home and Aid Society, "Illinois had been slow to appreciate the advances made by many of her sister states in the care of children."[4]

This vacuum of state care had not developed inadvertently. Before the Civil War, Chicago had established a municipal reform school that, under the superintendency of Reverend D. B. Nichols, resembled the early progressive regime of E. M. P. Wells of the Boston House of Reformation. In 1856 after fire destroyed the old prison-like structure that had housed the boys, Nichols inaugurated a "confidential system," with inmates filling nearly all institutional positions from gatekeeper to captain of the inmate police department. "We have no bars on our buildings, neither have we any lock-ups," reported Reverend Nichols. In 1862 the legislature authorized the position of Reform School Commissioner, and this officer screened all boys prior to their admission, frequently dismissing first-time offenders "on the promise to do better." Boys were also released on tickets of leave or given passes to visit their homes over the weekend.[5]

The Chicago Fire of 1871 incinerated the new reform school, but even before the Fire, the school's ability to receive dependent and delinquent children had been drastically curtailed by the effects of the O'Connell case. This decision made it impossible for the school to receive any children except those who had been convicted of felonies. Chicago circuit judge and later first judge of the juvenile court Richard S. Tuthill claimed that in the O'Connell case, the state supreme court "overthrew the whole prospect we then had of getting a chance to aid the boys."[6] As late as 1895, an earlier version of

4. Carl Kelsey, "The Juvenile Court of Chicago and Its Work," *Annals* of the American Academy 17 (1901), 119.

5. Wiley B. Sanders, ed., *Juvenile Offenders for a Thousand Years*, pp. 392–97. Also, see above, pp. 24–25.

6. Commercial Club of Chicago, *How Can Juvenile Offenders be Cared for and Reformed?* (Chicago, 1900), p. 57.

the juvenile court had been shelved by the Illinois legislature on the grounds that it might not be constitutional. Under these circumstances, the legal fraternity in Illinois, particularly the Chicago Bar Association, became concerned about the vacuum of state welfare power and sought a means to reassert the right of the state to assume parental power over delinquent children.[7]

In the absence of state reform schools, Illinois had authorized in 1879 the establishment of privately organized industrial schools that could receive both dependent and delinquent children. By 1887 four of these existed in the Chicago area, two Catholic and two Protestant, with each religion operating a boys' and a girls' school. But, like the earlier Chicago Reform School, the status of these schools was clouded by the results of a legal decision. In *County of Cook* v. *The Chicago Industrial School for Girls* (1888), the Illinois supreme court denied to "middleman" charitable organizations that did not actually operate industrial schools the right to receive delinquent children. Catholic groups such as the Chicago Visitation and Aid Society had interpreted the 1879 act as allowing them to place out delinquent Catholic children in unofficial—that is, unchartered— Catholic industrial schools. This decision technically blocked these Catholic charities from access to delinquent children of the Catholic faith and thereby threatened the entire quasi-official reformatory system. Also, officially recognized industrial schools were often full, and this meant that some children were either sent to jail or released. Occasionally, boys were sent to the state reformatory at Pontiac, an institution intended for young adult offenders. In short, by 1890 the Illinois system of handling delinquent children, haphazard at best, had virtually evaporated.[8]

The absence of a state system offended some people who were in positions to make amends. Foremost among these was John Peter

7. Julia Lathrop et al., *The Child, the Clinic and the Court* (New York: The New Republic, 1927), p. 292. Timothy D. Hurley, *The Origin of the Juvenile Court Law* (Chicago: Visitation and Aid Society, 1907), pp. 17–21. See also Grace Abbott, *The Child and the State,* 2 vols. (Chicago: University of Chicago Press, 1938), II, 330–32.

8. Fox, "Juvenile Justice Reform," *Stanford Law Review* 22 (1970), 1226–27. On industrial schools see above, pp. 114–15, and Anthony Platt, *The Child Savers,* pp. 110–13.

Altgeld (1848–1902), who as Governor of Illinois shocked conventional opinion by pardoning the men accused of instigating the Haymarket riot. Altgeld wrote *Our Penal Machinery and Its Victims* to protest the abusive treatment which children received in the jails of his state. "Remember," he concluded, "*brutal treatment brutalizes and thus prepares for crime.*" He made his protest meaningful by appointing Julia C. Lathrop (1858–1932), a resident of Jane Addams' Hull-House, to the Board of State Commissioners of Public Charities. Miss Lathrop carefully inspected all of the state's county jails and poorhouses, as well as its insane asylums, industrial schools, and institutions for the deaf, blind, and crippled. She focused her attention upon the plight of children held in jails or dumped in county almshouses. The 1898 report of the state commissioners expressed her concern:

> There are at the present moment in the State of Illinois, especially in the city of Chicago, thousands of children in need of active intervention for their preservation from physical, mental and moral destruction. Such intervention is demanded, not only by sympathetic consideration for their well-being, but also in the name of the commonwealth, for the preservation of the State. If the child is the material out of which men and women are made, the neglected child is the material out of which paupers and criminals are made.[9]

Like other incipient Progressive reformers, Julia Lathrop believed that children were the hope of the future and, as such, most in need of the state's solicitous care. Outraged by witnessing numerous abuses of this principle, she aroused other Illinois citizens who were soon making their own plans and pleas for reform. In 1895 the Chicago Women's Club sponsored the establishment of the John Worthy School, located in the Chicago House of Correction. The school provided juvenile delinquents with part-time instruction in basic subjects. It failed, however, to prevent the children from spending their free time with adult inmates. In 1898 Horace Fletcher (1849–1919), a nutritionist and advocate of free kindergartens in the Chicago public

---

9. John P. Altgeld, *Our Penal Machinery and Its Victims* (Chicago, 1886), p. 32. Illinois Board of State Commissioners of Public Charities, *Fifteenth Biennial Report* (1898), p. 63. Julia Lathrop, "The Background of the Juvenile Court in Illinois," in Lathrop et al., *The Child, the Clinic and the Court*, pp. 290–91.

school system, shocked public conscience with a tract reporting an encounter between a Chicago policeman and a four-year-old "baby crook" whom he had caught stealing cakes. Finally deciding to let the child go, the policeman barked, "If you git into my hands again I'll cut your ears off close ter yer head, and I'll sew yer mouth up so's yer can't eat no cakes, an' then I guess yer won't want ter steal 'em. Now git! yer little bastard, and *ter hell wid you!*"[10]

Outrage was translated into a concerted plan of action at the annual meeting of the Illinois Conference of Charities in 1898. Fletcher's story was widely discussed at the conference, which was devoted entirely to problems of state care of dependent and delinquent children. "Who are the children of the state?" asked Jenkin Lloyd Jones (1843–1918), conference president and a renowned Unitarian minister. "All children are children of the state or else none are," he answered himself. "The state is but the coordinated parentage of childhood, yielding to the inexorable logic of civilization that will compel co-partnership, co-operation, corporate life and conscience." After a great deal of debate, Frederick Wines, one of the foremost American penologists, proposed a plan of action. "What we should have, in our system of criminal jurisprudence, is an entirely separate system of courts for children, in large cities, who commit offenses which would be criminal in adults," he said. "We ought to have a 'children's court' in Chicago, and we ought to have a 'children's judge,' who should attend to no other business."[11]

With widespread support from the Chicago Bar Association and philanthropic reformers, the Illinois legislature unanimously passed in 1899 "An act to regulate the treatment and control of dependent, neglected and delinquent children." As the title indicates, the legislators were concerned with both juvenile delinquents and dependent and neglected children. Delinquents were children who violated "any law of this State or any City or Village ordinance." Dependency and neglect were broadly defined to mean

10. Horace Fletcher, *That Last Waif or Social Quarantine* (Chicago, 1898), pp. 27–28. John Worthy was superintendent of the Chicago House of Correction in 1895.

11. *Proceedings* of the Illinois Conference of Charities (1898), in Board of State Commissioners of Public Charities, *Fifteenth Biennial Report* (1898), pp. 282, 336.

any child who for any reason is destitute or homeless or abandoned; or dependent on the public for support; or has not proper parental care or guardianship; or who habitually begs or receives alms; or who is found living in any house of ill fame or with any vicious or disreputable person; or whose home, by reason of neglect, cruelty or depravity on the part of its parents, guardian or other person in whose care it may be, is an unfit place for such a child; and any child under the age of 8 years who is found peddling or selling any article or singing or playing any musical instrument upon the street or giving any public entertainment.

Whether children were categorized as dependent or delinquent, the court had the power to assign them to appropriate institutions. But the preference was not to send children to orphanages or industrial schools but to place them on probation either in their own or foster homes. As it applied to delinquent children, the Illinois act united extant legislation affecting juveniles in two states, Massachusetts and New York. It combined the concept of probation as developed in Massachusetts with several New York laws providing for special trial sessions and separate detention facilities for delinquents. The court was empowered to appoint "one or more persons of good character to serve as probation officers." There was, however, no provision for paying these officers, a deliberate omission based upon the belief that officers appointed through political influence would, according to *Charities* magazine, "render the law useless and inoperative."[12]

It is not unreasonable to assume that Illinois jurists and reformers, troubled by menacing legal precedents concerning the constitutional rights of juvenile offenders, were anxious to obviate this issue by creating a new adjudicating mechanism, a chancery or noncriminal court of equity which, by definition, would not have to be concerned with the rights of the accused child.[13] They desired that the parental

12. The Illinois act is reprinted in Bremner, *Children and Youth in America,* II, 507–11. On the Massachusetts system see above, p. 000. For the New York legislation see New York *Laws* (1877), ch. 428 (Albany, 1877), p. 486; and ibid. (1892), ch. 217 (Albany, 1892), pp. 459–60. Frank G. Soule, a Chicago insurance man, is given credit for making a survey of state laws affecting delinquent children which resulted in the Illinois law. See Hurley, *The Origin of the Juvenile Court Law,* p. 21; and *Charities* 10 (1903), 14–15.

13. According to Grace Abbott, "Our equity courts are the American substitute for the English High Court of Chancery, which was the keeper of the king's conscience in applying the principles of equity to cases in which the

powers, which reform schools had once enjoyed, now be extended to the entire legal process as it touched the delinquent. By emphasizing probation, the juvenile court was to be considered a place of aid and education, not punishment, despite the fact that it also had the power to relegate children to the discredited reform schools. "The fundamental idea of the Juvenile Court is so simple it seems anyone ought to understand it," said Timothy Hurley, President of the Chicago Visitation and Aid Society. "It is, to be perfectly plain, a return to paternalism. It is the acknowledgement by the State of its relationship as the parent to every child within its borders. Civilization for years lost sight of this relationship and as a consequence the utter demoralization of society was threatened."[14]

The juvenile court represented both a restatement and an expansion of the *parens patriae* doctrine. As such, it was enormously appealing. By 1909 a decade after the passage of the Illinois act, ten states and the District of Columbia had authorized localities to establish juvenile courts. Twelve other states followed suit in the next three years, and by 1925, all but two states, Maine and Wyoming, had juvenile court laws. In 1945 Wyoming at last completed the roster. There were, of course, noticeable differences between courts. In rural and small-town areas, the juvenile courts—when they existed at all—often involved little more than the county court judge hearing cases pertaining to juvenile delinquency on a day specially set aside for this purpose. Children were often incarcerated with adults prior to these hearings, and seldom were probation officers available to advise the judge or to accept responsibility for monitoring the children's activities following court appearance. In urban areas, such as Chicago, a judge of the circuit court was designated by fellow judges to serve full time as juvenile court judge. Special detention homes and a proba-

---

right rules of law alone would not result in justice. They exercised the prerogative of the crown or of the state as *parens patriae* in behalf of children whose welfare was in jeopardy" (*The Child and the State,* II, 331). See also Herbert H. Lou, *Juvenile Courts in the United States* (Chapel Hill: University of North Carolina Press, 1927), pp. 1–11; and Bernard Flexner, "The Juvenile Court—Its Legal Aspect," *Annals* of the American Academy 36 (1910), 49–56.

14. Hurley, p. 56. Hurley had reason to be pleased with the new juvenile court law because it restored the right of all Catholic charities to act as guardians for those Catholic children whom the court placed on probation; see above, p. 128.

tion staff supplemented the courts' work in varying degrees of thoroughness. Even in the cities, however, provisions existed in juvenile court laws which allowed judges to send serious offenders to jail. Judge Tuthill remanded thirty-seven children to the Grand Jury during the Chicago court's first full year of operation. Citing this fact, Sanford Fox has reminded us that the juvenile court, like the reform schools and refuges of the nineteenth century, concentrated on "salvageable offenders," leaving the truly difficult child to the "adult criminal system."[15]

Nevertheless, widespread establishment of juvenile courts in the early years of this century represented one of the proudest achievements of progressive reformers. In 1912 Grace Abbott, who was to serve as chief of the U.S. Children's Bureau from 1921 to 1934, believed that these tribunals had effected a historic breakthrough in public policy toward youthful crime. In her words, the child offender was no longer regarded "as a *criminal* but as a *delinquent*." Jane Addams, equally enthusiastic, recalled, "There was almost a change in mores when the juvenile court was established. The child was brought before the judge with no one to prosecute him and none to defend him—the judge and all concerned were merely trying to find out what could be done on his behalf. The element of conflict was absolutely eliminated and with it all notions of punishment as such with its curiously belated connotations." In a spirit not unlike that of the early refuge managers, Frederic Howe claimed that because of the court, "the budding crop of crime of the next decade will be largely diminished, at great saving to life and character, as well as to the purse of the community." Homer Folks, then secretary of the State Charities Aid Association of New York, spoke of the meaning of the Chicago Juvenile Court:

> Although some of its beginnings were had in some of the eastern states, its great progress and development, its distinctive character, its propaganda, all took their origin in the city of Chicago. And I think

15. A survey of the early development of juvenile courts is U.S. Congress, *Children's Courts in the United States,* 58th Cong., 2d sess. (1904), House Doc. 701. For a summary of juvenile court provisions for children in the rural West, see Elmer M. Coffeen, "Juvenile Courts and Social Work in Rural Districts of the Central West," *Annals* of the American Academy, 27 (1906), 189–92. On the persistence of criminal sanctions in juvenile courts, see Fox, "Juvenile Justice Reform," *Stanford Law Review* 20 (1970), 1191.

it is from this city that we have drawn some of the best ideas of what
the juvenile court should be and what it should do. . . . The central
idea . . . is that the juvenile court is the community pondering upon
the problem of the exceptional child.[16]

Protestant children's aid societies and their feminine allies in urban
women's clubs were especially influential in spreading the juvenile
court idea. Lucy L. Flower and Louise DeKoven Bowen mobilized
the Chicago Women's Club to play a key role in the establishment of
the Chicago court. Hannah Kent Schoff, president of the National
Congress of Mothers, led the campaign to get Pennsylvania to adopt
a juvenile court law in 1903, and her organization contributed to the
support of probation officers for the new court. Similarly, Charlotte
C. Eliot and the ladies of the Humanity Club of St. Louis helped to
secure a juvenile court for that city.[17]

So forceful were these ladies that a recent student of the juvenile
court has suggested that the child-saving movement was heavily influenced by maternal values and especially by middle-class women
who extended their housewifely roles into public service and used
their political and economic contacts to advance their cause. Another
scholar entitles his analysis "The Ladies of Chicago and the Creation
of the Juvenile Court."[18] This approach is misleading to a degree. We
have already noted the influential but low-keyed role played by the
entirely masculine Chicago Bar Association in gaining passage of the

16. Miss Abbott quoted in Sophonisba P. Breckinridge and Edith Abbott, *The
Delinquent Child and the Home* (New York: Russell Sage, 1912), p. 247.
Jane Addams, *My Friend, Julia Lathrop* (New York: Macmillan, 1935), p. 137.
Frederic Howe, *The City: The Hope of Democracy* (New York: Charles Scrib-
ner's Sons, 1913), p. 228. Homer Folks, "Cooperation of Public and Private
Agencies in Behalf of Truant, Wayward and Backard Children," NCET *Proceed-
ings* (1905), pp. 127–33. For a description of Folks's earlier efforts (1890s) in
Pennsylvania to place delinquents in private homes, see above, pp. 112–13. He
continued to believe that reform schools were prisons, intent on sabotaging
probation experiments. See Homer Folks, "Prevention and Probation," in
Savel Zimand, ed., *Public Health and Welfare: The Citizen's Responsibility*
(New York: Macmillan, 1958).

17. Hannah Kent Schoff, *The Wayward Child* (Indianapolis: Bobbs-Merrill,
1915), pp. 206–34. Hannah Kent Schoff, "Pennsylvania's Unfortunate Children," *Charities* 11 (1903), 425–28. Charlotte C. Eliot, "Before and After in St.
Louis," *Charities* 11 (1903), 430–32.

18. Platt, *The Child Savers,* p. 14. Hawes, "Society Versus Its Children" (Ph.D.
diss., University of Texas, 1969), p. 314.

Illinois juvenile court law. Additionally, Catholic philanthropic organizations, which provided some volunteer probation officers to the early juvenile courts, excluded female parishioners from this work altogether.

There is another factor. The preponderant figure of the first courts was the judge, and he was invariably a man who emphasized his masculinity in approaching delinquent children, especially boys. Judge Tuthill, the first juvenile court judge, described his approach: "I talk with the boy, give him a good talk, just as I would my own boy, and find myself as much interested in some of these boys as I would if they were my own." "It is the personal touch that does it," said George W. Stubbs, judge of the juvenile court in Indianapolis. "I have often observed that if I sat on a high platform behind a high desk . . . with the boy on the prisoner's bench some distance away, that my words had little effect on him; but if I could get close enough to him to put my hand on his head or shoulder, or my arm around him, in nearly every such case I could get his confidence."[19]

No one better illustrated the importance of "the personal touch" or, as he called it, "the artistry of human approach" than Benjamin Barr Lindsey (1870–1943), judge of the circuit court of Arapahoe County (Denver), Colorado. As a boy, Lindsey worked as a janitor and newsboy to support his family. When he began to read law, he was unable to grasp the technicalities and sophistries of the subject, and he became so discouraged that at one time he tried to kill himself. Sobered by the experience, Lindsey redoubled his efforts to master the legal profession, and in 1894 he was admitted to the Colorado bar.[20]

Lindsey's first case took him to Denver's West Side Jail to meet his clients. He described the encounter:

> At the end of a corridor I came in front of a cage on the floor of which were two small boys engaged in gambling with two grown

19. Tuthill quoted in Commercial Club of Chicago, *How Can Juvenile Offenders Be Cared for and Reformed?* p. 60. Stubbs quoted in U.S. Congress, *Children's Courts in the United States,* 58th Cong., 2d sess. (1904), House Doc. 701, p. xiii. See also Julian W. Mack, "The Law and the Child," *Survey* 23 (1910), 642; and Harvey H. Baker, "Procedure of the Boston Juvenile Court," ibid., pp. 643–52.

20. New York *Times* (March 27, 1943).

men. . . . I found that these boys had already been in jail more than 60 days and had learned to play poker from their older cell mates, a safe cracker and a horse thief, upon whom they had come to look as great heroes.[21]

Although Lindsey obtained freedom for these boys and others like them, he was unable to achieve any comprehensive reform until 1900, when he was appointed to the probate division of the circuit court as a result of his loyal service to the Democratic Party of Colorado.

At first Lindsey's probate court had no special legislation to enable him to discriminate in favor of juvenile delinquents. But, as he said, "It is not so much a question of law as a question of doing the thing." Lindsey's "thing" consisted not only of comradely talks with individual delinquents in court and private chambers, but also of "snitching bees" with gangs of boys—sessions in which youths confessed their peccadillos to the judge, who, in return, protected them from police harassment on condition of their future good behavior. Lindsey's approach inspired great loyalty and affection from youngsters, even those whom he finally had to send to the state reform school. "My dear friend," wrote Charles Wise, an inmate at the State Industrial School for Boys, "I would like to know how you are. I read your last letter. I was very glad to hear you were comming [*sic*]."[22] Lindsey confounded oppressive police officers who believed that he had "hypnotized" the boys of Denver. "Why couldn't they see how violence projected violence, hate projected hate?" he wondered.[23]

Lindsey brought a breath of fresh air to the study of juvenile delin-

---

21. Lindsey and Borough, *The Dangerous Life*, p. 49.

22. Lindsey quoted in U.S. Congress, *Children's Courts in the United States,* 58th Cong., 2d sess. (1904), House Doc. 701, p. xi. On "snitching bees" see Lindsey and Borough, *The Dangerous Life,* pp. 120–30; and Ben B. Lindsey, "The Reformation of Juvenile Delinquents through the Juvenile Court," NCCC *Proceedings* (1903), 206–30. Charles Wise to Ben Lindsey (December 17, 1902), Box 1, The Papers of Benjamin B. Lindsey, Library of Congress, Washington, D.C. See also Benjamin B. Lindsey, "Denver Juvenile Court," *Juvenile Record* (February 1902), pp. 9–10. For an analysis of Lindsey's social thought, see Peter Gregg Slater, "Ben Lindsey and the Denver Juvenile Court: A Progressive Looks at Human Nature," *American Quarterly* 20 (1968), 211–23.

23. Lindsey and Borough, *The Dangerous Life,* p. 168. See also Murray Levine and Adeline Levine, *A Social History of Helping Services* (New York: Appleton-Century-Crofts, 1970), pp. 209–17. As the Levines point out, Lindsey utilized the boys to do the work of the court in the community "thus encouraging a view of the court as an institution which helps and not only punishes."

quency as it was being carried on by ponderous academics at the turn
of the century. His replies to their letters asking him how to determine a "delinquent type" are delightful. To the University of Chicago
criminologist Charles Richmond Henderson he wrote, "I do not believe that the physical defect is often present, or at least responsible
for any misdemeanor, unless it might be, and frequently is, the case
that an empty stomach may prompt a boy to certain acts which otherwise he would not be guilty of." His naïveté cut pleasantly into the
pretentiousness of the scholarly approach, as this letter to G. Stanley
Hall demonstrates:

> I wish to say that the methods I have employed here have simply
> grown up as a result of my observations and experience, and I have
> up to this time purposely refrained from consulting or studying any
> sociological works for fear I might embibe [*sic*] some theory, pre-
> ferring to work things out from what seemed to me the practical
> standpoint, and after an experience of four years I am glad I have
> taken this course. . . . At the present time I am simply trying and
> hoping to learn.[24]

By "trying and hoping to learn" Lindsey was able to secure the
passage of a juvenile court law, a law punishing parents who neglected their children, and numerous other measures protecting the
children of Colorado. He became a leading figure in the Progressive
Party and championed many reform causes in what he called "the
larger fight." "More than through books I saw through the tears and
misfortune of these children, the defects and injustice in our social,
political and economic conditions, and I have to thank the child for
my education. . . . I owe more to the children than they owe to me."
Always the center of contention, Lindsey was disbarred in 1927 for
illegally accepting a gift in his capacity as judge. By the time that the
Colorado State Supreme Court had reinstated him in 1935, he had
moved to Los Angeles and been elected to the Los Angeles Superior
Court. Lindsey's later crusades—his advocacy of birth control and of
trial marriage—never dimmed his enthusiasm for the role of juvenile
court judge. "So much depends upon *personnel*," he wrote Father
Flanagan of Nebraska's Boys' Town in 1941. Almost forty years

24. Lindsey to Charles Richmond Henderson (August 29, 1904), Lindsey MS,
Box 2. Lindsey to G. Stanley Hall (September 27, 1904), ibid.

earlier he had written, "The Juvenile Court rests upon the principle of love. Of course there is firmness and justice, for without this there would be danger in leniency. But there is no justice without love."[25]

Lindsey's "personal touch" attracted advocates everywhere. Sir William Clarke Hall, who presided over one of England's first juvenile courts, also emphasized the importance of the magistrate's personality. "The most complete adaptability of the building, the wisest statutory provisions for procedure, the highest training and capacity of probation officers, the most perfect keeping of records will all go for little if the spirit that can animate the whole is absent," he wrote, adding, "The majority of people forget their own childhood with astonishing rapidity." James F. Hill of the Detroit Society for the Prevention of Cruelty to Children, one of Lindsey's zealous admirers, proposed amending juvenile court laws to require that the judge as well as the probation officer visit the home of the delinquent child.[26]

Many of Lindsey's contemporaries during the early days of the juvenile court believed that the new institution would need more than love or judicial personality in order to become an effective reformatory agency. Specifically, they believed that delinquency could be combated more efficiently by a professional probation bureaucracy than by a charismatic judge. Julian W. Mack (1866–1943), judge of the Chicago Juvenile Court from 1905 to 1907 and later a distinguished federal judge and Jewish leader, regarded Lindsey's success and popularity as threatening to the future development of the court. Mack and other reform and philanthropic leaders were cool toward Lindsey among themselves, although they continued to endorse his work in public. "Judge Lindsey cannot be imitated, because his work depends upon his personality," said Mack. "His real greatness is his work as his own chief probation officer. Now, if a judge happens to be fitted by nature to be the chief probation officer in his community, and if his community is of a size that he can combine the work of the judge and chief probation officer, that community is fortunate. But

25. Ben B. Lindsey, "My Lesson from the Juvenile Court," *Survey* 23 (1910), 652–56. Lindsey to Father Flanagan (November 25, 1941), Lindsey MS, Box 289. Ben B. Lindsey, "The Boy and the Court," *Charities* 13 (1904), 354.

26. William Clarke Hall quoted in Cadbury, *Young Offenders Yesterday and Today*, p. 83. James F. Hill to Lindsey (January 12, 1903), Lindsey MS, Box 1.

the lines of our work should not be laid out on the basis that we are going to find that unique personality in any of our communities." Lindsey himself encouraged the development of a probation system which he hoped would develop the Denver juvenile court into a full-fledged "institution of human relations," an agency not unlike later family courts. Nevertheless, Lindsey's warm and erratic personality seemed anathema to those attempting to construct a systematic and impersonal bureaucracy to serve urban courts.[27]

Probation had existed in various forms before the inception of the juvenile court, but it was radically extended in the wake of the court movement. And, like the court itself, probation systems varied considerably from one place to another. By 1902 Rhode Island, Indiana, Minnesota, and New Jersey had followed Massachusetts' example by passing state probation laws which provided for paid state agents to assist the juvenile courts. San Francisco and Washington, D.C., passed municipal ordinances for the same purpose. State laws also permitted courts in other cities—Chicago, Philadelphia, Boston, and New York for example—to utilize services of volunteers from the same child-saving societies, settlement houses, and municipal organizations which had campaigned to establish the juvenile court.[28]

Probation officers, whatever their sympathies for delinquent children, considered themselves servants of the judge of the juvenile court, not defenders of the rights of children. They gathered what they regarded as relevant facts and opinions on each case in order to help the judge make his disposition. Because children in juvenile court were no longer subject to criminal law, probation officers dismissed due process safeguards of that law as unnecessary or even injurious —an attitude which often obscured or eliminated the proof of facts

27. Julian W. Mack, "The Juvenile Court: The Judge and the Probation Officer," NCCC *Proceedings* (1906), pp. 123–25. For an unflattering view of Lindsey see Julian Mack to Julius Rosenwald (1925?), Papers of Julius Rosenwald, University of Chicago Library; see also Levine and Levine, *A Social History of Helping Services,* pp. 223–25, 227–29. Lindsey disavowed claims that he had originated the juvenile court and, in so doing, demonstrated a knowledge of the court's historical roots which was not shared by many of his contemporaries who were inclined to believe that they had created an entirely new institution. See above, p. 133, and *Survey* 24 (1910), pp. 741–42.

28. Emily E. Williamson, "Probation and Juvenile Courts," *Annals* of the American Academy 20 (1902), 259–67.

essential in establishing the court's authority to intervene in the circumstances. For their part, juvenile court judges saw nothing anomalous about returning children to the supervisory care of the same probation officer whose testimony had placed them at the court's mercy in the first place.[29]

At first, most juvenile courts relied upon volunteer juvenile probation officers whose importance was heavily emphasized. Their work, said one observer, "is the cord upon which all the pearls of the Juvenile Court are strung. It is the keynote of a beautiful harmony, without it the Juvenile Court could not exist." In fact, the "beautiful harmony" was often a set of balanced antagonisms between ethnic groups or between Protestant and Catholic child-saving societies. Frederic Almy, secretary-treasurer of the Charity Organization Society of Buffalo, described the careful ethnic and religious division of probation responsibility in his city:

> Of the ten probation officers in Buffalo all are unpaid for this special work, but two are truant officers, two are officers of the Charity Organization Society, and one is the head worker of Welcome Hall, a leading settlement. The city is divided into two districts, in each of which there are a Catholic and a Protestant female officer for the girls and younger boys, and a Catholic and Protestant male officer for the older boys. There are a Jewish officer and a Polish officer for the city at large.[30]

The development of the probation system in Chicago serves best to illustrate the delicate nature of voluntary support as well as the consequences of replacing volunteers with publicly paid "civil service" professionals. As we have already noted, the Chicago juvenile court initially had the enthusiastic support of all local philanthropic organizations. As a continuing token of their support, these groups sent

29. These procedures have been the focus of recent criticism of the juvenile court. See Maxine Boord Virtue, *Public Services to Children in Michigan* (Ann Arbor: University of Michigan Press, 1952), pp. 229–37. Mark H. Haller, "Urban Crime and Criminal Justice: the Chicago Case," *Journal of American History* 57 (1970), 629, notes that the growth of the probation system in Chicago increased juvenile delinquency proportionately. In 1913–14 twenty-three staff members were added, and the number of referrals increased by 50 percent.

30. Anon., "Third Day in Juvenile Court," *Juvenile Court Record* 2 (February 1901), 15–17. Frederic Almy, "Juvenile Courts in Buffalo," *Annals* of the American Academy 20 (July 1902), 279.

privately paid representatives to the juvenile court as probation officers. Indeed, the absence of representatives from the Italian colonies
caused Judge Tuthill to complain, "The number of Italian children
brought into the Juvenile Court is altogether out of proportion to
the Italian population in Chicago and thus far I have not been able
to get in close touch with the parents who are responsible for the
raising of these little ones." Tuthill urged "representative Italians of
Chicago" to appoint and support their own probation officers.
Timothy Hurley of the predominantly Irish Catholic Visitation and
Aid Society served as the court's principal probation officer. The
Protestant Illinois Childrens' Home and Aid Society also contributed
an officer.[31] The Chicago Women's Club, under the leadership of Lucy
Flower and Louise de Koven Bowen, provided the salary of Mrs.
Alzina Stevens, a Hull-House resident and the first female officer of
the court. In 1902 Mrs. Flower and Mrs. Bowen helped to found
the Juvenile Court Committee which not only mobilized financial
support for Protestant probation officers, but also established a detention home for children awaiting hearing in Chicago juvenile court.[32]

Timothy Hurley strongly supported this voluntary system of probation because he believed that it guaranteed children places in families
of their own religion if they could not be returned to their own homes.
"Atheists fight this here," he wrote to Ben Lindsey. The atheists he
was probably referring to were the Protestant club women of the
Juvenile Court Committee, the residents of Hull-House, and also
Judge Julian W. Mack, who was Jewish. In 1903 Mack had been
appointed to the Illinois Civil Service Commission. Two years later,
with the help of the Juvenile Court Committee, he helped secure
passage of an amendment to the juvenile court law providing for a
publicly supported probation force which was to be selected com-
petitively on the basis of a civil service exam. As a result of this test,

31. Chicago *Tribune* (November 11, 1902). Timothy D. Hurley, "Development
of the Juvenile Court Idea," *Charities* 11 (1903), 423–25. Hurley edited the
Juvenile Record, later the *Juvenile Court Record,* which was the official organ
of the Chicago Visitation and Aid Society.

32. Elisabeth Parker, "Personnel and Organization in the Probation Department of the Juvenile Court of Cook County, 1899–1903" (Master's thesis, University of Chicago, 1934), pp. 7–9. Louise de Koven Bowen, *Growing Up with
a City* (New York: Macmillan, 1926), pp. 103–106.

Henry W. Thurston, a sociologist at Chicago Normal School, replaced Hurley as chief probation officer. The remainder of the staff consisted solely of representatives from Protestant organizations. The "beautiful harmony" had been shattered.[33]

Hurley and the members of the Visitation and Aid Society had some reason to feel aggrieved. Under the pretense of civil service reform, they had been excluded from helping Catholic children appearing before the juvenile court, just as their ancestors had been prevented from assisting Catholic youths locked inside houses of refuge. Henry Thurston minimized religious differences, but Louise de Koven Bowen, one of the graders of the civil service exams, ridiculed the efforts of Catholic candidates, particularly one man who gave his qualifications as "having had charge of four boys who bid fair to be criminals, and made priests out all four." Mrs. Bowen was nearly mobbed during several speaking appearances.[34]

In 1907 Hurley took a measure of revenge when he was appointed to the Chicago circuit court and convinced his fellow judges to vote Julian Mack off the bench of the juvenile court. Hurley's enthusiasm for the legal prerogatives of the juvenile court had diminished considerably by this time. "Children and parents have constitutional rights and they must be observed," he said. "God, in his goodness and mercy, blessed parents with children, and before the court severs the relations of parent and child . . . greatest care should be exercised."[35]

Probation officers often exacerbated religious and ethnic tensions by assuming an authoritarian attitude toward probationers and their families, many of whom were both foreign-born and poor. "When my son is so ruthlessly torn away from me, it gives me much pain," a bereaved father wrote to Ben Lindsey, protesting the high-handed

33. Timothy Hurley to Ben Lindsey (January 1, 1903), Lindsey MS, Box 1. Parker, "Personnel and Organization in the Probation Department of the Juvenile Court of Cook County, 1899–1903," pp. 10–14.

34. *Survey* 23 (1910), 665. Bowen, pp. 115–18. As late as 1926, Hastings Hart described a reform school superintendent as "a Roman Catholic, but . . . a broad minded man." Hart to Graham Taylor (July 19, 1926), Taylor MS, Newberry Library, Chicago, Illinois. Taylor was founder of the Chicago Commons settlement.

35. *Charities* 18 (1907), 416–17. Timothy D. Hurley, "Necessity for the Lawyer in the Juvenile Court," NCCC *Proceedings* (1905), pp. 173–77.

methods of one officer. Homer Folks, the leading advocate of probation, defended the right of the court authority to enter the delinquent's
home as "the very essence of the probation system." Although Folks
believed that probation visiting must be friendly in order to be successful, he warned at the same time that it "must utilize to the fullest
degree whatever advantages there are in the shock caused by appre-
hension of the child, by the court proceedings and the judge's counsel." Probation, he concluded, "provides a new kind of reformatory,
without walls and without much coercion."[36]

Coercion, however, lurked close to the surface. Probation officers
emphasized the friendly aspect of visitation, but simultaneously they
felt compelled to threaten the delinquent and his family. "When
sterner treatment was demanded," said one officer, "the friendly ad-
viser became the official representative of the court with the demand
that certain conditions be observed or that the probationer be returned
to the court." "All right-minded people are willing to have boys and
girls have chances to do the right thing," wrote Henry Thurston, "but
after they persistently throw chances away the same people have a
right to insist that these young people be really controlled, even if it
takes a criminal court process to do it."[37]

Juvenile court judges and probation officers emphasized ideas and
displayed attitudes which would not have seemed unfamiliar to early
reform school officials. The judges and their lieutenants claimed that
their tribunals protected children from harsh institutional settings,
but they did not hesitate to threaten youths with the prospect of in-

---

36. Charles Wenske to Ben Lindsey (October 6, 1902), Lindsey MS, Box 1.
Trattner, *Homer Folks*, p. 92. Homer Folks, "Juvenile Probation," NCCC
Proceedings (1906), pp. 117–22. Folks helped to establish the New York State
Probation Commission in 1907 and served as its first president. The commission provided state control and supervision of probation work and by 1931 had
been emulated by twenty other states. The National Probation Association was
established in 1907.

37. Edith Jones, "Probation in Practice," *Charities* 17 (1907), 983. Thurston
quoted in *Charities* 20 (1908), 287–88. Hastings Hart, who by 1910 was director of the Department of Child Helping of the Russell Sage Foundation, supported similar sentiments; see Hart, "Report of the Committee on Children,"
NCCC *Proceedings* (1906), pp. 90–91; and Hart, *Preventive Treatment of Neglected Children* (New York: Charities Publication Committee, 1910). See also
Malcolm Dana, "Remedial Work on Behalf of Our Youth," NCCC *Proceedings*
(1895), p. 237.

carceration or to use home visitations and court sessions to scold
delinquents and their parents for failing to foresee-the consequences
of their misdemeanors. Judges like Ben Lindsey and Harvey H. Baker
and Frederick P. Cabot, of the Boston Juvenile Court, sent children
to reform school only as a last resort, but alternative dispositions were
often just as bad. In many jurisdictions, court detention facilities were
absent, and this meant holding children in jail while they waited court
appearances; even when detention homes were available, they often
resembled jails more than homes. "With its barred windows and
locked doors . . . the whole atmosphere of the place is wrong,"
wrote Mrs. Bowen of the Chicago detention home in 1925.[38]

In short, juvenile courts, even those with a panoply of supporting
staff and institutions, provided new bottles for old wine—ways of
supervising delinquent children which, while not formally incarcerating them, provided penal sanctions for persistent wrongdoers. The
charismatic approach of some early judges and the sheer amount of
organizational and promotional activity associated with the creation
of a seemingly novel tribunal obscured for a long while the juvenile
court's traditional attitude toward delinquent children and their parents. Far from limiting the parental power of the state, legal decisions
bearing on the constitutionality of the juvenile court increased or at
least sustained the *parens patriae* doctrine. The father of Mary Ann
Crouse, the girl whom the state of Pennsylvania refused to relinquish
in 1838, would have surely recognized the sentiments of this *obiter
dictum* which comprised part of *Commonwealth* v. *Fisher,* a 1905
decision upholding the parental function of the Pennsylvania juvenile
court:

> To save a child from becoming a criminal, or from continuing in a
> career of crime, to end in maturer years in public punishment and
> disgrace, the legislatures surely may provide for the salvation of such
> a child, if its parents or guardians be unable or unwilling to do so, by
> bringing it into one of the courts of the state without any process at
> all, for the purpose of subjecting it to the state's guardianship and
> protection.[39]

38. Louise de Koven Bowen, "The Early Days of the Juvenile Court," in *The
Child, the Clinic and the Court,* p. 309.

39. *Commonwealth* v. *Fisher,* 213 Pennsylvania 48 (1905). See also *Mill* v.
Brown, 88 Pacific Reporter 609 (Utah, 1907). For a unique decision, which

The Fisher decision became an often-cited precedent in subsequent cases involving the legality of juvenile court actions.

Parental delinquency laws passed during the first decade of the twentieth century (often as amendments to juvenile court laws) offered further indications of the persistence of the tradition of blaming parents for the faults of their children. Ben Lindsey berated "the careless father, unworthy as a man, dangerous as a citizen," and he influenced the passage of a Colorado law providing jail sentences and fines for parents who neglected their children. In Kansas, parents could be "fined in a sum not to exceed $1000, or imprisoned in the county jail for a period not to exceed one year, or . . . both" for contributing to or encouraging the delinquencies of their children.[40]

Legal decisions upholding the parental powers of the juvenile court, and parental delinquency laws themselves, originated in part because of the confusion and bickering that surrounded efforts to define the scope and function of the institution. We have already noted that the juvenile court, even in its early days, did not always proceed in an atmosphere of universal self-congratulation. But behind and beyond the arguments between rival philanthropic groups over the future of the court and probation lay more fundamental disputes. On the one hand, some lawyers and judges challenged the constitutional basis of the court, claiming that children were indeed being prosecuted for crimes and thus were entitled to protection against unfair loss of liberty as provided by the Bill of Rights. On the other, nascent social workers and reformers, whom Margaret Rosenheim has called "expansionists," while agreeing that the court's performance left much

---

declared a juvenile court act unconstitutional, see *Robison* v. *Wayne Circuit Judges,* 151 Michigan 315 (1908). Given the accessibility of juvenile court officials into the homes and affairs of delinquent children, the enthusiasm of progressive reformers for the family as a child-caring institution becomes more understandable. The 1909 White House Conference on the Care of Dependent Children, one of the last acts of Theodore Roosevelt's Presidency, resolved that children should not be deprived of home life "except for urgent and compelling reasons": 1909 *Proceedings* of the Conference on the Care of Dependent Children (Washington, D.C.: Government Printing Office, 1909), p. 5. See also Fox, "Juvenile Justice Reform," *Stanford Law Review* 22 (1970), 1191–92.

40. Benjamin B. Lindsey, "The Child, the Parent and the Law," *Juvenile Court Record* (May 1904), pp. 9–10. Colorado *Laws* (1905), ch. 81 (Denver, 1905), pp. 163–65. Kansas *Laws* (1907), ch. 177 (Topeka, 1907), pp. 277–80.

to be desired, insisted that the only remedy lay in further developing its constituent parts or in redefining its purposes through other agencies.[41]

Both critics—the lawyers and "the expansionists"—believed that the juvenile court had not fulfilled its initial promise. Judge Charles W. Hoffman, surveying Pennsylvania's juvenile court system for the U.S. Children's Bureau in 1927, found many children languishing in detention homes and county jails, despite the fact that state laws specifically forbade the incarceration of children. "What has the advanced legal status accomplished? Is it not clear that the juvenile courts are not functioning?" he asked. A survey of *Courts in the United States Hearing Children's Cases,* conducted in 1920 by Evelina Belden of the Children's Bureau, concluded in a similar vein: "In the majority of jurisdictions in the United States special provision for children coming before the courts has not yet been made." Nearly 30 percent of the children's cases brought before the courts of the United States in 1918 were tried by courts "not adapted to the handling of children's cases." "Statistics cannot adequately reveal the injury done these children through their association with adult offenders, their trial under the old criminal processes, and the absence of equipment for the study of their needs or for proper oversight and protection," said Miss Belden.[42]

Judges like Edward Lindsey of Pennsylvania and Edward F. Waite of Minnesota focused upon what they regarded as legal travesties visited upon the delinquent child. Lindsey found the juvenile court act of Pennsylvania "clearly in conflict with constitutional provisions and this conclusion can only be escaped by evasions." Sounding not unlike Justice Fortas in the recent Gault case (1967), Lindsey added, "Every child accused of crime should be tried and subject to neither punishment nor restraint of liberty unless convicted. No child should

41. Margaret K. Rosenheim, "Perennial Problems in the Juvenile Court," in Margaret K. Rosenheim, ed., *Justice for the Child* (New York: Macmillan, 1962), pp. 1–21.

42. Hoffman quoted in U.S. Children's Bureau, *Proceedings* of the Conference on Juvenile Court Standards, Publication 97 (Washington, D.C.: Government Printing Office, 1922), pp. 17, 15. U.S. Children's Bureau, Evelina Belden, *Courts in the United States Hearing Children's Cases,* Publication 65 (Washington, D.C.: Government Printing Office, 1920), pp. 12, 15.

be restrained simply because he has been accused of crime, whether he is guilty or not." Judge Waite also sounded a warning which has a contemporary ring:

> *The greater the conceded discretion of the judge, the freer he is from the vigilance of lawyers, the less likely is he to have his mistakes corrected on appeal,* so much the more careful should he be to base every judicial conclusion on evidence proper to be received in any court of justice. Otherwise the State's parental power which he embodies is prostituted, the interpreter of the law degenerates into the oriental kadi and the juvenile court falls into suspicion and disrepute.[43]

Other lawyers and reformers, however, saw the juvenile court's failure as emanating from more mundane causes. Court calendars were clogged with cases involving only destitution or neglect which, in their opinion, properly belonged to other agencies. Bernard Flexner (1865–1945), a corporation lawyer, and Roger N. Baldwin, a St. Louis social worker who later founded and served as first director of the American Civil Liberties Union, denounced this practice in their coauthored *The Juvenile Courts and Probation* (1914): "The presence of the dependent or destitute child in the court, presenting family or home conditions remediable simply by relief measures, is an injustice to the court, and a worse injustice to the child and to the family." Lack of differentiation resulted in overcrowding and the vaunted "personal touch" suffered. Courtroom appearances were shortened and probationary supervision likewise became perfunctory. "Having a child receive ten minutes of a judge's time in an open juvenile court hearing may result in just as much harm as that which he would have received in an adult court in years past," commented Prentice Murphy of the Children's Bureau of Philadelphia. Sociologist Thomas D. Eliot recognized the humane intent of judges who sought to provide children with medicine, shoes, clothes, and school books but contended that "if this be granted, no line can be drawn short of a court administering all the children's charities; as a sort of department of

---

43. Edward L. Lindsey, "The Juvenile Court from the Lawyer's Standpoint," *Annals* of the American Academy, 52 (1914), 145–47. On Waite see U.S. Children's Bureau, *Proceedings* of the Conference on Juvenile Court Standards, p. 56. A compendium of opinion on this subject is J. Prentice Murphy, "The Juvenile Court at the Bar," *Annals* of the American Academy 145 (1929), 80–97.

maladjusted children, many of whom might have been kept normal had the community shouldered the task in time."[44]

Some judges and other expansionists continued to believe that the juvenile court could serve as a community agency in the broadest sense. In 1907 the Illinois juvenile court law was amended at the urging of the Chicago Bar Association and the Chicago Women's Club in order to give the court jurisdiction over neglected children as well as juvenile delinquents. Two years later, the ladies of the Chicago Juvenile Court Committee reconstituted themselves as the Juvenile Protective Association, a more broadly conceived investigative group which undertook surveys of child labor and morals investigations of theaters, book stores, and bawdy houses. Judge Edward Shoen of Newark, New Jersey, reflected the expansionist mood when he proclaimed:

> The field of the juvenile court is the maladjusted child, whom the State is in duty bound to protect, correct, and develop; and the duty of this tribunal is to follow up the case by ascertaining all the facts and circumstances in the life of the child, to determine in what particulars that child has been deprived of essentials for a full moral and physical development. And if, as is common experience, it is found that certain essentials are lacking in the environment in which the child is being reared, the State, *in loco parentis,* acting through its instrumentality, the juvenile court, must provide the essentials of which the child has thus far been deprived.

No one took a grander view of the evolutionary progress of the juvenile court than Herbert H. Lou, an early historian of the court:

> In place of judicial tribunals, restrained by antiquated procedure, saturated in an atmosphere of hostility, trying cases for determining guilt and inflicting punishment according to inflexible rules of law, we have now juvenile courts, in which the relations of the child to his parents or other adults and to the state or society are defined and adjusted summarily according to the scientific findings about the

44. Bernard Flexner and Roger N. Baldwin, *Juvenile Courts and Probation* (New York: Century, 1912), pp. x-xi. Murphy, "The Juvenile Court at the Bar," p. 87. Thomas D. Eliot, "The Trend of the Juvenile Court," *Annals* of the American Academy 52 (1914), 154. Flexner and Baldwin originally submitted their book as a report to the National Probation Association. Flexner edited a special edition (February 5, 1910) of *Survey* magazine commemorating the tenth anniversary of the juvenile court.

child and his environments. In place of magistrates, limited by the outgrown custom and compelled to walk in the paths fixed by the law of the realm, we have now socially-minded judges, who hear and adjust cases according not to rigid rules of law but to what the interests of society and the interests of the child or good conscience demand. In place of juries, prosecutors, and lawyers, learned in the old conception of law and staging dramatically, but often amusingly, legal battles, as the necessary paraphernalia of a criminal court, we have now probation officers, physicians, psychologists, and psychiatrists, who search for the social, physiological, psychological, and mental backgrounds of the child in order to arrive at reasonable and just solutions of individual cases. In other words, in this new court we tear down primitive prejudice, hatred, and hostility toward the law-breaker in that most hide-bound of all human institutions, the court of law, and we attempt, as far as possible, to administer justice in the name of truth, love, and understanding.

As Margaret Rosenheim has pointed out, most juvenile courts, in the name of "truth, love, and understanding" operated under broad definitions of delinquency which implied that they could find remedies for children suffering from all degrees of want or trouble.[45]

There was, however, a recognition by certain figures in the juvenile court movement that the institution had been granted its extensive jurisdiction because alternative judicial and social agencies did not exist, particularly in regard to public services such as mothers' aid and placement of dependent children. Bernard Flexner and Roger Baldwin advocated one method of compensating for the deficiency—creating a family court to treat "the adult responsible for the child's condition." This tribunal could "deal more effectively with the family which produces the neglected or delinquent child, who is merely a factor in the larger and more complicated problem." The development of domestic relations courts, beginning in Buffalo in 1910 and dealing primarily with cases of nonsupport and desertion, commenced the movement toward family courts. In 1914 in Hamilton County (Cincinnati, Ohio), the juvenile court and the domestic relations court were joined to create the first official family court in the United States.

---

45. Shoen quoted in U.S. Children's Bureau, *Proceedings* of the Conference on Juvenile Court Standards, pp. 35–36. Lou, *Juvenile Courts in the United States,* p. 2. Rosenheim, "Perennial Problems of the Juvenile Court," in Rosenheim, ed., *Justice for the Child,* p. 12.

The aim of this court, according to Charles W. Hoffman, judge of the court and its foremost spokesman, was to provide "for the consideration of all matters relating to the family in one court of exclusive jurisdiction, in which the same methods of procedure shall prevail as in the juvenile court and in which it will be possible to consider social evidence as distinguished from legal evidence. In fact, providing for a family court is no more than increasing the jurisdiction of the juvenile court and designating it by the more comprehensive term of family court." Judge Willis B. Perkins of Michigan, writing in favor of integrated family and children's courts, said:

> It is no doubt true that the causes of juvenile delinquency and dependency, desertion and nonsupport, pauperism, divorce and marital dissensions, generally speaking, are all interrelated subjects. They cannot be treated separately.

Like Hoffman, Perkins advocated the widest jurisdiction for domestic relations courts, to include divorce and alimony, separate maintenance, adoption, and guardianship of children, bastardy cases as well as desertion and nonsupport cases. During World War I and throughout the 1920s, the family court and the domestic relations court increased the impact of the juvenile court by carrying out its function under different organizational guises.[46]

To some reformers in the emerging professions of social work and public welfare administration, the creation, expansion, and manipulation of courts hearing children's cases seemed somewhat beside the point when juvenile delinquency was considered as a social problem. Julia Lathrop and Homer Folks were more interested in understanding and combatting poverty, crime, and disease—the larger social problems of which delinquency was only one part. "All children need for successful rearing the same conditions: homes of physical and moral decency, fresh air, education, recreation, the fond care of wise fathers and mothers," said Julia Lathrop. "These essentials curtailed

46. Flexner and Baldwin, *Juvenile Courts and Probation,* p. vii. Charles W. Hoffman, "Social Aspects of the Family Court," *Journal of Criminal Law and Criminology* 10 (1919), 409–22. Willis B. Perkins, "Family Courts," *Michigan Law Review* 17 (1919), 378–81. See also Jacob T. Zukerman, "The Family Court—Evolving Concepts," *Annals* of the American Academy 383 (1969), 119–28.

at any point, the degree of human wastage grows with the curtailment. No institution, no probation system, no orders of court, can instantly produce from chaos these essentials." According to Homer Folks, the probation officer should regard the offense of the delinquent "as the joint product of his individuality and his environment and [the officer] seeks to influence both factors so that they will work together for good."[47] These reformers stressed the multiplicity and interrelationship of delinquency's causes. In 1917 Julia Lathrop wrote: "The time has passed, I believe, when we can consider any social problem apart from the problem of securing free opportunity for every normal individual to secure by earnest, trained effort a fair standard of life. This is a long, heavy task, but it does not make it shorter or easier to blink it."[48]

By definition, a long and heavy task requires for its completion skilled planning and organization. One step in the struggle to understand the social forces which underlay delinquency and other problems was the establishment of schools of philanthropy and social work. The New York School of Philanthropy, the first school for the professional training of social workers, was founded in 1898. In 1907 Sophonisba P. Breckinridge (1866–1948) and Edith Abbott (1876–1957) began their distinguished careers in social work administration as "Directors of the Department of Social Investigation" in Graham Taylor's Chicago School of Civics and Philanthropy. In 1917 the New York institution became the New York School for Social Work, while the University of Chicago adopted the Chicago School of Civics in 1920 and, in 1924, renamed it the School of Social Service Administration. As Roy Lubove has demonstrated, these schools were intended to convert social work from a voluntary activity to a profession requiring special investigative skills of its practitioners and, in so doing, to provide communities with caseworkers expert in identifying and aiding families and individuals in various conditions of need. Social workers would not only give their clients advice and economic

---

47. Lathrop quoted in Breckinridge and Abbott, *The Delinquent Child and the Home,* p. 10. Trattner, *Homer Folks,* p. 89.

48. Julia Lathrop to Lamar T. Beman (February 14, 1917), Record Group 102, Records of the U.S. Children's Bureau, National Archives, Washington, D.C.

assistance but also channel them to appropriate schools, hospitals, juvenile courts, and mental health clinics as each case warranted. In the voluntary field, caseworkers were usually located in family service agencies, the lineal descendants of the charity organization societies. In government, family social work was carried on by municipal, county, and state welfare departments. It was the hope of the early advocates of social work training that the development of community social service facilities might lessen the need for the juvenile court. Social workers would take the lead in assuming responsibility for locating more appropriate community agencies and directing children and families to them. From this point of view, the responsibility for reform work lay more in the community than in the court. "The juvenile court cannot work miracles unaided," wrote Sophonisba Breckinridge and Edith Abbott in 1912. "It cries out to the community for the co-operation of all its citizens in removing the conditions which are feeding into the court thousands of delinquent children every year."[49]

To facilitate community cooperation, schools of social work and public agencies of various types sponsored extensive surveys of individual municipalities in order to determine the availability of local resources and the extent of local problems and to stimulate corrective civic action. The pioneer American effort, the Pittsburgh Survey of 1907, was directed by Paul U. Kellogg and carried out by the staff of *Charities and the Commons* magazine. Kellogg made the first comprehensive application of the inductive method to social and economic questions as they related to individual wage earners. In his own words, the Pittsburgh Survey was "an appraisal . . . of how human engineering had kept pace with mechanical in the American steel dis-

49. Louise C. Wade, *Graham Taylor, Pioneer for Social Justice, 1851–1938* (Chicago: University of Chicago Press, 1964), pp. 161–85. Lubove, *The Professional Altruist*, pp. 22–156. Breckinridge and Abbott, *The Delinquent Child and the Home*, p. 177. Voluntary family service agencies formed the National Association of Societies for Organizing Charity (1911), which became the American Organization for Organizing Family Social Work (1919) and then the present-day Family Service Association of America (1946). See Harry L. Lurie, ed., *Encyclopedia of Social Work*, 15th ed. (New York: National Association of Social Workers, 1965), pp. 309–19. On the definition and dimensions of family service work in the 1920s, see Sophonisba P. Breckinridge, ed., *Family Welfare Work in a Metropolitan Community: Selected Case Records* (Chicago: University of Chicago Press, 1924).

trict . . . an attempt to throw light on these and kindred economic forces not by theoretical discussion of them, but by spreading forth the objective facts of life and labor which should help in forming judgment as to their results." By living among the "wage earning population" whose "inventory" they were taking, Kellogg and his colleagues consciously avoided sweeping generalizations when portraying their subjects and concentrated instead on explaining their problems in factual and statistical terms—what Robert Woods of Boston's Andover Settlement House called "piled up actualities."[50]

The Pittsburgh Survey was imitated at all levels of government from municipality to state. At first, these surveys were, like the Pittsburgh Survey, general studies of entire communities. By the 1920s, however, a number of surveys had been taken which appraised only one major phase of community life, an approach reminiscent of nineteenth-century studies of sanitation and housing. In addition to these problems, surveys concentrated on public education, recreation, employment, industrial relations, crime, and juvenile deliquency. As one index of a community's social health, delinquency was usually included in community surveys, but it found fuller expression in crime surveys. The Cleveland Crime Survey (1921), directed by Roscoe Pound and Felix Frankfurter, the Missouri Crime Survey (1926), directed by Raymond Moley, and Lawrence Veiller's 1923 study of *The Adolescent Offender* in New York City were the most prominent.

One specialized study, Edith Abbott and Sophonisba Breckinridge, *Truancy and Non-Attendance in the Chicago Schools* (1917), was intended to examine just one facet of juvenile delinquency. Much to their own surprise, however, the women found themselves considering a host of problems which bore indirectly but powerfully on the whole etiology of delinquency and of poverty in society. They wrote:

The present volume . . . has taken us beyond the juvenile court

---

50. Kellogg and Woods quoted in Allen Eaton and Shelby M. Harrison, *A Bibliography of Social Surveys* (New York: Russell Sage, 1930), pp. xvii–xix. It was obviously no coincidence that *Charities and the Commons* became *Survey* when Paul U. Kellogg became the magazine's editor in 1909. On Kellogg see Clarke A. Chambers, *Paul U. Kellogg and the "Survey": Voices for Social Welfare and Social Justice* (Minneapolis: University of Minnesota Press, 1971).

children with whom we began . . . for it was apparent that a study
of truancy would be of limited value without an inquiry into the
broader questions of non-attendance during the compulsory-attend-
ance period and the enforcement of the child labor laws which should
protect the children who are near the age when the required period
of school attendance comes to an end.

The study became less an inquiry into the truancy of school children
and more a plea for factory inspection laws, mothers' aid pensions
and higher wages and workmen's compensation for adult wage earners. Abbott and Breckinridge discovered that examination of the relationship between truancy and delinquency was incomplete without
a consideration of the effects of child labor upon both. When reduced
to individual cases, truancy often meant children pursuing legitimate
or illegitimate trades in order to help widowed mothers or disabled
or underpaid fathers to sustain the family. They concluded, "So long
as vast numbers of people find it so difficult, and at times impossible,
to provide adequate food and clothing for the children for whom the
state is providing education, just so long will many children find it
impossible to attend school regularly."[51]

The increasing number of child welfare studies in the early twentieth century illuminates Robert Wiebe's characterization of child care
as the touchstone of the progressive reform movement:

> If humanitarian progressivism had a central theme, it was the child.
> He united the campaigns for health, education, and a richer city en-
> vironment, and he dominated much of the interest in labor legislation.
> . . . The most popular version of legal and penal reform also empha-
> sized the needs of youth.

As poignant victims of exploitative forces and as embodiments of
hope for the future, children caused concerned citizens to make special efforts on their behalf. And for the first time, a significant effort

---

51. Edith Abbott and Sophonisba Breckinridge, *Truancy and Non-Attendance
in the Chicago Schools* (Chicago: University of Chicago Press, 1917), pp. vii,
352. A collection of articles on child labor in the early twentieth century is
included in Breckinridge, *The Child in the City*, pp. 273–312. On the campaign
for child labor reform which centered around the activities of the National
Child Labor Committee (1904), see Walter I. Trattner, *Crusade for the Children* (Chicago: Quadrangle Books, 1970). An excellent study of the campaign
in one state is Jeremy P. Felt, *Hostages of Fortune: Child Labor Reform in
New York State* (Syracuse: Syracuse University Press, 1965).

was made by the federal government when Congress established the U.S. Children's Bureau in 1912. Congress mandated the bureau "to investigate and report upon all matters pertaining to the welfare of children and child life among all classes of our people." During its first two decades, the bureau conducted over two hundred studies on a variety of subjects ranging from child labor and dependency to juvenile delinquency and maternal and infant mortality. Obviously, the objects of these studies were the children of the poor, not youths from "all classes of our people," but this fact should only increase our interest in the Children's Bureau approach.[52]

In its early days, the bureau was guided by female reformers who had already made reputations in the settlement house movement or in organized charity and social work. Julia Lathrop served as the first chief of the bureau (1912–1921), and she was followed by Edith Abbott's sister Grace, who served until 1934. Under their direction, the bureau conducted a number of studies of juvenile delinquency, most of which concluded by emphasizing the need to improve the facilities and services of the juvenile court in order to prevent delinquency.[53]

Children's Bureau reformers also saw delinquency as just one symptom of poor living standards or, in Neva Deardorff's words, "defective social organization." Proper treatment and prevention required study of "the whole child in his whole environment." Each child was to be studied and treated according to his or her particular psychic and social needs.[54] From this point of view, the juvenile court had a more

52. Robert H. Wiebe, *The Search for Order, 1877–1920* (New York: Hill and Wang, 1967), p. 169. A summary history of the Children's Bureau is Dorothy E. Bradbury, *Five Decades of Action for Children: A Short History of the Children's Bureau,* Publication 400 (Washington, D.C.: Government Printing Office, 1966).

53. Foremost among the early Children's Bureau studies of delinquency were Kate Holladay Claghorn, *Juvenile Delinquency in Rural New York* (Publication 32, 1918), Evelina Belden, *Courts in the United States Hearing Children's Cases* (Publication 65, 1920), Bernard Flexner and Reuben Oppenheimer, *The Legal Aspects of the Juvenile Court* (Publication 99, 1922), Helen R. Jeter, *The Chicago Juvenile Court* (Publication 104, 1922), Bernard Flexner, Reuben Oppenheimer, and Katherine P. Lenroot, *The Child, the Family, and the Court* (Publication 193, 1929), and Dorothy W. Burke, *Youth and Crime* (Publication 196, 1930).

54. Clarke A. Chambers, *Seedtime of Reform: American Social Service and Social Action* (Minneapolis: University of Minnesota Press, 1963), pp. 54–58.

limited function than other more ardent supporters of the institution
had claimed for it. It had no business, for instance, in administering
mothers' pensions or the placement of dependent children. Grace
Abbott castigated Judge Kathryn Sellers of the Washington, D.C.,
juvenile court for attempting to do this very thing. The court was, in
Miss Abbott's view, primarily a place where delinquent children were
sent "when the home and the school have failed to cure conduct difficulties." Making an explicit analogy between the hospital and the
juvenile court, she continued, "In many of the children brought to the
courts the disease of delinquency is so advanced that cure is impossible." Ideally, the court would serve as the place where psychologists,
psychiatrists, and other specialists concerned with the diagnosis of
youth problems both helped children and trained parents and teachers to understand the complex nature of juvenile delinquency. Miss
Abbott recognized that few courts were equipped to provide such
specialized services but defended the attachment of habit and child
guidance clinics to the court since, in her words, "it alone has the
authority to remove children from home and school if such treatment
is indicated by a careful study of the case." According to Sophonisba
Breckinridge, the court "helped to rescue the child from irresponsible parents and has pointed the way to a new relationship between
the family and the community."[55]

Other students of the juvenile court were not so sure. As early as
1914, Thomas Eliot advocated replacing the court with administrative
agencies which would center their activities around the public schools
in each community instead of the juvenile court. Grace Abbott herself grew steadily disillusioned with the juvenile court and eventually
concluded that it had been a failure "and that agencies entirely apart
from the Court should be developed." In 1934 she commended
Fiorello La Guardia for establishing, separate from the regular juvenile court, a municipal children's bureau which was designed to help
younger children whose "conduct problems" were just emerging. "We

55. Grace Abbott to Charles P. Sisson (January 15, 1931), Papers of Edith
and Grace Abbott, Manuscript Division, University of Chicago Library.
Grace Abbott, "Case Work Responsibility of Juvenile Courts," *Proceedings*
of the National Conference of Social Work (1929), pp. 158–59. Breckinridge
quoted from draft of her own paper on the juvenile court, prepared for the
1930 convention of the National Conference of Social Work, in Abbott MS.

need neighborhood health agencies similar to Child Health Centers which will easily be available to help parents, and others responsible for children in these problems," she wrote to him.[56]

Grace Abbott's disenchantment with the juvenile court is less intriguing than her first reasons for enthusiasm. What made her and others like her think that the juvenile court properly equipped with a social work staff and a subsidiary child guidance clinic could effectively combat "conduct problems" which could no longer be handled in the home and at school? To answer this question we need to consider the juvenile court from another point of view. By virtue of its administrative and legal power and its generally urban location —delinquents' personal histories were filed here and delinquents themselves could be studied here—the court served as a laboratory for the professional study of juvenile delinquency. Social and medical scientists flocked into this laboratory during the quarter century preceding the New Deal. The results of their researches informed Grace Abbott's approach and, more generally, laid the basis for modern attitudes toward juvenile delinquency.

56. Thomas D. Eliot, *The Juvenile Court and the Community* (New York: Macmillan, 1914). Grace Abbott to Edith V. Cook (August 3, 1936), Abbott MS. Grace Abbott to Fiorello La Guardia (March 31, 1934), Abbott MS. See also Grace Abbott, "The Juvenile Courts," *Survey* 72 (1936), 131–33. On school social work developing apart from the juvenile court, see Lela B. Costin, "A Historical Review of School Social Work," *Social Casework* (1969), pp. 439–53.

CHAPTER 6

Modern Theories of
Juvenile Delinquency, 1900–1940

E ARLY SCIENTIFIC STUDENTS of juvenile delinquency, particularly the criminal anthropologists and eugenicists, were not sanguine about the future careers of youthful wrongdoers. G. Stanley Hall's "recapitulation" theory portrayed delinquent behavior as a natural and passing phenomenon of growth in the male of the human species, but this concept had by definition little need for preventive programs. Early psychological testing seemed to aim at fixing permanently the identity of mentally and morally backward children, thereby implying that few remedies were available to help them.

Fatalistic explanations of human conduct and origins did not go uncontested. Psychologists like William James were generally optimistic about man's ability to help himself and to help others solve personal and social problems. From James's point of view, theories could not be used to hinder man from attempting to shape his environment. Adolf Meyer, a student of James's and, in 1895, pathologist at the Worcester State Hospital in Massachusetts, integrated this positive orientation into psychiatry. When Meyer began his work, the study of mental disease was largely concerned with seeking the causes of insanity and mental aberration through the dissection of the brains of former patients. Neuropathology was considered the key to the comprehension of mental disease, and psychoses were explained, according to Meyer, on the "exhaustion, poor nutrition, and metabolism level." Meyer's orientation was quite different. He saw the mind as a "living being in action; and not a peculiar form of mind stuff" and emphasized the need to study the wholeness of human behavior and to understand the uniqueness of the individual case. When his own mother became mentally ill, he theorized that many psychotic patients had a special history and at an earlier point in time had been sane. Thus, the psychiatrist's job was to discover what events accounted for an individual's misfortune in order to seek his or her readjustment to society.[1]

To help understand the life situations of his patients, Meyer felt the need to get outside of the state hospital setting, to study the individual's home and social environment. In 1898 he and his wife organized a rough system of psychiatric social work at the Pathological Institute (Ward's Island, New York). By visiting homes they gathered and organized information about each patient. These case histories enabled them to counsel patients more knowledgeably and to provide patients' families with information and aid regarding post-hospital adjustment. Meyer also urged that state hospitals sponsor the establishment of community clinics to serve as prophylactic measures for potential patients. "The institutions for the insane must indeed become the nucleus of a far reaching work for social and individual mental hygiene and mental readjustment," he said. However, the movement to found community clinics had to await the organization of the National Committee for Mental Hygiene (1909), a private group established by Clifford W. Beers, a former patient in a mental hospital.[2]

Meyer and other similarly inclined psychiatrists focused upon emotionally disturbed children as particularly appropriate subjects for their study and care. The Freudian psychiatrist William Alanson White described the reason for the emphasis:

1. Adolf Meyer, "Thirty-Five Years of Psychiatry in the United States and Our Present Outlook," *American Journal of Psychiatry* 8 (1928), 9–10, 21. See also Helen L. Witmer, *Psychiatric Clinics for Children* (New York: The Commonwealth Fund, 1940), pp. 10–27.

2. Adolf Meyer, "The Problem of the State in the Care of the Insane," *American Journal of Insanity* 65 (1909), 690. Witmer, *Psychiatric Clinics for Children*, pp. 18–19. On Beers see Albert Deutsch, *The Mentally Ill in America*, 2d ed. (New York: Columbia University Press, 1949), pp. 314–16; and Beers's autobiography, *A Mind that Found Itself* (London: Longmans, Green, 1908).

> If it is true that defects in the character make-up can be explained
> as originating in traits which were acquired in early childhood as
> reactions to certain factors in the child's environment, then the way
> is opened for an attempt to prevent such undesirable traits by an
> understanding of the child and a modification or elimination of those
> environmental factors which produce such results.

Meyer himself was drawn to the problems of children as he sought
to understand the total life situations of his psychotic patients at the
state hospital:

> In harmony with my dynamic conceptions of most mental disorders,
> I had to reach out, in my actual work, more and more toward a
> broader understanding of the patients, which led me to a study of the
> family settings, and by and by [about 1903], also of the place where
> the individual first becomes a member of the community, the school.[3]

Clinical and outpatient work with children was begun in Massachusetts in the 1890s, first by Dr. Walter E. Fernald at the Massachusetts School for the Feebleminded and then by Dr. Walter Chan-
ning at the Boston Dispensary. These children were generally feebleminded or even insane, but the new attitude in psychiatry with its
emphasis upon total behavior and the social and emotional genesis of
mental problems also encouraged the establishment of clinics and
special schools for less severely disturbed children who exhibited, in
Meyer's words, "traits of character that should serve as warnings to
be heeded." In 1896 the first broadly conceived clinic was founded
by University of Pennsylvania psychologist Lightner Witmer, who
located his institution within the psychology department. Witmer
focused particularly upon retarded school children, helping them to
stay in school and demanding that the schools themselves make extra
efforts to serve the special needs of exceptional children. A similar
spirit informed the work of Adolf Meyer in his new position as director of the Henry Phipps Psychiatric Clinic in Baltimore (1913)
and of Dr. E. E. Southard and his principal assistant, Mary C.
Jarrett, at the outpatient department of the Boston Psychopathic
Hospital (1912). Receiving emotionally disturbed children from
schools, juvenile courts, and social agencies, these clinics attempted

3. William A. White, "Childhood, the Golden Period for Mental Hygiene,"
Mental Hygiene 4 (1920), 261. Meyer, "Thirty-Five Years of Psychiatry," 16.

to adjust their problems on an individual basis without resorting to institutionalization.[4]

Juvenile delinquency is a legal category, not a psychological one. It does not describe the cause or the quality of a child's behavior but tells only that he has broken some law and because of this infraction has been brought into juvenile court. The initial expectation of juvenile court enthusiasts had been that distinctions based on kinds of behavior would be unnecessary. Court appearances coupled with probationary supervision would suffice to prevent further delinquency. It soon became apparent, however, that some children were immune to the normal appeals and proceeded unchecked on especially destructive or dangerous courses of action. One seven-year-old in the Chicago detention home poured kerosene over the children's beds and set fire to them. Other children repeatedly lied or stole for reasons which probation workers were unable to fathom. As a result, in 1909 the ladies of the Juvenile Protective Association organized a special committee, chaired by Julia Lathrop, to search for a specialist to investigate the causes of such behavior. Mrs. Ethel Sturges Dummer (1866–1954), a wealthy Chicago philanthropist, had offered to support this investigation for a five-year period. She called for "an inquiry into the health of delinquent children in order to ascertain as far as possible in what degrees delinquency is caused or influenced by mental or physical defect or abnormality with the purpose of applying remedies in individual cases whenever possible."[5]

On the advice of Adolf Meyer, William James, and James Rowland Angell, the committee selected William Healy (1869–1963), an English-born psychiatrist, to conduct the study. Healy had studied at Harvard College and Medical School and also at the University of Chicago Medical School, where he received his M.D. in 1900. After

4. Adolf Meyer, "What Do Histories of Cases of Insanity Teach Us Concerning Preventive Mental Hygiene during the Years of School Life?" *Psychological Clinic* 2 (1908), 95. On Lightner Witmer see Levine and Levine, *A Social History of Helping Services,* pp. 49–72. On Southard and Jarrett see Roy Lubove, *The Professional Altruist,* pp. 78–80; and E. E. Southard and Mary C. Jarrett, *The Kingdom of Evils* (New York: Macmillan, 1922).

5. Levine and Levine, p. 164. Deutsch, pp. 323–24. Circular letter of Ethel S. Dummer (January 2, 1909), Papers of Ethel Sturges Dummer, Schlesinger Library, Radcliffe College. The Juvenile Protective Association was formerly the Juvenile Court Committee; see above, pp. 140–41.

working as a physician at Wisconsin State Hospital and instructing in gynecology at Northwestern University Medical School, he did postgraduate research in Vienna, Berlin, and London in 1906 and 1907. Between 1903 and 1916 he was also an instructor and associate professor of nervous and mental diseases at the Chicago Polyclinic. In this capacity he came to the attention of Julia Lathrop and her committee. In 1909 the Juvenile Psychopathic Institute was founded, with Healy as the first director.[6]

More than any other man, Healy was responsible for channeling scientific study of juvenile delinquency away from sterile efforts to quantify its relationship to mental ability or bodily form. His work in Chicago and, after 1917, at the Judge Baker Foundation in Boston, stimulated the development of other clinics in Ohio (1915) and Michigan (1916) whose main purpose was to examine the psychological causes of juvenile misbehavior. Healy's work with children led psychologists in the mental hygiene movement to see, in the study of juvenile delinquency and youthful misbehavior, the best way of understanding crime and insanity generally. Psychologist Frankwood Williams recalled the principal discovery of the early investigations:

> Working with adult delinquents, or with adolescent delinquents, we seldom found that the delinquency was a recently developed or isolated matter, but merely an incident in a long series of delinquencies leading back into school life and childhood. . . . What actually we had to deal with, whether it was in the field of functional nervous and mental disease, delinquency, dependency, industrial unrest, was social maladjustment, due to faulty emotional development, which had its roots in childhood.[7]

In association with Dr. Thomas Salmon of the National Committee for Mental Hygiene, Healy helped to initiate and to promote the Commonwealth Fund's program to establish child guidance clinics in communities throughout the country. The purpose of these clinics was to serve the mental hygiene needs of all children. At first, they were organized in liaison with juvenile courts, but later they were usually founded in connection with hospitals, schools, or community family

6. In 1914 after Mrs. Dummer ended her support, control of the Institute passed to Cook County and, in 1917 to the State of Illinois. In 1914 it was renamed the Institute of Juvenile Research.

7. Frankwood E. Williams, "Finding a Way in Mental Hygiene," *Mental Hygiene* 14 (1930), 237–83.

service agencies where they could better serve children whose behavior problems required attention but not institutionalization. Child guidance clinics, together with habit clinics devoted to study and treatment of behavior problems of infancy, formed the dynamic core of the mental hygiene movement during the 1920s. By 1931, 674 psychiatric clinics existed, of which 232 were child guidance clinics employing either full or part time, a three-member team of psychologist, psychiatrist and social worker.[8]

William Healy could have hardly foreseen these developments when he began to study individual cases of children in the Chicago Juvenile Court. Indeed, by his own admission, he was still very much influenced by traditional scientific attitudes toward delinquency. As a charter member of the American Breeders Association (1903), he had been interested in the eugenic explanation of crime, and even in 1910, he spent a great deal of time measuring delinquents to see if they conformed to Lombroso's description of the born criminal.[9] Also, his belief that persistent delinquents were feebleminded led him initially to support their permanent institutionalizaton.[10]

Nevertheless, Healy refused to make an absolute correlation be-

8. Commonwealth Fund Program for the Prevention of Delinquency, *Progress Report, 1926* (New York: Joint Committee on Methods of Preventing Delinquency, 1926), p. 8. On child guidance clinics see George S. Stevenson and Geddes Smith, *Child Guidance Clinics: A Quarter Century of Development* (New York: The Commonwealth Fund, 1934); Witmer, pp. 52–62; Levine and Levine, pp. 231–78; and Joel D. Hunter, "The History and Development of Institutes for the Study of Children," in Lathrop, *The Child, the Clinic and the Court,* pp. 204–15. In 1921 Dr. Douglas A. Thom of Boston established the first habit clinic for the study of the behavioral problems of infants and small children. In *Everyday Problems of the Everyday Child* (New York: D. Appleton, 1927) and *Child Management* (Washington: Government Printing Office, 1925), Thom emphasized the need to understand the learning process in order to discover the genesis of behavior problems. Arnold Gesell, on the other hand, continued to believe that the age-behavior relationship was unaffected by environmental factors and was largely determined "at the conceptual union." See Kessen, *The Child,* pp. 208–11; and Arnold Gesell et al., *An Atlas of Human Behavior: A Systematic Delineation of the Forms and Early Growth of Human Behavior Patterns,* 2 vols. (New Haven: Yale University Press, 1934).

9. John C. Burnham, "Oral History Interviews of William Healy and Augusta Bronner," Houghton Library, Harvard University (1960, 1961), pp. 55, 73, 77. These interviews may not be directly quoted in print.

10. William Healy, "The Mentally Defective and the Courts," *Journal of Psycho-Asthenics* 15 (1910), 44–57. William Healy, "Mental Defects and Delinquency," NCCC *Proceedings* (1911), pp. 59–63.

tween mental defect and misconduct, and he believed that intelligence tests were unreliable indicators of mental quality because they failed to take into account individual emotional factors. He was dissatisfied with the attempts of psychologists such as Henry H. Goddard and Edward L. Thorndike to use intelligence tests to establish statistically the relationship between juvenile delinquency and mental backwardness. Psychology, he believed, should concentrate more upon introspection and reasoning than on searching for theoretical explanations based upon observable reactions to laboratory experiments. "Of general theory there is no lack," he said, "but when we come to that study of the individual which leads to clear understanding and scientific treatment, there is almost no guidance."[11]

To fill this void, William Healy used a broadly diagnostic approach, personally examining each child for physical defects as well as psychiatric symptoms and, in cooperation with court probation officers and community social workers, obtaining information about the child's home and school life. He also utilized intelligence tests which were administered by psychologist Augusta Bronner, who was his lifelong collaborator and second wife. Healy and Bronner then discussed each case informally, often conferring with interested social workers from public and voluntary agencies. These casual talks were the origin of the casework conference, a defining characteristic of the social work profession which Healy formalized during his later career. On the basis of diagnosis and discussion, Healy recommended to the judge of the Chicago Juvenile Court a specific course of treatment for each child.[12]

In 1917 Healy accepted the invitation of Judge Frederick P. Cabot of Boston to become the director of the Judge Baker Foundation (later the Judge Baker Guidance Center) in that city. There he was

11. Burnham, "Oral History Interviews," pp. 39–40, 161–65. William Healy, *The Individual Delinquent* (Boston: Little, Brown, 1915), p. 3.

12. John C. Burnham, "The New Psychology: From Narcissism to Social Control," in John Braeman, Robert H. Bremner, and David Brody, eds., *Change and Continuity in Twentieth Century America* (Columbus: The Ohio State University Press, 1968), pp. 364–66. Augusta Bronner wrote her doctoral dissertation at Columbia under the supervision of Edward L. Thorndike. She was much more cautious than he about the value of intelligence tests. See Augusta Bronner, *A Comparative Study of the Intelligence of Delinquent Girls* (New York: Columbia Teachers College, 1914).

able to treat children as well as to study them, and he received prom-
ises of close cooperation from local social work agencies and the
Boston Juvenile Court. Until his retirement in 1946, Healy remained
at the Judge Baker Center, refining and developing the methods of
helping delinquents that he began in 1909.[13]

The title of William Healy's first book, *The Individual Delinquent*
(1915), indicated his and Augusta Bronner's attitude toward juvenile delinquency. In the introduction he wrote, "Our main conclusion
is that every case will always need study by itself. When it comes to
arraying data for the purpose of generalization about relative values
of causative factors we experience difficulty." Typing or classifying
a delinquent "may be an impossible task," said Healy. The complexity and variability of the causes of delinquency led him to emphasize the importance of studying "youthful recidivists" in order to
understand the origins of their misbehavior; this knowledge would
lead in turn to comprehension of "the structural growth of whole
delinquent careers." "Just because the delinquent's character is the
result of a long-continued process of growth, one needs to regard him
as the product of forces, as well as the sum of his present constituent
parts; one must study him dynamically as well as statically, genetically
as well as a finished result," he added. In short, Healy and Bronner
were interested in the study of causations (etiology) not because they
wished to construct a theory or theories rationalizing juvenile delinquency but because they were concerned "with the eminently practical and specific points of what can be done with certain given individuals" under their charge.[14]

Healy always recognized the importance of environmental factors
in causing delinquency; he never doubted that social improvements

13. The Judge Baker Foundation was established with a bequest of $2,500,000
by George B. Tinkham, a Republican Congressman from Massachusetts. It
was named after Harvey Humphrey Baker (1869–1915), first judge of the
Boston Juvenile Court. Frederick P. Cabot (1868–1932) was the first president of the Foundation. In *The Delinquent Child* (New York: Century, 1932),
p. 51, Cabot characterized delinquency as "one of the natural outcomes of
those clashes of interest, prerogative and need that are inherent in living as a
social group."

14. Healy, *The Individual Delinquent,* pp. 5, 118, 4. William Healy, "Study of
Causation of Delinquency," NCET *Proceedings* (1917), p. 54. See also Burnham, "Oral History Interviews," pp. 164–65.

would lessen crime. Nevertheless, his ability to help children depended largely upon his skill as a psychiatrist, and he increasingly discussed environment in a familial or personal context and not as a broad social force. In his next book, *Mental Conflicts and Misconduct* (1917), he noted, "It comes out repeatedly in our histories that environment plays a great part, and particularly mental environment." Through psychiatric interviews he discovered "potent subconscious mental mechanisms working according to definite laws and . . . types of hidden early experiences which definitely evoke these mental processes that are forerunners of misconduct." These findings led him to believe that the common feature of delinquents' "psychological environment" was that they "never had any one near to them, particularly in family life, who supplied opportunities for sympathetic confidences."[15]

Healy and Bronner developed this theme most completely in *New Light on Delinquency and Its Treatment* (1936), "a comparison of the delinquent with a nondelinquent child in the same family." Here they concluded: "The father or mother either had not played a role that was admired by the child or else on account of the lack of a deep love relationship was not accepted as an ideal," and thus "the origins of delinquency in every case unquestionably represent the expression of desires and urges which are otherwise unsatisfied."[16] Healy and Bronner knew Freud's work and reflected it in their stress upon the subconscious motivation of conduct. They feared, however, that practitioners of Freudian psychiatry relied excessively upon the curative power of theorizing on dreams and probing the sexual nature of familial relationships.[17] Their rejection of extreme Freudianism

15. William Healy, *Mental Conflicts and Misconduct* (Boston: Little, Brown, 1917), pp. 324, ix, 327. Technically, Healy practiced orthopsychiatry, a preventive psychiatry concerned particularly with mental and behavioral disorders in children. This book was dedicated to E. E. Southard. See also Frederick H. Allen, "Psychic Factors in Juvenile Delinquency," *Mental Hygiene* 11 (1927), 764–74.

16. William Healy and Augusta Bronner, *New Light on Delinquency and Its Treatment* (New Haven: Yale University Press, 1936), pp. 1, 2, 10. See also James S. Plant, "The Search for Causes," *Social Work Year Book* (1933), pp. 35–40.

17. Burnham, "Oral History Interviews," pp. 218–20. For an example of the Freudian approach see John Christian Tjaden, *The Causes of Delinquency in*

coupled with their emphasis upon satisfactory family life as the key to preventing delinquency led Healy and Bronner to blame parents for causing the misbehavior of their children. Augusta Bronner pled for the authority to remove delinquent children from their homes and place them out, "a type of treatment that will remain much needed for long—indeed, until sufficient time has elapsed to make over unworthy or stupid parents, to teach them the principles of child-psychology, to alter in very fundamental ways a considerable share of mankind."[18]

In *Delinquents and Criminals: Their Making and Unmaking* (1925), Healy and Bronner were equally critical of reform schools and juvenile courts for failing to understand and to meet the needs of individual delinquents.[19] Only a few reform schools, such as the Whittier State School (California), were able to afford or were willing to provide the skilled professional staff necessary to treat children psychiatrically. Even the advances of these institutions were precarious. Under the leadership of Frederick Nelles, superintendent from 1914 to 1927, the Whittier School developed a Bureau of Juvenile Research whose staff not only provided psychological care for the (male) inmates but also began a program of statewide community education through child guidance clinic demonstrations. The Whittier Bureau also began the *Journal of Juvenile Delinquency* (1916), which was heavily weighted toward psychological and psychiatric studies of delinquent children. One staff psychologist emphatically claimed, *"The basic philosophy of correctional education has changed from the concept of punishment to that of adjustment through the understanding of individual differences."* During the 1930s, however,

---

Boys of Superior Intelligence (Des Moines, Iowa: Board of Control of State Institutions, 1923), pp. 12–13. Case "S-1" reads: "Apparently one of the dominating factors in this case is the hate aspect of the complex which in this subject has brought about an intense resentment to the father . . . the mother is over indulgent with the boy . . . she is periodically separated from her husband . . . she is willing to divorce him in order to live with the son."

18. Augusta F. Bronner, "The Contribution of Science to a Program for Treatment of Juvenile Delinquency," in *The Child, the Clinic and the Court,* p. 84.

19. William Healy and Augusta Bronner, *Delinquents and Criminals: Their Making and Unmaking* (New York: Macmillan, 1926), pp. 284–311.

state political interference forced the departure of knowledgeable administrators and reduced the school's budget. Repression and cruel punishment once again became prevalent—and to such a degree that in 1940, following the suspicious death of Benny Moreno, a Mexican inmate, the state was forced to appoint Ben Lindsey to make a special investigation of the institution. Lindsey's findings led to conviction of two staff members on charges of assault and battery.[20]

William Healy knew that most institutions for juvenile delinquents were either unable or unwilling to provide children with psychiatric care, but he was surprised to learn that this approach was not particularly effective, even at the Judge Baker Center. Sheldon and Eleanor T. Glueck's *One Thousand Delinquents: Their Treatment by Court and Clinic* (1934), written as part of the Boston Crime Survey, noted the high rate of recidivism among children treated at the center and by the Boston Juvenile Court. The Gluecks partially exonerated Healy by noting that the juvenile court often refused to follow his recommendations, especially when they suggested placing children in foster homes or institutions for the feebleminded. The study emphasized that just as delinquency was not caused by any single factor, rehabilitation could not occur in any one institution but required instead "a delicate multifaceted approach."[21]

Nevertheless, Healy was disappointed with the findings of the Crime Survey. In a meeting with Felix Frankfurter of the Harvard Law School, which had sponsored the study, he proposed to correct this failure by "an intensive clinical study and careful social supervision of a very small number of cases." And, in fact, the Judge

20. Norman Fenton et al., *The Delinquent Boy and the Correctional School* (Claremont, Calif.: Claremont College Guidance Center, 1935), p. 27; italics in original. Investigation of the Whittier School, Lindsey MS, Box 288.

21. Sheldon and Eleanor T. Glueck, *One Thousand Delinquents: Their Treatment by Court and Clinic* (Cambridge: Harvard University Press, 1934), pp. 228–33, 260–61. The Gluecks' study caused an outcry among social workers, judges, and probation officers; see esp. the review of Richard C. Cabot in *Survey* 70 (February 1934) and the subsequent correspondence in the magazine. "Delinquent children are hardened habitual thieves and are not going to be changed on any hypothesis that assumes that they are very much like the rest of us when we were small," wrote Cabot to Paul U. Kellogg, editor of *Survey*. See Cabot to Kellogg (January 31, 1934), Papers of Survey Associates, Social Welfare History Archives, University of Minnesota. A summary of the entire dispute is Thomas D. Eliot, "Suppressed Premises Underlying the Glueck Controversy," *Journal of Criminal Law and Criminology* 26 (1935), 1–12.

Baker Center, like many other child guidance clinics, became a referral point for congenial family service agencies as well as a treatment center for middle-class parents and children who sought it out. Extensive clinical therapy was featured and contact with the Boston Juvenile Court was minimized. Healy explained why child guidance clinics drew away from association with delinquency prevention programs:

> The conception that the guidance clinic may be of great aid in a program for the prevention of delinquency remains thoroughly valid, but indispensable for any such program is well-conceived, cooperative, social effort. . . . Whatever is undertaken, I am convinced . . . that any project for the prevention of delinquency will be confronted with the necessity for modification of the spirit or ideology of community life. . . . As it stands at present in most large communities, it is impossible for child guidance clinics, through their work with individual cases, to be playing any very important part in the prevention of delinquent and criminal careers.[22]

In his study of the emergence of social work as a profession, Lubove has noted that environmental explanations of dependency and delinquency became unfashionable among some social workers and psychologists in the late 1920s and the 1930s. During the Great Depression, when consideration of the social dimensions of crime and poverty was required, leading figures such as Virginia P. Robinson and Jessie Taft, both of the Pennsylvania School of Social Work, contended that personal problems generally and juvenile misbehavior particularly were caused mainly by conflicts within the family that confused the individual to the point that he or she was quite likely to indulge in one form or another of aberrant social conduct. According to the new "queens" of social work, this disorientation could be cured by psychiatric therapy. Thus, many family service agencies began to stress psychiatric counseling at the expense of social investiga-

---

22. Notes on a conference with William Healy (March 6, 1930), The Papers of Felix Frankfurter, Box 50, Library of Congress, Washington, D.C. William Healy, *Twenty-Five Years of Child Guidance,* Study 256 (Illinois Institute for Juvenile Research, Illinois Department of Public Welfare, 1934), pp. 14–15. See also Levine and Levine, *A Social History of Helping Services,* pp. 277–78. On the purposes and clientele of the therapy-oriented approach, see C. P. Oberndorf, "Psychotherapy in a Resident Children's Group," in K. R. Eissler, ed., *Searchlights on Delinquency* (New York: International Universities Press, 1949), pp. 165–73.

tion while special new institutions like the Montefiore School (1929) in the Chicago public school system were established to provide intensive psychiatric care for a small number of delinquent and emotionally disturbed children.[23]

Also indicative of interest in the psychiatric approach was the favorable reception accorded to the work of Freudian psychoanalysts Franz Alexander and August Aichorn. Geoffrey Steere has pointed out that the extent to which Freudianism characterized child-rearing manuals has been overestimated, but as an explanation of youthful misbehavior, it attracted many adherents. According to Alexander, poverty was an insufficient explanation of delinquency. Personal influences within the family were more significant as this summary of one of his early studies demonstrates:

> We have found that criminal behavior in the majority of cases is the expression of a protest against certain deprivations, a reaction of spite against certain members of the family, the expression of jealousy, envy, competition, and frequently a proof of masculinity. Often it originates from the stubborn wish for compensation for previous deprivations, or is the result of a sense of guilt and consequent need for punishment, similar to that found in the psychogenesis of neuroses. . . . In cases where actual deprivations due to social circumstances are present, these latter can easily replace previous emotional conflicts arising from the family situation.

Aichorn's, *Wayward Youth* (1935), an account of cases of individual reformation supposedly resulting from the application of Freudian methods in a German reform school during the Weimar Era, also found a wide audience.[24]

23. Lubove, *The Professional Altruist,* pp. 112–15. See also Carl R. Rogers, *The Clinical Treatment of the Problem Child* (Cambridge, Mass.: Riverside Press, 1939), pp. 340–47. Virginia Robinson advocated Freudian analysis, which stressed insight and interpretation, while Jessie Taft used relationship therapy which depended for its supposed success upon developing a healthy emotional bond between therapist and child. See Virginia P. Robinson, *A Changing Psychology in Social Casework* (Chapel Hill: University of North Carolina Press, 1930); Jessie Taft, *The Dynamics of Therapy,* 2d ed. (New York: Dover Books, 1962); and Jessie Taft to Ethel Dummer, n.d., Dummer MS, folder 232. Ethel S. Dummer was a leading supporter of the Montefiore School; see Dummer MS, folder 822.

24. Geoffrey H. Steere, "Freudianism and Child-Rearing in the Twenties," *American Quarterly* 20 (1968), 759–65. Franz Alexander, "Contribution of Psychological Factors in Anti-Social Behavior," *The Family* 13 (1932), 143–46.

William Healy continued to warn that psychoanalysis of delinquents and older criminals would do little good unless social and economic conditions were improved. His research, however, continued to stress other factors. After a study of children at the Judge Baker Center with Franz Alexander, he reemphasized his belief that crime would most likely be reduced "by a better understanding of the psychological processes which underlie human behavior in general and crime in particular." For Healy, and for most psychologists, the key to understanding delinquency was psychiatric study of the individual delinquent's attitude toward his or her familial environment.[25]

The number of girls being sent to reform schools in 1920 may not have been significantly affected by the fact that some scientists and social workers had gained a greater comprehension of their psychological problems. Nevertheless, at a few schools this new orientation toward delinquency, when combined with other factors, perhaps made the girls' lives less unpleasant than heretofore. Female delinquency often involved sexual offenses. In the Victorian era such moral lapses were regarded not as the way of all flesh but as signs of mental incapacity. Therefore, girls' reform schools were commonly thought of as storage bins for witless moral transgressors who, for their own protection, would have to be imprisoned during their child-bearing

---

August Aichorn, *Wayward Youth* (New York: Viking, 1935). See also Gisela Konopka, "Reform in Delinquency Institutions in Revolutionary Times: The 1920's in Germany," paper read before the Council of Social Work Education, Cleveland, 1969. On the influences of European psychoanalysis upon American thought, see Marie Jahoda, "The Migration of Psychoanalysis: Its Impact on American Psychology," *Perspectives in American History* 2 (1968), 420–45; Hendrik K. M. Ruitenbeck, *Freud and America* (New York: Macmillan, 1966); David Shakow and David Rapaport, *The Influence of Freud on American Psychology, Psychological Issues* (New York: International Universities Press, 1964); and John A. P. Millet, "Psychoanalysis in the United States," in Franz Alexander, Samuel Eisenstein, and Martin Grotjahn, eds., *Psychoanalytic Pioneers* (New York: Knopf, 1966), pp. 546–96.

25. William Healy, "Psychoanalysis of Older Offenders," *American Journal of Orthopsychiatry* 5 (1935), 27–28. Franz Alexander and William Healy, *Roots of Crime: Psychoanalytic Studies* (New York: Knopf, 1935), p. 3. In 1939 Healy and Benedict S. Alper, his colleague at the Judge Baker Center, surveyed the British borstal system and commented enthusiastically upon it. See Healy and Alper, *Criminal Youth and the Borstal System* (New York: Commonwealth Fund, 1941). For the inmate's point of view see Brendan Behan, *Borstal Boy* (New York: Knopf, 1959).

years. As we have noted, delinquent girls, because of the supposedly hereditable nature of their misbehavior, were particularly vulnerable to the alarmist conclusions drawn from intelligence tests.[26]

The first signs of a more sympathetic attitude toward female delinquency appeared before World War I. In 1908 Mary W. "Molly" Dewson (1874–1962), superintendent of the parole department, Massachusetts State Industrial School for Girls, denounced lengthy sentences based upon "mere lack of scholastic capacity." The female delinquent, she believed, could be reformed "by testing herself under real conditions." Although still feeling the need to detain "licentious girls," Molly Dewson and her successor, Edith N. Burleigh, placed most of the school's girls on parole as soon as possible. The Chicago Juvenile Protective Association, under the leadership of Jessie Binford, executive director from 1916 to 1952, rescued many girls from predicaments clearly not of their own making. "We must release virtue," said Jessie Binford, "not suppress vice."[27]

World War I mobilization with its rapid proliferation of military training camps and consequent social disorganization gave added importance to the need for protective work for girls. Investigators from the Juvenile Protective Association and from other wartime emergency groups such as the Committee of Protective Work for Girls (part of the Commission of Training Camp Activities in the War Department) vigorously denounced the flourishing prostitution near these bases. "It is an outrageous thing to take a woman's boy from under her influence and throw him into such a cess-pool as they have surrounding the boys at Camp Nichols," wrote a New Orleans business woman to Julia Lathrop. Doubtless, numbers of "uniform crazy" girls, whom self-appointed or official vice squads discovered in local cabarets dancing cheek to cheek with servicemen, suffered shame and ostracism in their local communities. But some women—mostly psy-

26. See above, pp. 98–99.

27. The Papers of Mary W. Dewson, Schlesinger Library, Radcliffe College, folders 3.3, 3.4, and 7; Elizabeth Glendower Evans and Mary W. Dewson, "Feeblemindedness and Juvenile Delinquency," *Charities* 20 (May 2, 1908), 183–93. During the New Deal, Molly Dewson headed the Women's Division of the Democratic National Committee. On Mrs. Evans see above, p. 69n. On Jessie Binford see Dummer MS, folder 451. See also Edith N. Burleigh and Frances K. Harris, *The Delinquent Girl* (New York: New York School of Social Work, 1923).

chologists and social workers—recognized the need for a new approach toward female delinquency. Mrs. Dummer developed in the course of her investigative work a humane sympathy for young prostitutes and girls whose escapades had led to premarital pregnancy. "If the unmarried mother were given comfort and courage instead of condemnation, the ranks of prostitution would be depleted," she wrote to Paul U. Kellogg of *Survey*. In another letter to Augusta Bronner, she equated female feeblemindedness and promiscuity to the "shell shock" suffered by soldiers in the war and believed that both conditions were curable. In 1921 Mrs. Dummer sponsored a conference on illegitimacy and female delinquency. Psychologist Marion E. Kenworthy, one of the principals, explained the new point of view:

> We must not lose sight of the fact that in the pregnancy itself we may find a potent factor for good. All women are endowed with a maternal instinct and as the physiological processes continue during the prenatal period we have certain psychological influences at work, and the maternal desires gradually unfold themselves. If through our efforts we furnish this mother with an unstigmatized opportunity to remain with her child, to assume the responsibility of its care, to have a normal outlet for the pent up love craving, we will discover that much of the libido (the hunger) finds a normal outlet through the sublimational channels of mother love.[28]

These sentiments were translated into concrete programs at a number of girls' reform schools. The foremost of these institutions were Sleighton Farms (formerly the girls' department of the Philadelphia House of Refuge), Samarcand Manor (North Carolina), the Texas State School for Girls, Sauk Center Reform School (Minnesota), and El Retiro (Los Angeles County). Superintendents such as Martha P. Falconer (Philadelphia), Carrie Weaver Smith (Texas), Fannie French Morse (Minnesota), and Miriam Van Waters (El Retiro)

28. Jean M. Gordon to Julia Lathrop (September 20, 1917), Record Group 102, Records of the U.S. Children's Bureau, National Archives, Washington, D.C. Ethel Dummer to Paul U. Kellogg (May 23, 1919), Dummer MS, folder 613. Dummer to Augusta Bronner (January 26, 1920), folder 463. Marion E. Kenworthy, "The Mental Hygiene Aspects of Illegitimacy," *Intercity Conference on Illegitimacy* (privately printed, 1921). Like William Healy, Mrs. Dummer supported prohibition as well as other authoritarian movement connected with the social upheavals during and after World War I. On September 9, 1920, she wrote to the Healys, "I hope you are both rejoicing at the progress in Italy." See Dummer MS, folder 579.

recruited idealistic college women to staff their institutions and established routines which emphasized education, cultural appreciation, and inmate self-government.[29] In a survey of girls' reform schools conducted for and supported by the bounteous Mrs. Dummer, Miriam Van Waters found "more knowledge of the delinquent girl, more sympathy, more of that greatness which reveals itself in the interpretation of human life, better theory and better practise in the problem of delinquency than we find outside in the general community."[30]

Miriam Van Waters (b. 1887) was the leading figure in the field of female corrections during the twenties and thirties. The daughter of an Episcopal minister in Portland, Oregon, she graduated from the University of Oregon and then attended Clark University, writing her Ph.D. dissertation (1914) on "The Adolescent Girl in Primitive Society." Awed at first by G. Stanley Hall, she came to believe that his view of delinquency was too rigid: "A prostitute is not a type," she is reported to have told him. After receiving her degree, Van Waters became Superintendent of the Frazer Detention Home in Portland and in 1916 moved on to a similar job at Juvenile Hall in Los Angeles. In 1920 she was appointed first superintendent of El Retiro.[31]

Miriam Van Waters once said, "All my life to the point where I entered into the understanding and treatment of delinquency and crime was but a preparation for a Christian Mission to offenders." This evangelical view combined an optimistic concept of the historical process with sympathy, even kinship, for the female delinquent and condemnation for society's frivolous or indifferent attitude toward juvenile delinquency. "Yes, I believe with you it is a tide—this affair of humanizing our ideas and our treatment of children, this restora-

29. Formal training for reform school staff members did not exist. Whatever advice these young women did receive was brief and to the point. "Remember two things, girls," Martha Falconer told two Oberlin graduates. "No sweaters [unhygienic] and no ducks and dollies [lesbianism with inmates]." Interview with Mrs. Karl De Schweinitz (October 17, 1968).

30. Miriam Van Waters, "Where Girls Go Right," *Survey Graphic* 1 (1922), 361–76.

31. Burton J. Rowles, *The Lady at Box 99* (Greenwich, Conn.: Seabury Press, 1962), p. 95. The title of Miriam Van Waters' biography refers to her postal address as superintendent of the Women's Reformatory, Framingham, Massachusetts, 1931–1957.

tion to them of their joy and faith in life," she wrote to Mrs. Dummer whose own ideas coincided so closely with hers that she became Miriam's personal benefactress. Miss Van Waters concluded of her early days at El Retiro, "Sometimes it would seem that all the thinking people are indifferent, so much is said, so little is done. But the joy of working with those glorious young rebels supports everything."[32]

Believing that reform school unrest was caused by the failure of administrators to feel "oneness" with their children, she created a "society of inmates" which emphasized group participation in government, choice of institutional occupation, and encouragement of self-expression through play, essays, and a school newspaper. El Retiro returned girls to respectable jobs in the community as soon as possible and, in order to facilitate community reintegration, maintained a "half-way" club and alumnae house in Los Angeles staffed by girl probationers and one supervisor. Margaret and Geraldine were representative cases:

> Margaret . . . was the oldest in a large family headed by a dissolute gang-foreman and a quarrelsome, complaining mother. Her home life was marked by coarseness and obscenity of language, and her personality by alternate melancholy and violence. At El Retiro it became probable that her behavior was the reaction made by her organism in seeking that which it really craved most, peace and security. She became an El Retiro homemaker. A troublesome asthma yielded to treatment based on quiet and contentment. Margaret is now Vice-president of the Alumnae club. She lives at home which has largely become rehabilitated through her efforts. The club affords her the necessary contact with other girls.

> Geraldine is a girl of eighteen, wrecked on the moving picture industry. She was seduced by an under-director in attempting to sell a

---

32. Rowles, *The Lady at Box 99,* p. 95. Van Waters to Dummer (June 12, 1920), Dummer MS, folder 818. Mrs. Dummer's autobiography, *Why I Think So* (Chicago: Clarke-McElroy, 1937), reflects her interest in mystical thought. She was influenced by the English seeress Mary Everest Boole, who taught (much like Georg Hegel), "that one must grasp whatever truth there was in the thought antagonistic to one's own before being sure of one's position." Concerning El Retiro, Mrs. Dummer wrote Miss Van Waters, "Our *vision* cannot fail, for it is part of necessary evolution, and the Life *Force* which has brought us up from the amoeba is not dependent upon any one person." Dummer to Van Waters (July 4, 1923), Dummer MS, folder 820.

scenario, and was passed from hand to hand until her health broke. Her experiences were unbelievably tragic and unbelievably common. Her health, self-confidence and charm were restored at El Retiro. She took to nursing, but the key to her interest in everything was affection. A professional man understood her real and genuine capacity and married her. She is an exceptional wife and mother. She too is a club member, proud of her school and eager to assist.

"We do not wish to shelter them until they are twenty-one," said Miriam Van Waters, "but to build up sufficient moral muscle for their protection in the world outside." Van Waters remained superintendent until 1924 when she became referee of the Juvenile Court of Los Angeles. In 1927 El Retiro, always the subject of unfriendly political probes, was converted into a conventional custodial institution.[33]

During the twenties, Mrs. Dummer's financial support freed Miriam Van Waters from the vicissitudes of El Retiro to pursue the enemies of humane treatment for female delinquents. In her survey of female reform schools (1922), she was harsh on the institutions which abused their inmates:

> (Virginia State School for Girls)
> They still thrash the girls, the Supt., a young healthy woman . . . applying the switches herself.

> (Delaware School for Girls)
> They horsewhip the girls. We must needs see these institutions for a type.

> (New Jersey School for Girls)
> Dr. Harris is too complacent for results. They are trying to do psycho-analysis, but they remind me of the friends of Hamlet,—they fret the girls, but do not play upon them.

Van Waters summarized, "Hardly an *old* institution is free from its historic riots with arson, flogging, jailing, hand cuffing and the like, and those who have passed through this horror and come to a better

33. Rowles, *The Lady at Box 99*, p. 135. "El Retiro—A School for Girls," Papers of Miriam Van Waters, Schlesinger Library, Radcliffe College, folder 543. Cases cited in Miriam Van Waters, draft of paper, "Special Problems with Girl Delinquents," in Survey Associates MS, correspondence with Van Waters. Interview with Van Waters (July 26, 1968).

method all agree 'no punishment.' If punishment is used at all, it ends eventually in brutality."[34]

Other observers supported these conclusions. Floyd Dell's "The Beating" (1914), a story of cruelty and degradation in a girls' reform school, was probably all too representative. Minnie, the protagonist, was a resigned victim of her fate:

> Minnie was not "queer." She would have made, under other circumstances, a dutiful wife for the same reasons that now made her an inmate of a Reform School. She had never been other than passive and acquiescent. She had never wanted to be "bad"—and wouldn't have been, if they had only let her alone. But the boys at the box factory and the tablet factory, who took her to the parks and nickel theaters, were insistent. She had never encouraged them; she had been merely apprehensively submissive. There was nothing beautiful about that.

Margaret Reeves, in her 1929 survey of girls' reform schools, concluded optimistically, "Self-expression has taken the place of repression." But many of the new institutions for girls, whose advent occasioned this survey, were located in the southern states and were founded specifically to incarcerate Negro girls. Here, reformation proceeded in the traditional way. Also, innovative superintendents such as Fannie French Morse in Minnesota were, more often than not, rebuffed by local school boards and community groups when they tried to integrate institution girls into regular programs.[35]

Miriam Van Waters' sympathy for institutionalized girls led her to distrust both criminally oriented juvenile courts which committed them and negligent parents who raised them. "We find the public filled with ideas of vengeance and cruel punishment. . . . One court refers to its 'felonies' and 'misdemeanors.' One judge reported that 'young criminals in this state are carefully looked after by the

---

34. Van Waters to Dummer (December 16, 1920), Dummer MS, folder 818. Ibid. (March 10, 1921).

35. Floyd Dell, "The Beating," in William L. O'Neill, *Echoes of Revolt: The Masses, 1911–1917* (Chicago: Quadrangle Books, 1966), pp. 63–67. Margaret Reeves, *Training Schools for Delinquent Girls* (New York: Russell Sage, 1929). Fannie French Morse to Julia Lathrop (March 25, 1921), Record Group 102, Records of the U.S. Children's Bureau, National Archives.

judges,' " she said.[36] Her suspicions of the court were confirmed by personal letters such as these from El Retiro girls:

> Dear Dr. Van Waters: . . . The Juvenile Court has so many cases that we are just treated like cattle—we go in one door of the court-room and out the other and have to do whatever the court says and sometimes without a chance. Is that justice?

> Dear Dr. Van Waters: . . . Why must we be taken away (?) My own mother has suffered *hell* and no doubt many others have. On account of courts, always courts. I think that if America is a *free* country lets have more *Liberty absolutely*.

> Dear Dr. Van Waters, Boys and girls should be taken away from home when their parents are not able to support them and when they are cruel to them but not when they have a home and their parents can take care of them.[37]

Despite the faith of these girls in their parents, Van Waters believed that the seeds of delinquency were sown in the home. "Why cannot . . . mother face Mary with calm affirmation of the family stand on questions of selfish pleasure, pre-nuptial chastity and industry?" she asked. "Because the mother herself has lost faith in old standards of virtue. . . . She recalls her own drab, misunderstood, frequently punished youth (when the Puritan home was losing its arts, crafts, its good cookery, and somber, rich coloring of the old faith, and there remained little of the spirit and very much of the letter of colonial Church and home discipline), so in her words, she 'wants Mary to have a good time.' " Parents had acquiesced in, even encouraged, the mechanization of civilization and thereby robbed the home of its "emotional and imaginative appeal" and their children of "legitimate energy-outlets." "It took as much mechanical ingenuity and self-control properly to prime the pump as to start the Ford, but the pump never got you into trouble," Van Waters observed, adding:

36. Miriam Van Waters, "The Juvenile Court from a Child's Viewpoint," in *The Child, the Clinic and the Court*, p. 224. Quotes taken from U.S. Children's Bureau, Publication 65, p. 42. See also Van Waters, "Socialization of Juvenile Court Procedure," *Journal of Criminal Law and Criminology* 13 (1922), 61–69.

37. Letters to Miriam Van Waters from El Retiro Girls, Van Waters MS, folder 541; italics in original of second letter. Names of girls, where given, have been withheld.

> Children should deal with the elemental things of the world—earth, stones, trees, animals, running water, fire, open spaces—instead of pavements, signboards, subdivided lots, apartment houses, and electric percolators. Civilization has been hardest on children.

In *Parents on Probation* (1927) she listed "Nineteen Ways of Being a Bad Parent" (for example, "A parent is bad who repudiates a child in dire need" and "A parent is bad who can not shelter a child from premature exposure to adult anxiety or perplexity"). One chapter was entitled, "I Would Rather Die Than Go Home."[38]

In 1929 Van Waters was appointed consultant to the National Commission on Law Observance and Enforcement (The Wickersham Commission) and prepared one part—*The Child Offender in the Federal System of Justice*—of the commission's final report.[39] She discovered that the federal government had few responsibilities concerning juvenile delinquents but had met even these few tasks poorly or not at all. Child offenders brought before federal courts (mostly for violations of postal laws or federal laws on prohibition, motor vehicles, immigration, and white slavery) were treated like adults; juvenile court procedures did not exist in these tribunals. Often delinquents were detained in wretched U.S. district court jails and then sentenced to federal penitentiaries or state reformatories that had contracted with the Bureau of Prisons to receive them. Of these "schools" she said:

> The best of the institutions houses the children in large groups, uses basements for living and play rooms, employs disciplinary measures such as silence at meals, marching, formal routine, and flogging; inmates are frequently at the mercy of boy captains; the worst is not to be distinguished from the prison.

38. Miriam Van Waters, *Youth in Conflict* (New York: New Republic, 1925), p. 77. Van Waters, "The Juvenile Court from a Child's Viewpoint," pp. 221–22. Van Waters, *Parents on Probation* (New York: New Republic, 1927), pp. x, xii.

39. This study was made under joint auspices of the commission and the (1930) White House Conference on Child Health and Protection. Judge Frederick P. Cabot, Chairman of the Conference's Committee on the Socially Handicapped, called for a nationwide program of individualized treatment of delinquency in which "The services of the Federal Government are essential in affording thorough fact finding, research, and education." See *White House Conference on Child Health and Protection, 1930* (New York: Century, 1931), p. 353.

Individualization of treatment has not been accomplished.[40]

Van Waters' work on the Wickersham Commission revived efforts to restructure federal policy on juvenile delinquency. As early as 1912, George Wickersham, then attorney general in the Taft administration, proposed to return federal offenders to state juvenile courts, but Congress refused to appropriate the necessary funds. In 1922 the United States Children's Bureau reported on the plight of juvenile offenders against federal laws, but this too was ignored by the national legislature. Similarly, Congress—and particularly southern Representatives—refused to modify the juvenile court law for the District of Columbia to provide more humane and discrete disposition and better education for the mostly black children whom it served. Opposing such an act in 1916, Georgia Congressman William S. Howard shouted, "I am opposed to taxing my people in Georgia to give all sorts of high faluting curleycues in the way of education to a crowd of Washington niggers that is of no benefit to them."[41]

In 1932 shortly after Miriam Van Waters' investigation for the Wickersham Commission, Congress remedied one shortcoming of the federal judicial system by providing for surrender of juvenile violators of federal laws to state authorities if the delinquents had also broken state law. In 1938 this act was supplemented by legislation allowing federal courts to use juvenile court procedures when dealing with children. That same year the juvenile court for the District of Columbia was finally modernized.[42]

40. National Commission on Law Observance and Enforcement, Report 6, *The Child Offender in the Federal System of Justice* (Washington, D.C.: Government Printing Office, 1931), pp. 2–5, 106.

41. *Congressional Record,* 62d Cong., 3d sess. (1913), pp. 1786–89. U.S. Children's Bureau, Ruth Bloodgood, *The Federal Courts and the Delinquent Child,* Publication 103 (Washington, D.C.: Government Printing Office, 1922). *Congressional Record,* 64th Cong., 1st sess. (1916), p. 6745. Kathryn Sellers, Judge of the Juvenile Court of the District of Columbia, was not regarded as a friend of enlightened treatment for juvenile delinquents. Mrs. Dummer found her "too weird for words," and Grace Abbott, chief of the Children's Bureau from 1921 to 1934, tried to have her replaced. See Dummer to Van Waters (July 14, 1922), Dummer MS, folder 822; and Grace Abbott to Charles P. Sisson, Assistant Attorney General (January 15, 1931), Abbott MS. For a favorable picture of Judge Sellers and the District of Columbia court see Raymond W. Murray, "The Delinquent Child and the Law" (Ph.D. diss., Catholic University of America, 1926).

42. For a summary of federal legislation involving juvenile delinquents before World War II, see Abbott, *The Child and the State,* II, 432–37.

With her appointment as superintendent of the Framingham Reformatory in 1931, Miriam Van Waters moved into the field of adult corrections. She did not lose interest in juvenile delinquents, however, or in the problems of youth as a whole. From 1935 to 1941 she served as secretary of the American Youth Commission, a nongovernmental organization established in 1935 by the American Council on Education and composed of major national educational associations and institutions. In addition to collecting information about the needs of youth, the commission conducted studies of New Deal agencies such as the Civilian Conservation Corps and the National Youth Administration in order to increase the agencies' ability to employ and to educate more youths.[43] The study of delinquency was only a small part of the American Youth Commission's work. Nevertheless, Van Waters' contribution to this segment was unmistakable:

> Older societies to be sure gave youth many adult life opportunities, such as work and community participation. But we give almost unlimited personal freedom without supervision, then when youth fails we punish them with more penal severity than any other civilized democracy.[44]

While William Healy was exploring the origins of delinquency in terms of individual mental conflicts and Miriam Van Waters was attempting to improve the institutional care of delinquent girls, academic sociologists who taught at the University of Chicago or who had been trained there were critically examining the environmental bases of many social problems including juvenile delinquency. The "Chicago School" was founded by Albion W. Small (1854–1926), first dean of the graduate school, chairman of the sociology department (1894–1926), and first editor of the *American Journal of Sociology* (1895). Small shaped the development of academic sociology in the United States by adhering more consistently than his rivals to the positivist

43. See American Council on Education, American Youth Commission, *Next Steps in National Policy for Youth* (Washington, D.C.: American Council on Education, 1941); and Lewis L. Lorwin, *Youth Work Programs: Problems and Policies* (Washington, D.C.: American Council on Education, 1941). A recent study is Bruce Flack, "The American Youth Commission" (Ph.D. diss., The Ohio State University, 1969).

44. Van Waters, "Delinquency and Youthful Crime," Van Waters MS, folder 47½. See also folder 480.

spirit of Auguste Comte. This tradition demanded the systematic sub-ordination of imagination to observation in the investigation of human society and the formulation of the laws controlling human institutions and functions. Sociology was not a point of view but described instead the empirical method of integrating data into a theoretical framework of discoveries about mankind. The pioneers of American sociology at other universities—Lester Frank Ward (Brown), William Graham Sumner (Yale), Edward A. Ross (Stanford and Wisconsin)—eschewed the inductive approach of the positivists in order to debate the theory of evolution and its application to the study of man and society. They utilized this doctrine for diametrically opposite ends—Sumner, to argue against government participation in programs of social and economic amelioration; Ward and Ross, to rally support for governmental action against the abuses of big business. But all three scholars seemed more interested in winning converts than in encouraging systematic and independent study of society. Small, on the other hand, emphasized "open, modest searching in the spirit of an inductive science." This approach meant removing sociology from direct concern with the task of alleviating immediate problems of human welfare and the consequent severing of relationships between schools of sociology and social welfare.[45]

The division or split was never made final, even at Chicago. Edith Abbott and Sophonisba Breckinridge of the University's School of Social Service Administration continued to promote research on modes and customs of urban life through their participation in the interdepartmental Local Community Research Committee. On the other hand, Robert Ezra Park (1864–1944) and Ernest Watson Burgess (1886–1966), leaders of the sociology department in the twenties, inclined strongly toward active participation in humanitarian programs. "We cannot separate the beginnings of urban sociology from the perennial battle to wipe out the slums," wrote Nels Ander-

---

45. On the development of sociology as a science see Robert E. Park, "Sociology and the Social Sciences," *American Journal of Sociology* 26 (1921), 401–24. The history of the Chicago School and its rivals is discussed in Robert E. L. Faris, *Chicago Sociology, 1920–1932* (Chicago: University of Chicago Press, 1970), esp. pp. 123–30. Franklin H. Giddings of Columbia established the most durable rival to Chicago by emphasizing the application of statistical methods to sociological research.

son, an early Burgess student.[46] Albion W. Small admired the muck-raking of Lincoln Steffens and the settlement work of Jane Addams and Graham Taylor, but he established the sociology department around men such as William I. Thomas (1863–1947) and George Herbert Mead (1863–1931) whose interest in social problems was not in their immediate alleviation but in empirical analysis of the processes which underlay social disorganization. Ellsworth Faris, Small's successor as chairman, summarized the sociologists' view of the proper framework and purpose for their inquiries:

> An objective science does not concern itself immediately with welfare. In order to be efficient it must be disinterested. But science, or knowledge, is always in the service of ends, and the ultimate justification of science, certainly the science of human nature, will be the service it can render to human welfare.[47]

As the early leaders of the department, Mead and Thomas were responsible for translating these objectives into scholarly achievement. Mead, the lesser known of the two, was instrumental in defining the study of social psychology. In opposition to the behaviorist psychology of John Watson and others, he and Charles Horton Cooley of Michigan described the self as originating in the social process and as the result of imaginations which the individual constructs of other persons and objects. While not denying that there was an instinctive basis for behavior or that physiological conditioning occurred among men as well as animals, Mead saw human behavior largely as the result of the self concept which the individual acquired from society. William I. Thomas, the dominant figure in the department, left a lasting legacy to later scholars through his active pursuit of material for research and his theoretical discussions on the meaning of attitudes and imagery as causes of behavior. According to Thomas, men defined objects in terms of their attitude toward it and not in light of the objective reality of the physical things. Accordingly, the subjective aspects of human life assumed equal importance with the purportedly

46. Anderson quoted in Charles N. Glaab and A. Theodore Brown, *A History of Urban America* (New York: Macmillan, 1967), p. 249.

47. Faris quoted in his son's book, R. E. L. Faris, *Chicago Sociology*, p. 131. See also Ellsworth Faris, *The Nature of Human Nature* (New York: McGraw-Hill, 1937), p. 4.

objective accounts of behaviorist psychology. On the value of personal statements in determining the reality of the social situation, Thomas provided the memorable line: "If men define situations as real, they are real in their consequences."[48]

Thomas' major work was *The Polish Peasant in America,* a prodigious labor involving eight years of collecting material in both Poland and the United States.[49] Written in collaboration with Florian Znaniecki, a Polish philosopher, the volumes utilized a wide range of sources—newspaper accounts, public documents, institutional records, family letters, and autobiographies, published and unpublished. Thomas and Znaniecki analyzed Polish peasant society in transition, in rural Poland and, following emigration, in the slums of Chicago. The two scholars discovered that Polish families were disintegrating under the impact of city life. Industrial urban societies placed no value upon those social canons—female chastity, cultivation of domestic arts, economic solidarity of the household—which bound family and community together in the old country. With no relevant traditions to impart to their children, parents either taught them nothing or, in order to relieve family poverty, encouraged their children's delinquencies.[50]

Thomas studied the whole range of social problems confronting the Polish peasant in Chicago, and, naturally, one of these was juve-

48. On Mead see Anselm Strauss, ed., *George Herbert Mead on Social Psychology* (Chicago: University of Chicago Press, 1964). Morris Janowitz's introduction in Janowitz, ed., *W. I. Thomas on Social Organization and Social Personality* (Chicago: University of Chicago Press, 1966), contains a brief, but informative biography of Thomas, pp. ix–xviii. After Thomas left Chicago in 1918, as the result of prosecution for a morals offense, he worked briefly on the Americanization studies sponsored by the Carnegie Corporation, and from 1920 to 1923 he was provided with research funds and living expenses by Ethel Dummer, surely the lady bountiful of delinquency study. Mrs. Dummer also aided Thomas and his second wife, Dorothy Swaine Thomas, in preparing *The Child in America* (New York: Knopf, 1928), a survey of child study programs in the United States and Canada. See also Kimball Young, "Contributions of William Isaac Thomas to Sociology," *Sociology and Social Research* 47 (October 1962–July 1963).

49. William I. Thomas and Florian Znaniecki, *The Polish Peasant in Europe and America,* 2d ed., 2 vols. (New York: Knopf, 1927). This work was originally published in five volumes, 1918–20, by the University of Chicago Press (vols. I–II) and Richard G. Badger (vols. III–V).

50. Thomas and Znaniecki, *The Polish Peasant in Europe and America,* II, 1776–78, 1800–1802.

nile delinquency. In exploring delinquency in cultural context, he drew upon records of the juvenile court of Chicago to demonstrate the amorality rather than the immorality of the immigrant children's behavior. "Joe and John Kasperek" read one case. "In July, 1913, John and Joe left home separately. After 8 days John was picked up by an officer, but Joe was gone 5 weeks. . . . John frequently stayed home and looked after the younger children, but Joe was wilder and was soon sent to an institution. . . . John was picked up later and sent to the Parental School also. The parents did not go to see the children or send them any clothes, though ordered to do so by the court. The father pretended he did not know where they were. When they were released Joe and another boy broke into a drygoods store and stole some things. . . . John about the same time was arrested for stealing $1 from his father and leaving home." Without the close social controls of the village, immigrant girls sometimes turned to prostitution, not only to avoid the meaningless drudgery of housework or factory employment, but also to obtain nice clothes and other luxuries whose availability they constantly saw advertised. "Nettie Wieczorek" was one case:

> She has been soliciting for 3 months on the streets downtown. . . . She seems to know all the routine and the ways, mentions several "rich hotels" where they had 2 beds in a room with bath connected . . . (Court): Did you want to do this sort of thing? (Nettie): Why no, I did not. (Q): Who first induced you to do that? (A): Della Fox. (Probation Officer): She had gone down to the Beach with Della one time and she said the other day she did not want to do house work because it was so much easier to make money that way.

Another record included this letter from Marien Stepanek to her mother:

> Dear Mother, I am feeling fine. Everything is all right, don't worry about me. I am leading high life because I am an actress. I got swell clothes and everything, you wouldn't know me. . . . I want you to write a letter and say youll forgive me for not telling the truht . . . sent the letter to me this way General Devilry Miss Marion Stephan.[51]

In *The Unadjusted Girl* (1923), Thomas used case records and studies of reformatories in New York and Boston as well as the

---

51. Ibid., pp. 1780, 1805–1806, 1906–1907.

records of the Chicago Juvenile Court. He confirmed his belief that two factors accounted for much female delinquency: the disintegration of immigrant peasant culture in an urban environment and the girls' expectations for an affluent life—hopes which could be fulfilled only by illegal or amoral means.[52] But Thomas knew that tentative explanations for delinquency often became deterministic theories, and therefore he pointed out instances of youthful immigrants and immigrants' children who resisted temptations to become delinquent. "We overweight the standpoint acquired by our particular experience and our preconceived line of approach," he said. Eschewing debate on the etiology of delinquency, he asked, "How can we call certain experiences 'causative factors' in a delinquent group when we do not know the frequency of the same factors in a non-delinquent group?"[53]

In explaining juvenile delinquency, Thomas differed from Mead and later Chicago students by emphasizing the individual delinquent's wish for recognition as the principal cause of his or her behavior. Rejected by socialized individuals, the delinquent sought out other outcasts with whom he formed a gang whose collective behavior was also delinquent. According to Thomas, this group fulfilled the delinquent child's need for status, and henceforth it served as the principal means of defining his behavior. Thomas, for example, recognized that juvenile delinquency was often the consequence of gang activity, but he viewed this delinquency as having its roots in the psychological problems of individual gang members.[54]

Thomas inspired Park and Burgess, leaders of the second generation of Chicago sociologists, by the vigor and scope of his research.

---

52. William I. Thomas, *The Unadjusted Girl* (Boston: Little, Brown, 1923), pp. 98–150. In an introduction to a later edition of this book, Michael Parenti notes that many of Thomas' findings anticipated Daniel Bell's explanation of crime among second generation ethnics. Parenti commented, "Actual destitution and hunger counted for less than the disparity experienced between a circumscribed and confining reality on one hand, and the often illusionary lures of high mass-consumption society on the other." *The Unadjusted Girl,* Torchbook Edition (New York: Harper and Row, 1967), p. xviii.

53. William I. Thomas, "Situational Analysis: The Behavior Pattern and the Situation," in Janowitz, *W. I. Thomas,* pp. 161–62.

54. Faris, *Chicago Sociology,* pp. 14–15. Harry M. Shulman, "A Social Science View of Delinquency Causation and Control," in Frank J. Cohen, ed., *Youth and Crime* (New York: International Universities Press, 1957), p. 138.

Under their direction, students scoured the city to investigate the processes and styles of urban life. The scope of these students' researches was as broad as the range of city life itself, and here it is possible only to discuss the significant studies of juvenile delinquency and to mention works on the related pathologies of urban life. Still, the list is impressive, including not only the studies of Frederic M. Thrasher (1892–1962), Clifford R. Shaw (1896–1963), and Henry D. McKay (b. 1899), which were concerned directly with juvenile delinquency, but also the investigations of Nels Anderson (hobo life), Walter C. Reckless (vice), Edwin H. Sutherland (white-collar crime), and John Landesco (organized crime). Burgess and his student, Roderick D. McKenzie, stimulated the development of the science of human ecology, the study of spatial relationships between man and man as conditioned, among other factors, by man's habitat. From this point of view, Ernest R. Mower and E. Franklin Frazier proceeded to examine family problems and, in particular, the acute degree of family disorganization in certain urban areas. Frazier, a black scholar, concentrated on the problems of the Negro family. Under Park's direction, Norman S. Hayner studied the sociology of hotel life with particular emphasis upon the consequences of mobility and detachment upon the behavior of single persons and transients. In the tradition of William I. Thomas, Louis Wirth investigated the Chicago Jewish ghetto, documenting the disintegrative and integrative forces in the lives of the residents.[55]

The Chicago sociologists of the twenties and thirties regarded juvenile delinquency as essentially a social problem. Unlike Thomas and the psychologists who dwelt on individual mental problems as the major cause of delinquent behavior, they viewed the juvenile delinquent primarily as a person with status in his own circle. The delinquent's behavior was "the product of social interaction with his fellows." Therefore, gang delinquency in its urban context became the focus of their researches. The environmental setting was key. Park wrote:

Village gangs, because they are less hemmed about by physical structures and social inhibitions of an urban environment, ordinarily do

55. The literature of urban behavior research is discussed in Faris, *Chicago Sociology*, pp. 64–87.

not become a social problem, certainly not a problem of the dimensions and significance of those which constitute so obvious and so
obdurate a feature of city life.[56]

According to Park and Burgess, the differential growth of the city
and its population explained the development and activity of delinquent gangs. Rapid commercialization and industrialization of land
near the urban core deteriorated surrounding neighborhoods—the
homes of successive waves of immigrant groups. The families that attained a degree of affluence moved to suburbs or outlying areas, taking with them the cultural, religious, and political organizations that
had socialized life in the old neighborhood. Poorer families, excluded
from the suburbs because of the increased value of the residential
land, found themselves victimized by urban landlords and land spec-
ulators who refused to improve inner city property in anticipation of
the day when these holdings could be sold at a profit for further
commercial or industrial development. Thus the neighborhoods of
the central city residents turned into slums and centers of organized
crime—drug pushing, prostitution, and illegal betting. Family disorganization accorded with social disorganization, and young persons
modeled their behavior after the criminal and deviant persons and
groups who increasingly dominated the neighborhood. The prevalence
of delinquent gangs in these areas was as natural as the dominance of
nondelinquent gangs in the suburbs. The neighborhood's disintegration was hastened and then prolonged by the absence of legitimate
community organizations able to resist organized crime and by the
corrupt and symbiotic relationship between criminal elements and
venal politicians and city officials.[57]

This theory of urban decay and development was most fully applied
to the examination of juvenile delinquency by Clifford R. Shaw,
Henry D. McKay, and Frederic M. Thrasher. Shaw and McKay con-

---

56. Ernest W. Burgess, "The Study of the Delinquent as a Person," *American
Journal of Sociology* 28 (1923), 657–80. Park quoted in his introduction
to Frederic M. Thrasher, *The Gang: A Study of 1313 Gangs in Chicago*
(Chicago: University of Chicago Press, 1927), p. ix. See also Ernest W.
Burgess, "Juvenile Delinquency in a Small City," *Journal of Criminal Law
and Criminology* 6 (1916), 724–28.

57. See Robert E. Park and Ernest W. Burgess, eds., *The City* (Chicago:
University of Chicago Press, 1925).

centrated on describing the neighborhoods of delinquents and on recounting the careers of delinquent boys, while Thrasher penetrated delinquent gangs and analyzed their activity. Clifford R. Shaw made a number of studies—*Delinquency Areas* (1929), *The Jack-Roller: A Delinquent Boy's Own Story* (1930), *The Natural History of a Delinquent Career* (1931), and (with Henry D. McKay) *Social Factors in Juvenile Delinquency* (1931). Shaw and McKay utilized truancy records of the Chicago Board of Education and case histories of the Chicago Juvenile Court and the Institute for Juvenile Research (formerly Healy's Psychopathic Laboratory) to prove graphically and statistically that juvenile delinquents were not distributed uniformly over the city "but tend to be concentrated in areas adjacent to the central business district and to heavily industrial areas." Their other findings flowed from this thesis:

> Rates of truancy, delinquency, and adult crime tend to vary inversely from the center of the city. . . . This radial pattern may not be characteristic of all cities, and even in Chicago there are several deviations from this pattern. . . . While all cities may not show the same pattern of distribution as Chicago, it is probable that all will reveal marked differences in concentration between local areas.

> Another striking finding . . . is the marked similarity in the distribution of truants, juvenile delinquents, and adult criminals in the city.

> It is interesting to note that the main high rate areas of the city . . . have been characterized by high rates over a long period . . . [and] that relatively high rates have persisted in certain areas notwithstanding the fact that the composition of population has changed markedly.

> Delinquents living in areas of high delinquent rates are more likely to become recidivists.[58]

58. Clifford R. Shaw and Henry D. McKay, *Social Factors in Juvenile Delinquency* (Washington, D.C.: Government Printing Office, 1931), p. 383. Clifford R. Shaw, *Delinquency Areas* (Chicago: University of Chicago Press, 1929), pp. 198–204. In *Social Factors in Juvenile Delinquency,* Volume II of the Report on the Causes of Crime by the National Commission on Law Observance and Enforcement (Wickersham Commission), Shaw and McKay confirmed their conclusions with comparative analyses of six other cities (Philadelphia; Cleveland; Richmond, Va.; Denver; Seattle; and Birmingham, Ala.); see pp. 383–93. Another relevant study by a Chicago student is Leonard S. Cottrell, "Juvenile Delinquency among the Negro Groups of Chicago" (Ph.D. diss., Chicago, 1929).

After physically locating delinquency areas, Shaw and McKay conducted a situational analysis of the problem—a study of juvenile delinquency in relation to the social situation in which it occurred. They believed that the behavior of delinquent children could not be understood apart from the various social groups to which they belonged. These groups—families, clubs, schools, and gangs—subjected every child, delinquent or not, "to an increasing number and variety of personalities to which he must make some sort of adjustment. In the process of adjustment . . . the child's attitudes and behavior trends are gradually built up." In socially disorganized areas, crime and delinquency became "more or less traditional aspects of life," which were transmitted to the young through personal and group contacts. Thus juvenile delinquency was the normal way of life or "a traditional group pattern."[59]

Frederic M. Thrasher's *The Gang* demonstrated how some juvenile gangs developed into delinquent ones and then transmitted their norms of delinquent behavior to younger children. Drawing upon the records of private social agencies as well as those of the Chicago Juvenile Court and its allied institutions, Thrasher described and categorized activities of various types of gangs. He emphasized that membership in a delinquent gang was both natural and satisfying for a boy living in the disorganized areas. The boy himself was in most cases psychologically normal and was seeking only normal sociability in gang membership. Gangs became delinquent as they emulated the deficient and deviant organization of group life which characterized slum life as a whole. Thrasher's discussion of the behavior of delinquent gangs such as "The Murderers" and "Joe's Gang," is representative:

> [The Murderers] . . . a gang of thirty Polish boys, who hang out in a district known as The Bush.
> The pastimes of the boys were loafing, smoking, chewing, crap-shooting, card-playing, pool and bowling. . . . The new members who had been taken in from time to time were congenial spirits who had shown ability to elude the police or gameness in a fight.
> A favorite rendezvous of the gang was a large sand pile near the

59. Shaw and McKay, *Social Factors in Juvenile Delinquency*, pp. 4, 387. Shaw, *Delinquent Areas*, p. 9.

railroad tracks. Here they had great fun camping, flipping (derailing) freights, and pestering railroad detectives. . . .

They broke into box cars and "robbed" bacon and other merchandise. They cut out wire cables to sell as junk. They broke open telephone boxes. They took autos for joyriding.

[Joe's Gang] Originating with a dozen adolescent truants in the vicinity of Halsted and Harrison streets, Joe's Gang has been a solid group. Its members have initiative and a sense of honor toward each other and those who have befriended them. They went straight for some time, owing to the efforts of teachers and social workers, but they have now become a hold-up and beer-running outfit.

. . . Several of them pulled off a $100,000 robbery in a Loop jewelry store. Joe drove a wagon that bombed a building under construction on the North Side.[60]

Both Thrasher and Shaw, but particularly the latter, went beyond court and agency records to obtain the gang boy's own story, believing that court officials and other child welfare specialists often failed to help the delinquent because they interpreted his life by their own standards or interests and with "a total disregard of the boy's personality and his role in his own social group and juvenile community." "We robbed the Jews on Maxwell Street," one boy confided to Thrasher. "We'd go into a china store and ask how much a plate was and then drop it. Then the Jew would throw plates. My mother sold some suits to a Jew. The gang followed in a Hudson and robbed the suits." Shaw recorded another boy's own story:

When I was ten the gang started to robbin' stores and homes. We would jimmy the door or window and rob the place. I always stayed outside and gave jiggers. The big guys went in and raided the place. They showed me how to pick locks, jimmy doors, cut glass, and use skeleton keys and everything to get into stores and houses. Every guy had to keep everything a secret and not tell anybody or he would be beat up and razzed. The police were enemies and not to be trusted.[61]

---

60. Thrasher, *The Gang,* pp. 50–55.

61. Frederic M. Thrasher, "Social Attitudes of Superior Boys in an Interstitial Community," in Kimball Young, ed., *Social Attitudes* (New York: Henry Holt, 1930), p. 263. Thrasher, *The Gang,* p. 76. Clifford R. Shaw, *The Jack-Roller: A Delinquent Boy's Own Story* (Chicago: University of Chicago Press, 1930), p. 11.

The autobiography of Stanley, *The Jack-Roller*, recorded by Shaw and his associates over a five-year period, showed most fully the ubiquitous debasement of life in the delinquency areas and in the detention homes and reform schools largely populated by children from the slums.[62] Driven from his home at age six, Stanley became a vagrant and a petty thief and was sent in succession to the juvenile detention home of the Chicago Juvenile Court, St. Charles School for Boys, and eventually the Illinois State Reformatory at Pontiac. In each of these institutions Stanley's general demoralization, his hatred for the law, and his enthusiasm for breaking it were reinforced by inmates who became his companions and fellow criminals upon release. In the detention home he recalled, "I was really awed by the bravery and wisdom of the older crooks. Their stories of adventure fascinated my childish imagination, and I felt drawn to them. My timid spirit (you remember I was only eight) wanted to go out and achieve some of the glories for myself." Two years later "the glories" led Stanley to St. Charles, where he learned, much like Josiah Flint Willard of an earlier day, that "to squawk on a fellow-prisoner is an unpardonable sin and only the lowest characters will squawk. But there were boys who would squawk and they would usually become boy officers. . . . They were not fit to be associated with decent boys." Stanley also discovered a good deal about sexual perversion which he later used to his advantage as a jack-roller: "The bullies would attack the younger boys in the dormitories and force them to have relations. Some of the boys caught venereal disease and had to be treated. . . . I knew little boys who had sex relations with four or five older boys every night. It was easy in the dormitory to slip into another boy's bunk." Committed to St. Charles for a second time Stanley summarized his view of life:

> Crime and imprisonment were becoming more a matter of business, and I didn't worry and feel tender-hearted. I was beginning to be hard-hearted, sarcastic, and resigned to rough treatment. Besides, I was becoming an old timer and the young guys were beginning to look

62. Commenting on this work, Shaw said: "The story should be read with a view to getting insight into the boy's attitudes, typical reactions, and the social and moral world in which he lived. From this standpoint . . . rationalizations, prejudices, exaggerations are quite as valuable as objective description." See Shaw, *The Jack-Roller*, p. 47n. A jack-roller beat up drunks and homosexuals and then robbed them.

up to me and regard me as a hard-boiled gunman of wide experience.[63]

In discussing delinquent careers and delinquent areas, Shaw and
McKay were careful to qualify their description by considering cultural factors which could modify or intensify the exposure which individual children received from the delinquent culture of the neighborhood. By introducing the concept of differential association, Shaw
avoided explaining juvenile delinquency only in terms of disintegration of certain urban areas. He reminded his readers that conventional
groups pursuing legitimate goals continued to exist in most neighborhoods and competed with delinquent groups for the attention of local
children. The extent to which the child identified with one type of
group or the other determined whether he would engage in criminal
or conventional pursuits. Louis Wirth added perspective to this concept by applying it to the relationship of cultural conflict to juvenile
delinquency. Obviously referring to *Delinquency Areas,* Wirth said:

> We may be able to determine statistically that certain regions in the
> city have more delinquency than others, but we will not be able to
> interpret the localization of crime adequately until we see that in
> each area we may be dealing with a different community and that in
> each community we may find a different set of conflicting strains
> of cultural influences and mutually referring groups.

Delinquency rates, Wirth believed, varied directly with the cultural
sanctions for such activity within different immigrant groups. He
agreed, however, that the emotional security of gang life made it
"easier for the individual to meet culture conflict situations with a
delinquent form of behavior."[64]

---

63. Shaw, *The Jack-Roller,* pp. 57, 67, 69, 73. Stanley, according to Shaw,
eventually reformed. In *The Natural History of a Delinquent Career* (1931),
Shaw related the story of Sidney Blotzman, a young man whose criminal
activity continued unchecked by social agencies, reform schools, and prisons.
On Willard see above, pp. 108–109, 120–21.

64. Shulman, "A Social Science View of Delinquency Causation and Control,"
in Cohen, ed., *Youth and Crime,* pp. 129–30. Louis Wirth, "Culture Conflicts
and Misconduct," *Social Forces* 9 (1931), 488–89. See also Albert J. Reiss, Jr.,
ed., *Louis Wirth on Cities and Social Life* (Chicago: University of Chicago
Press, 1964). Sutherland extended the concept of differential diagnosis to
cover white collar crime (fraud, bribery, restraints of trade, monopoly, etc.).
See Edwin H. Sutherland, "White Coller Criminality," *American Sociological
Review* 5 (1940), 1–12.

The Chicago sociologists saw juvenile delinquency as the break-down of the machinery of spontaneous social control, and for them the community represented the logical starting place for remedial plans. Robert Park explained:

> It is in [the] community with its various organizations and its rational schemes for control of the individual, and not elsewhere, that we have delinquency. Delinquency is, in fact, in some cases the measure of the failure of our community organizations to function.

This emphasis upon indigenous community organizations as the key to prevention contrasted with the demand for child welfare legislation which resulted from the earlier urban investigations such as the Pittsburgh Survey (1908–1914). Thrasher demanded "a definitely organized and thoroughgoing preventive program in the local community from which the bulk of delinquents and criminals are produced." He believed that this program should utilize the "services of and cooperation among all preventive agencies existing in the given community" and that it should include "*all* children in the delinquency area, especially *all* the maladjusted and those likely to become delinquents."[65]

The Chicago Area Project, established in 1934 under Clifford Shaw's leadership and the sponsorship of the sociology department of the Illinois Department of Juvenile Research, provided Shaw and McKay and their students with the opportunity to test the findings of their studies. The project staff included residents of neighborhoods in delinquency areas, and they were encouraged to form local organizations that, among other things, attempted to socialize delinquent groups (mostly male gangs) by encouraging their participation in legitimate recreational and vocational activities.

Like the present-day community action programs sponsored by the federal government, the Chicago Area Project attempted to sustain the autonomy of these local groups and, as a result, was accused of promoting disorder and undermining the woᵣk of municipal officials and social workers. Such criticism did not overly trouble the Chicago sociologists. Their concern was for the people of the de-

65. Robert E. Park, "Play and Juvenile Delinquency," *Playground* 18 (1924), 96. Frederic M. Thrasher, "Juvenile Delinquency and Crime Prevention," *Journal of Educational Sociology* 6 (1933), 500–509. See also Thrasher, *The Gang,* pp. 361–63. On the social surveys see above, pp. 152–53.

linquency areas, whom they saw as victims of the urbanization process. Cut off from communication with their fellows and bereft of
spokesmen in government, slum area residents needed help only to
begin the reestablishment of group life. At this point, indigenous
leadership would shoulder the burden of channeling neighborhood
life into legitimate pursuits. In short, Chicago sociologists viewed
the prevention of juvenile delinquency as only one part of the greater
struggle to humanize the city. For Robert Park, the task centered
around "the problem of achieving in the freedom of the city a social
order and a social control equivalent to that which grew up naturally
in the family, the clan and the tribe."[66]

During the first third of the twentieth century, explanations of juvenile delinquency acquired the patina of professionalism. Psychiatrists,
following the example of William Healy, emphasized the causal significance of individual mental problems while University of Chicago
sociologists stressed the importance of forces intimately related to the
urbanization process. At first, psychiatrists based their remedies upon
clinical diagnoses but relied upon community-based child guidance
clinics employing social workers to sustain treatment. Evaluations
questioning the effectiveness of this approach led Healy and others
to stress clinical therapy at the expense of liaison with community
groups and institutions. Sociologists studied the processes of urban
disintegration and its effects upon the family and group life of children. Seeing delinquency as primarily a group activity, they studied
at first hand the structure of delinquent gangs. These scholars also
organized programs of crime and delinquency prevention as one part
of a larger program to reconstruct and socialize group life in slum
areas. Miriam Van Waters appreciated and even conducted some
scholarly analysis of juvenile delinquency. But she is best known as
the woman who influenced a re-evaluation of the treatment and status
of delinquent girls. With the help of like-minded women, she promoted a broadly humane and evangelical program, the principal aim
of which was to win greater sympathy and understanding for girls
whose delinquencies often involved moral offenses.

66. Solomon Kobrin, "The Chicago Project—A Twenty-Five Year Assessment,"
Annals of the American Academy of Political and Social Sciences, 322 (1959),
20–29. Park quoted in Glaab and Brown, *A History of Urban America*, p. 251.

Conclusion

T HE YEAR 1940 represents several landmarks in the history of juvenile delinquency in the United States. In that year the American Law Institute approved a model Youth Correction Authority Act, which provided guidelines for state governments to utilize in order to integrate administratively institutions and agencies responsible for handling child, adolescent, and young adult offenders. It was also the year of the fourth White House Conference on Children, appropriately entitled *Children in a Democracy* to reflect the concern of the participants that the future of democracy in a world grown unfriendly to it "depends in large measure upon the welfare of our children."

I am terminating my discussion here, for, in my judgment, during the war and postwar periods the literature of the subject grows so large and diverse that it requires treatment in another book. Indeed, even before 1940, the cascade of articles and books on various aspects of juvenile delinquency—gangs, child guidance clinics, juvenile courts, and probation systems—threatens to inundate the student. In the modern era especially, the history of attitudes and policies toward juvenile delinquency becomes an indication of trends in research and treatment.

On the programmatic level, many of the recent developments in the study and prevention of delinquency have followed contours laid out by William Healy, the Chicago sociologists, and other pioneers of the professional approach. Before 1960 the majority of research and prevention programs interpreted delinquency in terms of individual personality problems, although intensive studies of gang delinquency were also carried out. The Highfields Project, established by the state of New Jersey in 1950, was only the most notable of programs emphasizing intensive self-analysis and psychiatric counseling to promote "adjustment." At the Judge Baker Center, Healy and his successor, George Gardner, continued to investigate misbehavior in terms of malfunctioning family relationships and personality disorders. The Gluecks recalled Lombroso with their detailed study of *Physique and Delinquency* (1956). Investigating delinquency under the rubric "Children Who Rebel," the Midcentury White House Conference on Children concluded, "Antisocial acts are symptoms of some kind of emotional conflict."

Throughout the forties and fifties, Chicago and Chicago-trained sociologists continued to stress the social origin and context of delinquent behavior. They did not gain the opportunity, however, to implement preventive programs on a widespread basis until the establishment of the President's Committee on Juvenile Delinquency and Youth Crime (1961) and the subsequent passage of the Juvenile Delinquency and Youth Control Act. Strongly influenced by the ideas of sociologists Richard A. Cloward and Lloyd E. Ohlin, the President's Committee, chaired by Attorney General Robert Kennedy, channeled funds to foundation projects such as the Ford Foundation's "grey areas" program, and Mobilization for Youth, a community redevelopment project on the Lower East Side of New York City. Both these and later federal programs were informed by the belief that delinquency was a group phenomenon resulting largely from the perception of ghetto children that the existing structure of economic opportunity left them little chance to attain legally a decent standard of living. Sentiment correlating the relationship between crime control and economic opportunity became so pervasive that programs of delinquency prevention were de-emphasized in favor of broader antipoverty programs, like the Community Action Program in the Office of Economic Opportunity and the Model Cities program. The importance of strengthening neighborhood and local organizations has also been stressed in state plans like the California Youth Authority's probation subsidy program and by the President's Commission on Law Enforcement and Justice (1967). Illustrating the anti-institutional trend, Dr.

Jerome Miller, Massachusetts Commissioner of Youth Services, closed the nation's oldest state reform school (the Lyman School, formerly the Massachusetts Reform School for Boys) in 1972 as part of a state plan to phase out custodial institutions in favor of various community-based efforts.

The general quality of organized care for delinquent children has remained abysmally low. A genre of literature, both popular and scholarly, has periodically confirmed this fact. A sampling might include Paul Tappan, *Delinquent Girls in Court* (1947), Albert Deutsch, *Our Rejected Children* (1950), Benjamin Fine, *1,000,000 Delinquents* (1955), Joan Colebrook, *The Cross of Lassitude* (1967), and Lisa A. Richette, *The Throwaway Children* (1969). Howard James's *Children in Trouble* (1970) is one of the latest studies pointing up the failure of treatment. Remorsefully documenting the persistence of child abuse in reform schools and detention homes, James also describes successful preventive projects, although he found few enough of these. In the course of his research, he discovered several children serving jail sentences.

In retrospect, James's account seems not only familiar but predictable—the logical outcome of deeply rooted attitudes and policies toward delinquent children in particular and criminal and poor people in general. Juvenile delinquency has always described one of several labeling processes which have marked the transition of American society from rural and family-centered origins to the differentiated, mass-organized, and urban-based style of contemporary life. The concept of delinquency has served the twofold purpose of identifying poor urban children in terms of their deviant and criminal activities and fixing the parents of these children for the major share of the blame. Lately, the term juvenile delinquency has been used to describe shoplifting and drug offenses—committed by children from prosperous suburbs. Affluent parents have come to realize that they can no longer guarantee their children immunity from the system of juvenile justice so long reserved for the children of the less favored. Recent protest over the inadequacy of delinquency prevention programs stems in part from middle-class parents experiencing for the first time the effects of the reform school and the juvenile court upon their children. Still, before the 1960s, juvenile delinquency has seldom defined kinds of youthful misbehavior or crime shared by youths in all segments of society, and the children of the well-to-do continue to enjoy some of the exemptions of their status.

The sorting-out function of delinquency applies equally to programs of treatment that have been organized, for the most part, like sieves—to teach "industrious" or "socialized" habits to those children who would learn them and to pass along the remainder to the adult penological system. In both cases, youthful inmate experience has helped children to perform future social roles, either as apprentices and factory workers or as convicts.

These judgments, although harsh, are indicated by this study. Initial rules of care and discipline, for example, were not established by the Pestalozzian E. M. P. Wells who sought to reform children by appealing to intellect and by encouraging active participation in institutional affairs. Rather, the standard was set by Nathaniel Hart and Stephen Allen of the New York Refuge, both of whom saw reformation in terms of habituating the child to subservient modes of conduct.

Later developments sustained the dominance of this approach. Cottage reform schools, modeled to recreate family government, became miniature houses of refuge. The paradigm for the late nineteenth century was not Wichern's *Rauhe Haus*, where the aim was to develop in a domestic setting the individual's capacity for love and understanding, but the Ohio Reform School, where Colonel Adams proclaimed the importance of subordinating the child's will. Similarly, the liberal ideas of Charles Loring Brace and Samuel Gridley Howe, exemplified in the placing-out policy of the New York Children's Aid Society, were not widely copied, while the New York House of Refuge and its imitators continued to spread and develop. In the later nineteenth century, state boards of charity were more representative than "Daddy" George's unique system of inmate self-government. Although state boards were organized in part to eliminate egregious features of institutional life, they became distinguished for coordinating and differentiating the various institutions of charity and correction in order to facilitate efficient categorization and storage of social rejects.

Following the example of state boards, juvenile courts expanded the scope of delinquency care and softened its edges but offered less of a fundamental change in "mores" than Jane Addams had supposed. Here, the relevant figure was Julian Mack, who encouraged the development of a civil service bureaucracy to serve and expand the court and probation staff. The main effect was to create a less explicitly custodial but equally stigmatizing method of treatment which meshed with the discredited, though still useful, reform school system. In this context, Ben Lindsey with his "personal touch" was a passing phenomenon. Miriam Van Waters and the sociologists of the Chicago Area Project also tried to reverse the trend of identifying children as delinquent. Their efforts, which concentrated instead upon reintegrating children with their families and communities, were notable for their humanity but fragile and exceptional for the same reason. Discouraged by the loss of El Retiro, Miriam Van Waters grew fond of quoting the anarchist Kropotkin: "Men are everywhere better than the institutions they have built about them."

This observation is confirmed in another way. In many respects, the ultimate authorities on juvenile delinquency have always been the delinquent children themselves. Better than their keepers, they judged the efficacy of reform school programs. For the most part, their judgment, too, has been unfavorable. From the anonymous children who confided to Elijah Devoe, to the accounts of Josiah Flint Willard and Stanley the jack-roller, the tale has been one of drudgery and debasement. Institutions and juvenile courts smothered decent instincts and encouraged further crime and deviance.

To summarize: over the course of the past century and a half, dominant and more affluent social groups have developed juvenile correctional systems whose principal effect has been to stigmatize certain youths drawn largely from the poorer population in larger urban areas. Secondarily, there has been the hope that the example of youthful outcasts would discourage crime and deviant behavior on the part of those children who were also stigmatized, but only for their deprived condition. Administrators and promoters of correctional systems have always professed that their schemes would save children from future crimes by reorienting their habits and thus facilitating their return to society as law-abiding citizens. Nevertheless, the operating premises of institutionalization have been indictment and differentiation leading logically to adult criminal status. When challenged on this point by explanations stressing the social victimization of delinquent children, defenders of existing programs have altered them in degree but not questioned the ultimate rationale of treatment based upon stigma and separation. Thorough investigations of the social pathologies underlying crime and delinquency have been made, but these have never resulted in a sustained and broad-based commitment to revitalize family and community government at the expense of institutional systems.

The absence of such a commitment is reflected in both the persistence of familiar forms of juvenile delinquency and the advent of new forms of protest. Groups of young male delinquents, now called "rat packs," still prowl the streets of New York and other large cities preying upon vulnerable citizens and businesses. Other ghetto gangs, however, which once warred violently against each other or engaged in petty crimes, have organized programs of protest. They have directed their anger and energies at the political and social system itself by confronting officials with evidence of the inferior health care, housing, and schooling that is their lot. Some youths, disenchanted or bored with conventional society, have sought to escape its clutches by founding communes which, in diverse ways, seek to recreate social life on a family-centered or small group basis. If past experience is any guide, however, these efforts will not realize widespread success as long as the ideological descendants of Stephen Allen control the resources needed to reorganize the social structure from which our thorns and thistles grow.

Bibliographical Essay

IN THE MANUSCRIPT and document collections listed below, I am noting only the place of my own research. Some of the documents may also be found at other libraries and depositories. For a detailed list of historical sources on juvenile delinquency, the reader may wish to consult the bibliography of my Ph.D. dissertation, "Attitudes and Policies toward Juvenile Delinquency in the United States, 1825–1935," The Ohio State University, 1969.

The two principal guides to the history of the relationship between public policy and Anglo-American children are Grace Abbott, ed., *The Child and the State*, 2 vols. (Chicago: University of Chicago Press, 1938) and Robert H. Bremner et al., eds., *Children and Youth in America*, 3 vols. (Cambridge: Harvard University Press, 1970–   ). A more specialized collection which emphasizes English as well as American policies toward juvenile delinquency is Wiley B. Sanders, ed., *Juvenile Offenders for a Thousand Years: Selected Readings from Anglo-Saxon Times to 1900* (Chapel Hill: University of North Carolina Press, 1970). Two bibliographical studies are Augustus Frederick Kuhlman, comp., *A Guide to Material on Crime and Criminal Justice* (New York: H. W. Wilson, 1929) and P. S. de Q. Cabot, comp., *Juvenile Delinquency: A Critical Annotated Bibliography* (New York: H. W. Wilson, 1946). See also Dorothy Culver, comp., *Bibliography of Crime and Criminal Justice, 1927–1937*, 2 vols. (New York: H. W. Wilson, 1934, 1939).

Houses of Refuge, 1825–1860

The basic documents on the refuge movement are the *Annual Reports* of the institutions themselves. *Annual Reports* and special reports of the [New York] Society for the Prevention of Pauperism as well as *Annual Reports* of the [New York] Society for the Reformation of Juvenile Delinquents are available at the Widener Library, Harvard University. The

Papers of the New York House of Refuge (Syracuse University Library) are especially comprehensive. Reports of the Boston House of Reformation (1826) are included in the annually published Boston *City Documents* (Massachusetts State House Library). *Annual Reports* of the Philadelphia House of Refuge and miscellaneous institutional documents are at the Widener. Other relevant collections include the Papers of Stephen Allen and the Papers of John Stanford, both at the New-York Historical Society. Elijah Devoe's *The Refuge System* (New York, 1848) is part of the Sprague pamphlet collection, located at the Harvard Divinity School Library. The following primary sources may be found at the Widener: *Proceedings* of the 1857 and 1859 Conventions of Managers and Superintendents of Houses of Refuge and Schools of Reform; Joseph Curtis, *Examination of Subjects Who Are in the House of Refuge in the City of New York* (Albany, 1825); John Griscom, *A Year in Europe,* 2 vols. (New York, 1823); John H. Griscom, *Memoir of John Griscom* (New York, 1859); Edward Everett Hale, T. V. Moore, and A. H. Grimshaw, *Prize Essays on Juvenile Delinquency* (Philadelphia, 1855); Samuel L. Knapp, *The Life of Thomas Eddy* (New York, 1834); Catherine M. Sedgwick, *Memoir of Joseph Curtis, A Model Man* (New York, 1858).

Recent published work dealing with the refuge movement includes Robert S. Pickett, *House of Refuge: Origins of Juvenile Justice Reform in New York State, 1815–1857* (Syracuse: Syracuse University Press, 1969) and David J. Rothman, *The Discovery of the Asylum: Social Order and Disorder in the New Republic* (Boston: Little, Brown, 1971). Raymond A. Mohl, Jr., "Poverty, Public Relief and Private Charity in New York City, 1783–1825" (Ph.D. diss., New York University, 1967), has been published in revised form as *Poverty in New York, 1783–1825* (New York: Oxford, 1971). A related work, published too late for inclusion in this study, is Carroll Smith Rosenberg, *Religion and the Rise of the American City: The New York City Mission Movement, 1812–1870* (Ithaca: Cornell University Press, 1971). Several articles are significant: Sanford J. Fox, "Juvenile Justice Reform: An Historical Perspective," *Stanford Law Review* 22 (1970), 1187–1239; Clifford S. Griffen, "Religious Benevolence as Social Control, 1815–1860" in David B. Davis, ed., *Ante-Bellum Reform* (New York: Harper and Row, 1967); Michael Heale, "Humanitarianism in the Early Republic: The Moral Reformers of New York, 1776–1825," *Journal of American Studies* 2 (1968), 161–75; W. David Lewis, "The Reformer as Conservative: Protestant Counter-Subversion in the Early Republic," in Stanley Coben and Loren Ratner, eds., *The Development of an American Culture* (Englewood Cliffs, N.J.: Prentice-Hall, 1970); Keith Melder, "Ladies Bountiful: Organized Women's Benevolence in Early Nineteenth Century America," *New York History* 48 (1967), 231–55. A provocative dissertation is Peter G. Slater, "Views of Children and of Child Rearing during the Early National Period: A Study in the New England Intellect" (Ph.D. diss., University of California, Berkeley, 1970).

Preventive Agencies and Reform Schools, 1850–1890

Annual Reports of preventive agencies, including those of the New York Association for Improving the Condition of the Poor, the New York Children's Aid Society, the New York Juvenile Asylum, the New York Catholic Protectory, and the Boston Children's Aid Society, are located at the Widener Library. The unpublished records of the Boston Children's Mission are in the office of the Parents' and Children's Services of Children's Mission, 329 Longwood Avenue, Roxbury, Boston. Reports of state reform schools are usually found in the annual documents of individual states. One of the most complete depositories of the documents of all of the states is located in the annex of the Massachusetts State House Library. In addition to *Annual Reports* of individual institutions, state documents contain *Annual Reports* of boards of state charities in states where these agencies existed. The Papers of Samuel Gridley Howe (Houghton Library, Harvard University) contain several of his unpublished essays on juvenile delinquency. The Papers of Elizabeth Gardiner Evans (Mrs. Glendower Evans) (Schlesinger Library, Radcliffe College) are also important. Institutional collections include the Papers of the New York State Agricultural and Industrial School (formerly the Western House of Refuge), located at the Syracuse University Library, and the Papers of the Lyman School (formerly the Massachusetts State Reform School for Boys), now located at Clark University, Worcester, Mass.

Reports and proceedings of major penal and philanthropic groups provide a wealth of information on reform schools and preventive programs during the nineteenth century. The most valuable of these are The *Proceedings* of the National Conference of Charities and Correction; the *Proceedings* of the Boston Prison Discipline Society, the *Pennsylvania Journal of Prison Discipline, Reports* of the New York Prison Association, and the journal of philanthropy *Lend a Hand.* Alexander Johnson, comp., *A Guide to Proceedings of the National Conference of Charities and Correction, 1874–1907* (1908) is a useful bibliographical guide.

A major compendium of opinion on nineteenth-century reform schools is Enoch C. Wines and Theodore W. Dwight, *Report on the Prisons and Reformatories of the United States and Canada* (Albany, N.Y., 1867). Wines, *The State of Prisons and of Child Saving Institutions in the Civilized World* (Cambridge, Mass., 1880) is informative about European and English reform schools, as is Henry Barnard, *Reformatory Education: Papers on Preventive, Correctional, and Reformatory Institutions and Agencies in Different Countries* (Hartford, Conn., 1857).

Primary accounts of reform school and philanthropic work which proved especially valuable include John Augustus, *A Report of the Labors of John Augustus* (Boston, 1852); Charles Loring Brace, *The Dangerous Classes of New York and Twenty Years' Work Among Them* (New York, 1872); Emma Brace, ed., *The Life of Charles Loring Brace: Chiefly Told in His Own Letters* (London, 1894); William P. Letchworth, *Technologic Training in Reform Schools* (Buffalo, 1884); George C. Needham, *Street Arabs and Gutter Snipes: The Pathetic and Humorous Side of Young Vagabond Life in the Great Cities* (Boston, 1884); Bradford K. Peirce, *A Half Century with Juvenile Delinquents* (New York, 1869).

Published studies of reform schools are not plentiful. An acute analysis of the origins of the Massachusetts Boys Reform School is part of Michael B. Katz, *The Irony of Urban School Reform: Educational Innovation in Mid-Nineteenth Century Massachusetts* (Cambridge: Harvard University Press, 1968). James Leiby, *Charities and Correction in New Jersey* (New Brunswick, N.J.: Rutgers University Press, 1967), describes the history of the reform school in that state. Leiby's work and Gerald N. Grob's *The State and the Mentally Ill* (Chapel Hill: University of North Carolina Press, 1966), add greatly to our understanding of state government efforts to organize charitable and penal institutions. Informative studies of preventive philanthropy are Miriam Langsam, *Children West: A History of the Placing-Out System in the New York Children's Aid Society, 1853–1890* (Madison: University of Wisconsin Press, 1964); Harold Schwartz, *Samuel Gridley Howe: Social Reformer, 1801–1876* (Cambridge: Harvard University Press, 1956); William R. Stewart, *The Philanthropic Work of Josephine Shaw Lowell* (New York: Macmillan, 1911), a still useful study. R. Richard Wohl's article "The 'Country Boy' Myth and Its Place in American Urban Culture: The Nineteenth Century Contribution," *Perspectives in American History* 3 (1969), includes a brilliant analysis of the ideas of Charles Loring Brace.

A number of dissertations have focused on juvenile delinquency in the nineteenth century. One of these, Joseph M. Hawes, "Society Versus Its Children: Nineteenth Century America's Response to the Challenge of Juvenile Delinquency" (Ph.D. diss., University of Texas, 1969), has been published as *Children in Urban Society: Juvenile Delinquency in Nineteenth Century America* (New York: Oxford, 1971). Other recent studies are Thomas M. Bennett, "William Pryor Letchworth and His Work in Child Saving" (Master's thesis, The Ohio State University, 1967); Robert I. Cooper, "William Rhinelander Stewart and the Expansion of Public Welfare Services in New York State, 1882–1929" (Ph.D. diss., City University of New York, 1969); Allen S. Horlick, "Counting-Houses and Clerks: The Social Control of Young Men in New York, 1840–1860" (Ph.D. diss., University of Wisconsin, 1969). Philip H. Hosay, "The Challenge of Urban Poverty: Charity Reformers in New York City, 1835–1890" (Ph.D. diss., University of Michigan, 1969). Hilda Jane Zimmer-

mann, "Penal Systems and Penal Reforms in the South since the Civil
War" (Ph.D. diss., University of North Carolina, 1947), has information
on the treatment of delinquent children. Two other studies ought to be
mentioned because they focus upon contemporaneous efforts to prevent
juvenile delinquency in England: John P. Resch, "Anglo-American Efforts
in Penal Reform, 1850–1900: The Work of Thomas Barwicke Lloyd
Baker" (Ph.D. diss., The Ohio State University, 1969); and Harriet W.
Schupf, "The Perishing and Dangerous Classes: Efforts to Deal with the
Neglected, Vagrant and Delinquent Juvenile in England, 1840–1875"
(Ph.D. diss., Columbia University, 1971).

Scientific Explanations of Juvenile Delinquency, 1880–1910

Reports of the U.S. Immigration Commission and the anthropological
studies of Arthur MacDonald may be found in the annually published
documents and reports of the U.S. Congress. An excellent collection of
relevant medical and scientific journals is located at the Countway Library
of the Harvard Medical School. The Vineland (N.J.) Training School
Bulletin is available at the New York Public Library. Other principal pri-
mary sources are Stanley P. Davies, *Social Control of the Feebleminded*
(New York: National Committee for Mental Hygiene, 1923); Richard L.
Dugdale, *"The Jukes": A Study in Crime, Pauperism, Disease and Heredity*
(New York, 1877); Henry H. Goddard, *The Kallikak Family* (New York:
Macmillan, 1912); G. Stanley Hall, *Adolescence*, 2 vols. (New York:
D. Appleton, 1905); and Hall, *Youth: Its Education, Regimen, and
Hygiene* (New York: D. Appleton, 1906).

The following contemporary studies ought to be taken into account:
John D. Davies, *Phrenology: Fad and Science* (New Haven: Yale
University Press, 1955); John and Virginia Demos, "Adolescence in Historical Perspective," *Journal of Marriage and the Family* 31 (November
1969); Mark H. Haller, *Eugenics: Hereditarian Attitudes in American
Thought* (New Brunswick, N.J.: Rutgers University Press, 1964); John
Higham, *Strangers in the Land: Patterns of American Nativism, 1860–
1925* (New Brunswick, N.J.: Rutgers University Press, 1955); Dorothy
Ross, *G. Stanley Hall: The Psychologist as Prophet* (Chicago: University
of Chicago Press, 1972); Barbara M. Solomon, *Ancestors and Immigrants: A Changing New England Tradition* (Cambridge: Harvard University Press, 1956).

Crises and Changes in Institutional Care, 1880–1910

State documents and legislation (Massachusetts State House Library)
continue to provide information on developments in institutional care and
on the origins of state probation programs. *Proceedings* of the National

Conference of Charities and Correction also remain useful. *Proceedings of the National Conference for the Education of Truant, Backward, Dependent, and Delinquent Children* and the National Prison Association, and the *Annual Reports* of the U.S. Bureau of Education and the Commissioner of Labor are available at the Widener Library as they are at most larger libraries. The Widener also houses a substantial collection of early military school catalogues. Valuable manuscript collections include the Papers of Rutherford B. Hayes (Hayes Memorial Library, Fremont, Ohio). The Papers of the Ohio State Reform and Industrial School for Girls and the Ohio Boys Industrial School (Ohio Historical Society, Columbus, Ohio) are significant. The Papers of the George Junior Republic (Olin Library, Cornell University) fully portray life at the Republic and the ideas of "Daddy" George.

A revealing summary of opinions on the treatment of dependent and delinquent children is the National Conference of Charities and Correction's *History of Child Saving in the United States* (Boston, 1893). Sophonisba P. Breckinridge, ed., *The Child in the City* (Chicago: Chicago School of Civics and Philanthropy, 1912), is also informative. Josiah Flynt, *My Life* (New York: The Outing Company, 1908), provides one of the first inside accounts of reform school life. On the George Junior Republic see Earle D. Bruner, *A Laboratory Study in Democracy* (New York: Doubleday, 1927), and William R. George, *The Junior Republic* (New York: D. Appleton, 1910). The place of vocational education in reform school routines is discussed in David Snedden, *Administrative and Educational Work of the American Juvenile Reform School* (New York: Columbia University Press, 1907). John Henry Smyth's views on reform schools for Negro youths are available in two articles: "Negro Criminality," *The Southern Workman and Farm Record* 24 (1900), 625–31, and "Moral and Christian Influences of Reformatories," NCCC *Proceedings* (1899). See also the list of sources on Negro crime and delinquency in Monroe N. Work, *A Bibliography of the Negro in Africa and America* (New York: H. W. Wilson, 1928), and Elizabeth W. Miller and Mary L. Fisher, comps., *The Negro in America*, 2d ed. (Cambridge: Harvard University Press, 1970).

Jack M. Holl, *Juvenile Reform in the Progressive Era: William R. George and the Junior Republic Movement* (Ithaca: Cornell University Press, 1971), is an excellent monograph. Walter H. Drost, *David Snedden and Education for Social Efficiency* (Madison: University of Wisconsin Press, 1967), and Walter I. Trattner, *Homer Folks: Pioneer in Social Welfare* (New York: Columbia University Press, 1968), are penetrating biographies. James A. McLachlan's *American Boarding Schools* (New York: Charles Scribner's Sons, 1970) is a fascinating study of the development of institutions to socialize and discipline the sons of advantaged families.

The Juvenile Court, 1899–1940

Juvenile court laws may be consulted separately as state laws or, beginning in 1912, in the relevant publications of the U.S. Children's Bureau. One of the most complete surveys is Children's Bureau Publication 193, *The Child, the Family and the Court* (1929). Other significant federal government publications are U.S. Congress, *Children's Courts in the U.S.,* 58th Cong., 2d sess., House Doc. 701 (1904) and *Proceedings* of the Conference on the Care of Dependent Children, 1909 (Washington, D.C.: Government Printing Office, 1909). Legal cases cited may be located at the Harvard University Law School Library and other major law libraries. The Papers of Benjamin B. Lindsey (permission required, Library of Congress) are rich not only in correspondence among the juvenile court's leading spokesmen, but also in Lindsey's unpublished writings on delinquency. The Lindsey manuscripts contain many issues of the *Juvenile Court Record,* an invaluable compendium of early opinion on the court, edited by Timothy D. Hurley of the Chicago Visitation and Aid Society. The Papers of Grace and Edith Abbott (University of Chicago Library) provide much information regarding professional social workers' views of the juvenile court and programs of delinquency prevention. The Papers of Jane Addams (Swarthmore College Peace Collection; microfilm copy of correspondence, Schlesinger Library, Radcliffe College) and Graham Taylor (Newberry Library, Chicago, Illinois), excellent sources on the settlement house movement, do not include much specific material on juvenile delinquency. The Papers of Julius Rosenwald (University of Chicago Library) are also of limited value in this respect.

The juvenile court never lacked publicity, particularly in the years before World War I. I found the following studies the most useful: Edith Abbott and Sophonisba P. Breckinridge, *Truancy and Non-Attendance in the Chicago Schools* (Chicago: University of Chicago Press, 1917); Sophonisba P. Breckinridge, ed., *Social Work and the Courts: Select Statutes and Judicial Decisions* (Chicago: University of Chicago Press, 1934); Sophonisba P. Breckinridge and Edith Abbott, *The Delinquent Child and the Home* (New York: Russell Sage, 1912); Louise de Koven Bowen, *Growing Up with a City* (New York: Macmillan, 1926); Thomas D. Eliot, *The Juvenile Court and the Community* (New York: Macmillan, 1914); Bernard Flexner and Roger N. Baldwin, *Juvenile Courts and Probation* (New York: Century, 1912); Timothy D. Hurley, *The Origin of the Juvenile Court Law* (Chicago: Visitation and Aid Society, 1907); Julia Lathrop et al., *The Child, the Clinic and the Court* (New York: The New Republic, 1927); Benjamin B. Lindsey and Rube Borough, *The Dangerous Life* (New York: Horace Liveright, 1931); Herbert H. Lou, *Juvenile Courts in the United States* (Chapel Hill: University of North Carolina Press, 1927). Of the periodicals, Paul U. Kellogg's *Survey* magazine provides the most comprehensive coverage of juvenile court activities.

Anthony M. Platt, *The Child Savers: The Invention of Delinquency* (Chicago: University of Chicago Press, 1969), focuses on the origins of the Chicago juvenile court. Margaret K. Rosenheim, ed., *Justice for the Child* (New York: Macmillan, 1962) has essays on the history of the court. Charles Larsen's study of Ben Lindsey, *The Good Fight* (Chicago: Quadrangle Books, 1972), was published after this study had been completed. The changing nature of social welfare work is ably delineated in Roy Lubove, *The Professional Altruist: The Emergence of Social Work as a Career, 1880–1930* (Cambridge: Harvard University Press, 1965), and Clarke A. Chambers, *Seedtime of Reform: American Social Service and Social Action, 1918–1933* (Minneapolis: University of Minnesota Press, 1963). Walter I. Trattner, *Homer Folks,* continues to be valuable. Clarke A. Chambers, *Paul U. Kellogg and the "Survey": Voices for Social Welfare and Social Justice* (Minneapolis: University of Minnesota Press, 1971), was released too late for inclusion in this study. Ellen Ryerson, "Between Justice and Compassion: The Rise and Fall of the Juvenile Court" (Ph.D. diss., Yale University, 1970), is another recent work.

Modern Theories of Juvenile Delinquency, 1900–1940

The pioneers of modern attitudes—William Healy, Miriam Van Waters, the Chicago sociologists—contributed to both federal and state studies and reports, but their most significant writings were either commercially published or are available in manuscript collections. The Papers of Miriam Van Waters (Schlesinger Library, Radcliffe College) and Ethel S. Dummer (Schlesinger Library, Radcliffe College) increase understanding of female delinquency prevention programs and of the ideas of psychologists and sociologists interested in helping children. The Papers of Mary W. Dewson (Schlesinger Library, Radcliffe College) contain some information on efforts to end repressive treatment in one state (Massachusetts). The Papers of Felix Frankfurter (Library of Congress) have correspondence between Frankfurter and both Miriam Van Waters and Sheldon and Eleanor Glueck. The Papers of William Healy and Augusta Bronner have not been collected, but some of their correspondence may be found in the Dummer and Frankfurter collections. John C. Burnham's interview with Healy and Bronner (Houghton Library, Harvard University) is especially enlightening. The Papers of the Survey Associates (Social Welfare History Archives, University of Minnesota) contain correspondence relating to various programs of delinquency prevention and particularly to Healy's work at the Judge Baker Center (Boston). The Papers of the Abbott sisters are again important, as are the reports and publications of the Children's Bureau. The Papers of the Children's Bureau, Record Group 102

(National Archives, Washington, D.C.) are revealing of the ideas of Julia Lathrop and Grace Abbott.

Modern scholarly study of juvenile delinquency dates from William Healy's first significant work, *The Individual Delinquent* (Boston: Little, Brown, 1915). Many of the ideas of Healy, Adolf Meyer, and others appear earlier in medical journals, such as *Psychological Clinic* and the *Journal of Psycho-Asthenics,* which may be found in the Countway Library of the Harvard Medical School. Other major works by Healy are *Mental Conflicts and Misconduct* (Boston: Little, Brown, 1917) and, with Augusta F. Bronner, *Delinquents and Criminals: Their Making and Unmaking* (New York: Macmillan, 1926), and *New Light on Delinquency and Its Treatment* (New Haven: Yale University Press, 1936). The major evaluation of Healy's work is Sheldon and Eleanor Glueck, *One Thousand Delinquents: Their Treatment by Court and Clinic* (Cambridge: Harvard University Press, 1934). Studies by contemporaries of Healy's that describe the origins of psychiatric analysis of juvenile delinquents, are Carl L. Rogers, *The Clinical Treatment of the Problem Child* (Cambridge, Mass.: Riverside Press, 1939); George S. Stevenson and Geddes Smith, *Child Guidance Clinics: A Quarter Century of Development* (New York: The Commonwealth Fund, 1934); Helen R. Witmer, *Psychiatric Clinics for Children* (New York: The Commonwealth Fund, 1940). Miriam Van Waters' works include *Youth in Conflict* (New York: New Republic, 1925), *Parents on Probation* (New York: New Republic, 1927), and *The Child Offender in the Federal System of Justice,* Vol. VI in the report of the National Commission of Law Observance and Enforcement [Wickersham Commission] (Washington, D.C.: Government Printing Office, 1931). Among the contributions of the Chicago school of sociology which bear principally on juvenile delinquency are Clifford R. Shaw's studies, *Delinquency Areas* (Chicago: University of Chicago Press, 1929), *The Jack-Roller: A Delinquent Boy's Own Story* (Chicago: University of Chicago Press, 1930), and, with Henry D. McKay, *Social Factors in Juvenile Delinquency,* Vol. II of the Wickersham Commission report (Washington, D.C.: Government Printing Office, 1931); William I. Thomas, *The Unadjusted Girl* (Boston: Little, Brown, 1923); Frederic M. Thrasher, *The Gang: A Study of 1,313 Gangs in Chicago* (Chicago: University of Chicago Press, 1927).

Albert Deutsch, *The Mentally Ill in America,* 2d ed. (New York: Columbia University Press, 1949), and Murray and Adeline Levine, *A Social History of Helping Services* (New York: Appleton-Century-Crofts, 1970), discuss the origins of clinics for delinquent children in the context of the mental hygiene movement. Roy Lubove, *The Professional Altruist,* has bearing on this subject too. Geoffrey Steere, "Changing Values in Child Socialization: A Study of United States Child Rearing Literature, 1865–1929" (Ph.D. diss., University of Pennsylvania, 1964), provides another perspective. Burton J. Rowles, *The Lady at Box 99* (Greenwich, Conn.: The Seabury Press, 1962), is the biography of Miriam Van Waters. Bruce Flack, "The American Youth Commission" (Ph.D. diss., The Ohio State University, 1969), analyzes Miss Van Waters' role in the New Deal project. Robert E. L. Faris, *Chicago Sociology, 1920–1932* (Chicago: University of Chicago Press, 1970), is a useful guide to the history of the discipline in the United States.

Index

Abbott, Edith, xiii, 151, 182; and juvenile court, 152; and study of delinquency 153–54; *Truancy and Non-Attendance in the Chicago Schools,* 153–54

Abbott, Grace, xiii; *The Child and the State,* xiii; and child guidance clinics, 156; and juvenile court, 131, 133, 156–57; and U. S. Children's Bureau, 155

Abdy, Edward, 18

Adams, Colonel C. B., as reform school superintendent, 103, 109, 199

Addams, Jane, 183; on causes of delinquency, 83, 126; and juvenile court, 133, 200; *The Spirit of Youth and the City Streets,* 83

Adler, Polly, 3

"Adolescent Girl in Primitive Society, The" (Van Waters), 174

Adolescent Offender, The (Veiller), 153

African Free School Society (New York City), 7

Aichorn, August, *Wayward Youth,* 170

Alabama "reformatory for Negro boys," 122

Alabama State Federation of Colored Women's Clubs, 122

Alexander, Franz, 170; at Judge Baker Center, 171

Alger, Horatio, 62–63

Allan, George H., 45

Allen, Joseph, as reform school superintendent, 55

Allen, Stephen, 4, 9, 199, 201; and causes of delinquency, 16, 70; and New York House of Refuge, 6, 15, 18, 23, 26, 28

Almshouses, children in early, xxiii–xxiv; boards of state charities condemn, 66–67, 129; and houses of refuge, 8–10

Almy, Frederic, 140

Alper, Benedict S., 171

Altgeld, John P., 128–29; *Our Penal Machinery and Its Victims,* 129

American Bible Society, 7, 50

American Breeders' Association, 93; and William Healy, 163

American Civil Liberties Union, 147

American Council on Education, 181

American Journal of Sociology, 181

American Law Institute, 196

American Medical Association, 87

American Sunday School Union, 4, 7; and Horace Mann, 33

American Youth Commission, 181

Ames, Marcus, as reform school superintendent, 59

Amsterdam House of Correction (1595), xx–xxi

Anderson, Nels, 182–83, 187

Andover Settlement House (Boston), 153

Angell, James Rowland, 161

Anthropology, criminal: and delinquency, 84–90, 100; and juvenile court, 89; origins of, 83–84; and reform schools, 85–86, 90. *See also* Boas, Franz; MacDonald, Arthur

213